THE V

ALSO BY RAJ PATEL

Stuffed and Starved: The Hidden Battle
for the World Food System

THE VALUE OF NOTHING

HOW TO RESHAPE MARKET SOCIETY AND REDEFINE DEMOCRACY

Raj Patel

Portobello

Published by Portobello Books Ltd 2009
This paperback edition published 2011

Portobello Books Ltd
12 Addison Avenue
London
W11 4QR

A CIP catalogue record is available
from the British Library

9 8 7 6 5 4 3 2

ISBN 978 1 84627 218 9

www.portobellobooks.com

Printed and bound by
CPI Group (UK) Ltd, Coydon, CR0 4YY

CONTENTS

PART ONE

Nowadays people know the price of everything and the
value of nothing.

—OSCAR WILDE, *The Picture of Dorian Gray*

(ONE)

THE FLAW

> Now I a fourfold vision see,
> And a fourfold vision is given to me;
> 'Tis fourfold in my supreme delight,
> And threefold in soft Beulah's night,
> And twofold Always. May God us keep
> From Single vision, & Newton's sleep!
> —WILLIAM BLAKE, *"Poems from Letters"*

If war is God's way of teaching Americans geography, recession is His way of teaching everyone a little economics.

The great unwinding of the financial sector showed that the smartest mathematical minds on the planet, backed by some of the deepest pockets, had not built a sleek engine of permanent prosperity but a clown car of trades, swaps and double dares that, inevitably, fell to bits. The recession has not come from a deficit of economic knowledge, but from too much of a particular kind, a surfeit of the spirit of capitalism. The dazzle of free markets has blinded us to other ways of seeing the world. As Oscar Wilde wrote over a century ago: "Nowadays people know the price of everything and the value of nothing." Prices have revealed themselves as fickle guides: The 2008 financial collapse came in the same year as crises in food and oil, and yet we seem unable to see or value our world except through the faulty prism of markets.

One thing is clear: The thinking that got us into this mess is unlikely to rescue us. It might come as some consolation to know that even some of the most respected minds have been forced to puzzle over their faulty assumptions. Perhaps the most pained admission of ignorance happened in a crowded room in front of the House Committee on Oversight and Government Reform when, on October 23, 2008, Alan Greenspan described the failure of his worldview.

Greenspan was one of the acknowledged legislators of the world's economy over the past nineteen years in his role as chairman of the Federal Reserve. A card-carrying member of the free market brigade, he used to sit at the feet of Ayn Rand who, although largely unknown outside the United States, remains influential long after her death in 1982. Her 1957 book *Atlas Shrugged*, in which heroic business moguls fight the scourge of government officials and union organizers, has once again scaled the best-seller lists. Regarding altruism as "moral cannibalism," Rand was the cheerleader for an extreme free market libertarian school of thought, which she called "Objectivism." Drawn into her circle by this heady philosophy, Greenspan earned himself the nickname "the Undertaker" for his jolly demeanor and dress sense. When Greenspan chose a career in government, it was rather like a hippie joining the marines, a lapse that his former friends could never forgive. Despite this, Greenspan remained largely faithful to Rand's philosophy, continuing to believe that egoism would lead to the best of all possible worlds, and that any form of restraint would result in disaster.

At the end of 2008, Greenspan was summoned to the U.S. Congress to testify about the financial crisis. His tenure at the Fed had been long and lauded, and Congress wanted to know what had gone wrong. As he began to read his testimony, Greenspan looked exhausted, his skin jowly and sagging, as if the vigor that once kept him taut had all been spent. But he came out swinging. In the first round, he took aim at the information he'd been working with. If only the input had been right, the economic models would have worked, and the predictions would have been better. In his words,

> a Nobel Prize was awarded for the discovery of the pricing model that underpins much of the advance in derivatives markets. This modern risk management paradigm held sway for decades. The whole intellectual edifice, however, collapsed in the summer of last year because the data inputted into the risk management models generally covered only the past two decades, a period of euphoria. Had instead the models been fitted more appropriately to historic periods of stress, capital requirements would have been much higher and the financial world would be in far better shape today, in my judgment.[1]

This is a garbage-in-garbage-out argument: The model worked just fine, but the assumptions about risk and data, based only on the good times past, were faulty and so the output was correspondingly wrong. Greenspan's nemesis on the panel, Henry Waxman, pushed him to a deeper conclusion, in this remarkable exchange:

> WAXMAN: The question I have for you is, you had an ideology, you had a belief that free, competitive—and this is your statement—"I do have an ideology. My judgment is that free, competitive markets are by far the unrivalled way to organize economies. We have tried regulation, none meaningfully worked." That was your quote. You had the authority to prevent irresponsible lending practices that led to the subprime mortgage crisis. You were advised to do so by many others. And

now our whole economy is paying the price. Do you
feel that your ideology pushed you to make decisions
that you wish you had not made?

GREENSPAN: Well, remember, though, what an ideology
is. It's a conceptual framework with [*sic*] the way people
deal with reality. Everyone has one. You have to. To
exist, you need an ideology. The question is, whether
it is accurate or not. What I am saying to you is, yes, I
found the flaw, I don't know how significant or permanent it is, but I have been very distressed by that fact.

WAXMAN: You found a flaw?

GREENSPAN: I found a flaw in the model that I perceived
is the critical functioning structure that defines how
the world works, so to speak.

WAXMAN: In other words, you found that your view of the
world, your ideology, was not right, it was not working.

GREENSPAN: Precisely. That is precisely the reason I was
shocked, because I had been going for 40 years or more
with very considerable evidence that it was working
exceptionally well.

The flaw, to be clear, wasn't a minor one of shoddy data. Nor was it
the bigger Black Swan problem that writers like Nassim Taleb discuss, a problem of failing to account for highly unlikely events that,
should they happen, involve catastrophic consequences. Greenspan's
flaw was more fundamental still. It warped his view about how the
world was organized, about the sociology of the market. And Greenspan is not alone. Larry Summers, the president's senior economic
advisor, has had to come to terms with a similar error—his view that
the market was inherently self-stabilizing has been "dealt a fatal
blow."[2] Hank Paulson, Bush's treasury secretary, has shrugged his
shoulders with similar resignation. Even Jim Cramer from CNBC's

Mad Money admitted defeat: "The only guy who really called this right was Karl Marx."[3] One after the other, the celebrants of the free market are finding themselves, to use the language of the market, corrected.

The extent of Greenspan's admission has passed most of us by. If you trawl the op-ed pages of the financial press, you'll find plenty of analysis that fits Greenspan's first gambit, with pundits offering stories about how risk was incorrectly priced (which it was), how the lack of regulation allowed the panic to feed back into the financial system (which it has), how the incentive structures rewarded traders who were able to push financial risk far into the future (which they did) and how free market ideologues removed the sorts of circuit-breaking policies that might today have helped (and they did that too). But these are all it-could-have-been-fixed-if-we'd-planned-better responses. I am not sure that we're able to comprehend what Greenspan's admission might really mean for us. It would be too big a shock to have the fundamentals of policy in both government and the economy proved wrong, and to have nothing with which to replace them.

It's as if one day, you were to wake up and find yourself transformed into a cockroach.[4] This is the premise of Franz Kafka's novella *Metamorphosis*. In the first sentence, a young salesman named Gregor Samsa wakes up, after a night of bad dreams, to find that he has turned into an enormous bug. Gregor Samsa's response is revealing, telling us a little bit more about ourselves than we'd like. For what does Samsa do when he discovers he's a bug? He doesn't scuttle from his room screaming, or ponder how this happened, or what his transformation means, and what he might become tomorrow. His response is essentially this: "Poor me! How am I going to keep my job?"

Which is almost exactly how we've reacted to this economic crisis.

While no one has yet woken up in the body of a bug, we have all found ourselves in a world turned upside down, where everything we were told was to our advantage has turned out to be its opposite. Greenspan's "flaw" has profound repercussions—to understand it fully would mean a complete reappraisal of the way we conduct our lives. We would need not only a new way of mooring our expectations of our society and our economy, one based on richer assumptions about human nature, but also a different ideology governing the exchange of goods and services.

Prices do some heavy ideological lifting in Greenspan's world. They provide a way to see and know the collective wants and resources of our small planet. This is Friedrich Hayek's economic philosophy, in which prices are the tendrils through which wants and needs are communicated. Science fiction fans will already be familiar with what this looks like. In *The Matrix*, liberated humans (and the programs who hunt them) can see the world in its raw form, as a digital rain of symbols and signs. This is the science fiction that governs economic fact. Data pelting down monitors is what the masters of the universe on the global financial exchanges stare at, their eyes darting from screen to screen, trying to see through the world and profit from it. In *The Matrix*, the signs were a simulation of the real world, hiding more than they revealed. The trouble is that this unreliable digital ticker tape has now become a central prop in the drama of modern commerce.

Consider the fate of Volkswagen, which at the end of October 2008 managed briefly to become the world's most valuable corporation without having to sell a single vehicle. With the economy still in free fall, traders on stock-market floors were taking a dim view of Volkswagen. They looked at their screens and concluded that, just like every other auto manufacturer, Volkswagen was heading for tough times. Imagine you're a trader who feels in your bones that the stock price can only fall. One way to cash your hunch in is to sell Volkswagen stock today, and buy it back when the price falls. Since you don't walk around with Volkswagen stock falling out of your pockets, you'll turn to someone who does, like an institutional investor. You borrow their stock, for a price, and promise to return all of it very soon. The institutional investor is happy because they make money from lending out the stock, which they will get back in one piece. You're happy because you can sell this stock, wait for the price to fall, buy it back and, with the profit, not only pay back the institutional investor, but make the next installment on your yacht in Monaco. This practice is called "shorting."

The trouble was that Volkswagen's rival, Porsche, had started quietly buying Volkswagen stock, aiming to secure 75 percent of the company. When the scale of Porsche's buying spree came to light, it became rapidly clear that there was little of the company left to trade. With Porsche sucking up all the shares, the price for Volkswagen didn't drop. Traders were selling borrowed stock to Porsche, and when Porsche announced its intentions to hold the stock, traders panicked. This led to a "short squeeze," a flocking of investors looking to cover the ill-conceived bets that they'd paid for with stock that they didn't own. They'd wagered that Volkswagen's price, like that of any other car company in a recession, would fall. When it became clear that even if Volkswagen wasn't doing well in the car market, its share price was nonetheless defying gravity, the speculators rushed to buy before the price went any higher.

Their combined purchases drove the price of shares up further. So high did the price rise that Volkswagen entered the DAX 30 index of the largest corporations on the German bourse. This triggered another buying spree, driven not by stock-market gamblers, but by their polar opposites—conservative institutional investors. Pension funds, for instance, invest with an eye to long-term returns; they prefer a slow and certain accumulation of wealth rather than risky bets. One way that they keep their portfolio on an even keel is to buy shares in nothing but blue chip corporations, ones that are guaranteed to be least susceptible to the shocks that stocks are heir to, ones that are in the top, say, thirty corporations traded in the open market. When Volkswagen joined the ranks of the DAX 30, a flock of institutional investors automatically wanted in. So they bought Volkswagen shares at whatever price they could find them. The result? The price per share went from €200 to €1,000 in a week—an increase in company value of €300 billion (£244 billion; $386 billion). It made Volkswagen, briefly, bigger than Exxon-Mobil (with a book value of a mere $343 billion). And for this, the company didn't raise a finger.

In the end, the rules on the DAX were changed, the price settled down and, in 2009, Volkswagen bought Porsche. It is easy enough to tell this story as one where institutional investors got caught with their pants down, where there was imperfect information about the size of the market, where the rules of different short-run and long-run games tangled. But look more closely. Underwriting this version of the story is a conceptual structure that lies beneath every story of excess and crash. The very notion of a bubble relies on the premise that when the bubble pops, things return to a normal state, a situation of price reflecting value more accurately. This is the story told after every boom and bust, from the South Sea Bubble of 1720 to the housing catastrophe of 2008. There's a widely shared opinion that normality will ultimately return to the world economy—but it's a consensus view that rests on a story where bubbles are exceptions to the standard (and successful) procedures of market valuation. If those procedures themselves were flawed, as Greenspan suggests, then our faith in a gentle return to earth is misplaced, for there is and never has been any solid ground beneath our feet.

There is a discrepancy between the price of something and its value, one that economists cannot fix, because it's a problem inherent to the very idea of profit-driven prices. This gap is something about which we've got an uneasy and uncomfortable intuition. The uncertainty about prices is what makes the MasterCard ads amusing. You know how it goes—green fees: $240; lessons: $50; golf club:

$110; having fun: priceless. The deeper joke, though, is this: The price of something doesn't measure its value at all. This prickly intuition has become entertainment. An alien from another planet would find it strange that one of the most popular TV shows in dozens of countries is one that trades on the confusion around what something's worth: *The Price Is Right*. In the show, the audience is presented with various consumer durables, and asked to guess the retail price of each. Crucially, you don't win by correctly guessing how useful something is or how much it costs to make—prices are poor guides to use and true costs of production. You win by developing an intuitive sense of what corporations believe you're willing to pay.

In the world of fund management, the systematic confusion surrounding what something is worth has made some people very rich. Traders' salaries are linked to the returns above expected rates for the risk they take on, the so-called alpha that they contribute to the returns. Think of a bet on a coin flip, with odds of two to one. I bet $1 that I will hit heads, and every time I do, I get $2. In the long run, I'd expect a dollar bet with those odds to return a dollar because I'll come up heads about half the time. But if I'm returning $1.50 on the bet, I'm making magic happen. This magic gets turned back into coins that I get to keep, through bonuses and increased salary. This is a tough trick to pull off because there are only a handful of ways to create added value in fund management—I can pick undervalued stocks that outperform expectations, I can nurture innovations that change the rules of the game, or I can create new bespoke assets that institutional investors might like. So we would expect alpha to be rare, and it is, but driven by the desire to cash in, there were many who created *fake* alpha through bets that appeared to produce consistently good returns despite having a small built-in chance of catastrophic loss. If the expected value of this loss were factored in, the alpha would disappear. But the risks were ignored and bonuses flowed. The frat boys who ran the economy, and profited from its poor regulation, made billions. They were paid today for outcomes that they predicted would happen in the future, using a "mark to model" accounting practice that essentially allowed them to book today what they projected they'd earn tomorrow.[5] This practice was justified on the grounds that "markets know best."

That markets should know best is a relatively recent article of faith, and it took a great deal of ideological and political work to make it part of governments' conventional wisdom. The idea that markets are smart found its apotheosis in the Efficient Markets Hypothesis, an idea first formulated by Eugene Fama, a Ph.D. student in the University of Chicago Business School in the 1960s. In the ideological foundations it provided for financiers, it was a mighty force—think of it as *Atlas Shrugged*, but with more equations.

The hypothesis states that the price of a financial asset reflects everything that a market knows about its current and future prospects. This is different from saying that the price actually *does* reflect its future performance—rather, the price reflects the current state of beliefs about the odds of that performance being good or bad. The price involves a bet. As we now know, the market's eye for odds is dangerously myopic, but the hypothesis explains why economists find the following joke funny:

> Q: How many Chicago School economists does it take to change a lightbulb?
> A: None. If the lightbulb needed changing, the market would have already done it.

The problem with the Efficient Markets Hypothesis is that it doesn't work. If it were true, then there'd be no incentive to invest in research because the market would, by magic, have beaten you to it. Economists Sanford Grossman and Joseph Stiglitz demonstrated this in 1980, and hundreds of subsequent studies have pointed out quite how unrealistic the hypothesis is, some of the most influential of which were written by Eugene Fama himself.[6] Markets can behave irrationally—investors can herd behind a stock, pushing its value up in ways entirely unrelated to the stock being traded.[7]

Despite ample economic evidence to suggest it was false, the idea of efficient markets ran riot through governments.[8] Alan Greenspan was not the only person to find the hypothesis a convenient untruth. By pushing regulators to behave as if the hypothesis were true, traders could make their titanic bets. For a while, the money rolled in. In the mid-1990s, the *Financial Times* felt able to launch a monthly supplement, entitled *How to Spend It*, to help its more affluent readers unburden themselves. The magic of the past decade's boom also touched the middle class, who were sucked into the bubble through houses that were turned from places of shelter into financial assets, and into grist for the mill of the financial sector. But ordinary homeowners couldn't muster the clout that banks could: Governments enabled the finance sector's binge by promising to be there to pick up the pieces, and they were as good as their word. When the financiers' bets broke the system, the profit that they made from these bad bets remained untouchable: The profit was privatized, but the risk was socialized. Their riches have cost the whole world dear, and yet in 2009 the top hedge fund managers have had their third-best year on record. George Soros is, in his own words, "having a very good crisis," and staff at Goldman Sachs can look forward to the largest bonus payouts in the firm's 140-year history.[9]

What this suggests is that the rhetoric of "free markets" camouflages activities that aren't about markets at all. Goldman Sachs employees are doing well because their firm turned some distinctly nonmarket tricks. *Rolling Stone* journalist Matt Taibbi has recently revealed, with characteristic verve, how Goldman Sachs has bought the U.S. government. In the Obama administration's economic team,

Wall Street has a generation of finance-friendly appointees, from Treasury Secretary Tim Geithner, who arranged a historic $29 billion loan to persuade JPMorgan Chase to acquire Bear Stearns during his tenure as chair of the Federal Reserve Bank of New York; to Larry Summers, who earned $5.2 million by working one day a week for a couple of years in a large Wall Street hedge fund. Their new positions in the White House make them the Tarzans of the economic jungle. Wall Street has reason to be pleased. Goldman had invested heavily in AIG, the insurance giant whose financial products division had brought the ninety-year-old giant to bankruptcy. With the 2008 AIG rescue, the $13 billion that Goldman invested was repaid at full face value. Investors in Chrysler, by contrast, stand to get twenty-nine cents for every dollar they invested.[10]

Anyone concerned with democracy should be worried that the seam between Wall Street and the government is almost invisible. At the very least, it raises serious reasons to doubt that the institutions that facilitated the crisis can clean up their mess. Nassim Taleb points to the absurdity here: "People who were driving a school bus (blindfolded) and crashed it should never be given a new bus."[11] The problem is that because both our economy and to a larger extent our politicians aren't really subject to democratic control, the bus drivers are always going to be graduates of the same driving school.[12]

Despite the ongoing hijack of government by Wall Street, a word that hasn't been heard in over a generation is being uttered by politicians: "regulation." It's true that Goldman Sachs and others are profiting handsomely from the collapse, but there is nonetheless a growing sense among politicians that the market may have been allowed too free a rein. Naomi Klein's devastating critique *The Shock Doctrine* demonstrates how disasters were turned into platforms for rabidly free market policies, and it's an analysis that explains the post–World War II era and today's ongoing financial plunder, from California to Wall Street to the City of London, very well. But there is a recognition among the public and some politicians that today's economic crisis is a failure of free market thinking, and not a warrant for more. In response to popular outcry, politicians around the world seem ready to discuss how to regulate and restrain the market. The question is, can they, and, if they can, in whose interests will this regulation work?

From its inception, the free market has spawned discontent, but rare are the moments when that discontent coalesces across society, when a sufficiently large group of people can trace their unhappiness to free market politics, and demand change. The New Deal in the United States and the postwar European welfare states were partly a result of a consortium of social forces pushing for new limits to markets, and a renegotiation of the relationship between individuals and society. What's new about this crisis is that it's pervasively global,[13] and comes at the last moment at which we might prevent a global climate catastrophe. But the breadth and depth of both these crises reflect how profoundly our society has been transfixed by free market culture. To understand how this will affect us in the twenty-first century, we need to understand how it began, and to ask why today's markets look the way they do.

THE STORY OF THE STORY OF STUFF

On the weekends and holidays when I helped out in my family's convenience store, I most enjoyed being sent to the stockroom to refill shelves, which meant finding sweet things in the labyrinth of boxes and shelves, and then using the price gun on them. The gun itself was a mechanical plastic device about as big as this book, and when I squeezed the trigger it stamped and spat out a small sticker with whatever number you'd set on its dial. I spent many happy hours pulling the trigger, toting it like a Glock for junior capitalists,

tickering out random prices and generally making a nuisance of my-
self by setting the price of Mars bars to £999.99. The best thing,
though, was a game where I set the price to 0.01p and ran around
trying to tag my brother.

What tickled my ten-year-old self is what also makes phrases like
"Joe would sell his mother to go to the football game" funny. While
Joe may very much want to see the game and there may be no
more valuable person in his life than his mother, he can't *actually*
make the trade. My brother wasn't worth 0.01p, and the notion that
he might be exchanged for that, or for anything else, was the source
of my own private comedy. But this same idea that price labels can
be attached to everything is not only one of which our politicians
and business elites seem uncommonly fond, it can also lead to public tragedy.

In 1920, two German professors, Karl Binding and Alfred Hoche,
caused a sensation with the publication of their *Permission for the
Destruction of Life Unworthy of Life*. They presented an argument for
killing "incurable idiots, empty human husks, useless eaters, whose
ballast lives" might be jettisoned so as to allow the nation to soar ever
higher. They clinched their argument with an extended calculation
of the cost of care, which they summed up as "a massive capital in
the form of foodstuffs, clothing and heating, which is being sub-
tracted from the national product for entirely unproductive purposes."[14] Their calculus was impeccable but their conclusions were
repugnant.

The immediate objection to this is that it's horrifying to put a
price on human life. Yet governments and corporations routinely do
exactly this: The British government, like the U.S. health industry,
calculates what it costs to provide a treatment against the years of
life the treatment saves because, with limited resources, they want
to make sure they're saving as many lives as possible. Joseph Stiglitz
and Linda Bilmes estimated the cost of American lives lost in the

Iraq War by using a standard U.S. governmental and actuarial figure of $7.2 million per life as part of their calculation of the total costs of the war to the United States: in excess of $3 trillion. Applying just that valuation of human life to Iraq, the cost of the war to Iraqi civilians is $8.6 trillion. There's still something rather unsavory about this, even if no one is actually suggesting trading a human life for $7 million dollars.[15] But Professors Binding and Hoche took it a step further. They suggested that not all human life is worth the same, and that society as a whole could save money by killing the mentally ill. Finally, they proposed that the full force of the government should be put behind their recommendations. All of this, of course, provided the intellectual foundations for Nazism, but the practice of turning people into commodities whose lives might be bought or extinguished according to profit isn't unique to National Socialism. Most of Europe and the United States have profited from slavery in one form or another.

Times have, however, changed, and although human trafficking is widespread in the twenty-first century, with a value in 2006 estimated at $42 billion, there are few parts of the world where the notion is still favorably entertained. There are no more legal markets in people and it is generally agreed that this is a good thing. Indeed, there are now even prohibitions on the way we can place *ourselves* into markets. We are not, for instance, legally allowed to sell our organs. Give them away, yes. Sell, no.

The history of slavery shows not only that the set of things allowed into markets can change but also that decrees establishing what belongs in markets can be revoked. Once, slavery was allowed. Now it isn't. In other words, there is nothing *natural* about buying and selling things for profit, and allowing markets to determine their value. Before commodities can be bought and sold, they have to become objects that people *think* can be bought or sold. Most of the things that we buy and sell weren't always commodities in the way we understand them today—land, music, labor, care, people and food once had a much more ambiguous status. These things *became* commodities through complicated and layered processes, to be exchanged in markets with very specific attributes. In 1944, a dissident Hungarian writing in Britain in the middle of the Second World War published one of the most penetrating examinations of how this worked.

Karl Polanyi's book *The Great Transformation* is a history of eighteenth- and nineteenth-century England, with a long discussion of what sounds like a bit of eighteenth-century arcana, the Speenhamland laws. These were English "poor laws" designed to relieve the worst aspects of rural poverty by providing a form of welfare linked to the price of bread. Polanyi's argument, however, is about much more than pre-Victorian safety nets—he makes the case that markets and the society around them are bound together. Contrary to Greenspan's philosophy, Polanyi suggests that capitalism needs society's institutions in a very particular way. In order for markets to work, society needs to license the turning of things into commodities that can be bought and sold within the economy. Hence Polanyi's choice of title. The "transformation" describes how the most powerful groups in society tried to turn land and labor into "fictitious commodities," into things that were in principle very different from the goods that had previously been exchanged in markets.

It may sound odd to think about land or labor as fictitious when the heart of contemporary working life beats to the rhythm of paychecks and rent, but that's a measure of how "great" the transformation was. It transformed social arrangements so dramatically that it is impossible to think of them in any other way. In other words, the transformation not only changed society, it also changed *us*, by changing the way we see the world and our place in it.

The great transformation demanded a great deal of social upheaval. In order to buy and sell land, the people who were previously using it had to be evicted. This happened through the sometimes violent process of enclosure, where peasants were evicted from common land and consigned to cities where they might find income through selling their labor, and provide demand by becoming consumers. In other words, the great transformation required that the social rules governing land and work be entirely rewritten—and through this transformation, entirely new things became eligible for ownership, and for pricing. The process hasn't stopped. The engineers of new financial products work at the bleeding edge of this transformation in the twenty-first century. So do the makers of the cap-and-trade policies designed to solve climate change, in which the right to pollute becomes a commodity.

What Polanyi offers is a way of understanding not only why the economy and society are part of the same set of processes, but also why we erroneously believe that market and society are separate. The culture of profit-driven markets, what Polanyi calls the myth of the self-regulating market, turns out to need society far more than it pretends to—but the myth that economy and society are two distinct realms needs to be widely propagated if the self-regulating market is to spread farther. We generally think it unwise for one conjoined twin to operate on another, but what the market myth fosters is the belief not only that the twins are separated, but that one is the doctor, and one the patient.

In times of crisis, the myth becomes far easier to see through. After all, the failure of the banks could have spiraled into total economic meltdown were the public sector not there to catch it. Capitalism can no more bail itself out than it can stand on its own shoulders. The market has always depended on society, which is why the language of "too big to fail" simply means "so big that it can depend on society to pick it up when it topples." The logic of laissez-faire always needs a social base, and this is why Polanyi does not separate the way we live into "government and the free market"—for him, it's simply "market society."

By the same token, the market society is embedded in the natural world, which the myth of the self-regulating market equally tries to deny. Human civilization depends on Earth's ecology, even though we're literally exploiting it to death—by some estimates, human activity has raised extinction rates for other species by one thousand times normal levels.[16] In the relentless enclosure of the natural world, we have destroyed our planet and, if the quiet whispers among many climate scientists are to be believed, it may already be too late to do anything about it.[17] The perpetual quest for economic growth has turned humankind into an agent of extinction, through the systematic undervaluing of the ecosystemic services that keep our Earth alive. In the words of Herman Daly, one of the pioneers of ecological economics,[18] "Current economic growth has uncoupled itself from the world and has become irrelevant. Worse, it has become a blind guide."[19] In short, the economy takes a great deal for granted, for free, and is constitutionally unable to pay for it.

ANTON'S BLINDNESS

Seeing the world through markets has got us in trouble. Yet the great transformation has been so profound that it is hard to imagine that we might value, and manage, the world in any other way than by pricing it, and letting the free market sort it out. We cling to the myth of self-regulating markets, no matter how imperfect they are, because without them we feel we would be lost. We've only one compass when we think about what things are worth, and even if it rarely points north, it permits the fantasy that we know where we're going.

It's as if, collectively, we suffer from Anton's blindness. Named for the Austrian neurologist Gabriel Anton (1858–1933), this is a rare medical condition that can occur after a stroke or traumatic brain injury, in which its sufferers are blind, but possessed of a fervent belief that they can see. Doctors treating the condition, also known as Anton-Babinski syndrome, are confronted by patients who insist there's nothing wrong with them despite experiencing strange hallucinogenic episodes. Patients see unexplained phenomena—one patient reported seeing a new village outside her window that she couldn't recall being built, and on another occasion seeing a girl in her house who needed food.[20] People with Anton's blindness explain their bruises and injuries as a result of clumsiness or absentmindedness, not deficient vision. Their twisting confabulations, in which they rationalize their injuries, provide a way of diagnosing the disease. Insisting that free markets can light up our world, and making excuses when they fail spectacularly, is no less a confabulation than pretending to see when you are blind.

The clinical category into which Anton's blindness falls is called anosognosia—a word invented by the French neurologist Joseph Babinski (1857–1932) and derived from the Greek for "lacking knowledge about disease." It happens not just with a false sense of sight, but with other faculties too. Three anosognosiac patients with left-side paralysis were put in front of a mirror and asked to raise their arms. The arms stayed put but the patients insisted that they were moving. A research assistant who wasn't paralyzed was placed in a chair next to them. He was asked to raise and lower his hand, but he didn't. Two out of the three patients insisted that they saw him raise and lower his hand.[21] Anosognosias like Anton's blindness aren't merely individual afflictions—they're social too, transforming not only the way we see ourselves, but the very possibility of seeing others as they are. Seeing the world through markets not only distorts our sense of our selves, but projects our own disability onto everyone else.

As a metaphor, Anton's blindness helps us appreciate why it is so hard to understand today's economy. We're trapped by a culture and politics that insist that unfettered markets are the way to value the world properly, that we can through the unrestricted exercise of supply and demand make the world more perfect. This is not only delusional—it also distorts the way we see other people. Seeing fellow human beings as mere co-consumers blinds us to the deeper connections between us, and distorts our political choices. As a consumer of food, you can either proclaim your objections or refuse to buy—voice or exit.[22] There's no space to renegotiate so that everyone gets to eat, no way to become a co-producer—there're only the possibilities of supplicating for change, or walking away. I heard a young protester outside the Iranian embassy in London recently use this impoverished political vocabulary of consumerism. She said that she was part of a demonstration there to insist, in the wake of Iran's election fraud, that the government "make it right"—as if the government were experiencing a failure of customer service, which might be addressed by giving appropriate feedback to someone's supervisor.

I am not, however, arguing for a world without markets. The idea of a market as a place in which people with diverse needs exchange goods is one that can be found in every human civilization. What characterizes today's markets is exchange driven not by needs, but by profit.[23] It is pure ideology to think that the best way for society to function is to let markets seek profit, and that the best way for markets to function is with minimal interference. The terms on which markets operate are set by the powerful; our tragedy is to have let this happen. The blindness, the anosognosia here, is our faith in a faculty that routinely betrays us—in the demonstrably false promise that profit-driven markets can point to true value.

Which raises the question of how we are to heal ourselves. History shows that the cure cannot come from government alone, but requires change from within market society. As Polanyi makes clear, the birth of the free market required a great deal of violence, but he also observed something else: People fought back. The Speenhamland laws were introduced because of the anger of a rural public suffering the rapacity of enclosure. Poor laws are not an example of how self-regulating markets turn new things into stuff that might be bought and sold—they are a response to society's demands in the age of self-regulating markets. Polanyi showed how people fought back *against* the expanding market. In this back and forth, Speenhamland provided an example of what Polanyi called the double movement. On the one hand, transforming land and labor into things that might be bought and sold required widespread disenfranchisement—this is the first movement. The second movement is a response from society, which seeks to heal the wounds that the self-regulating market has inflicted. And both these movements happen within the framework of the market society.

Although the relative strength of movement and countermovement varies, this isn't a tug-of-war between markets pulling society forward into the future, and countermovements yanking it back into the past. Countermovements are built out of the politics that people have to hand, and with those politics and associations, entirely new institutions are built like the New Deal in the United States, or the welfare state in Europe. Social change, according to Polanyi's model, isn't a one-step-forward-one-step-back process, a sort of collective Charleston where, after a lot of motion, you end up where you started. It's more like an infinite symphony, with one movement building from the previous one.

Today's countermovements will tweet and blog, using the latest ideas and technology, as well as old-fashioned direct action, to fight for a different and sustainable world. The future will be shaped by our will to imagine a different kind of market society, and new ways of valuing the world without resorting to the tic of free markets. The outline of our twenty-first-century countermovement is the subject of the second part of this book, which looks at how global social movements and organizations are limiting the power of markets and its most powerful agents, and in so doing redefining how democracy might work. But before we can overcome our current blindness, we need to understand more clearly how the culture of the free market affects us, how things become stuff to be bought and sold and how we have all become the blind seers of modern market society—consumers.

(TWO)

BECOMING *HOMO ECONOMICUS*

> 'Tis the time's plague, when madmen lead the blind.
> —WILLIAM SHAKESPEARE, *King Lear*

MILL'S MONSTER

Market society doesn't simply turn things into commodities—it makes its own culture and ideas about human nature and social order. The embodiment of this culture is a man no one has ever met. He was created by one of the key exponents of classical political economy in the nineteenth century, John Stuart Mill, who intended for his creation to shine a light through the fog of human inconstancy, to find a deeper truth about us all.

In forging new scientific ways of thinking about the world, Mill believed that a couple of simplifying assumptions could reveal a deeper reality about how people interacted and behaved. In the same way that "geometry presupposes an arbitrary definition of a line, 'that which has length but not breadth,'" Mill thought that social sciences could use an abstract model to make assumptions about people:

> Just in the same manner [as geometry] does Political Econ-
> omy presuppose an arbitrary definition of man, as a being

who invariably does that by which he may obtain the
greatest amount of necessaries, conveniences, and luxu-
ries, with the smallest quantity of labour and physical self
denial with which they can be obtained in the existing
state of knowledge.[1]

Mill's reasonable assumption was that, in general, people don't waste
resources, and they use them as best they can to get what they want,
but the creature Mill formulated has taken on a life of its own. Meet
Homo economicus, Economic Man, animated by the desire to make
the best of what he has in order to get what he wants. Mill acknowledged the shortcomings of the simplifying assumptions, and cau-
tioned that it was only "in the abstract" that the results from using
this method could be considered true. A page later in his essay
"On the Definition of Political Economy," though, he seems to con-
tradict himself by suggesting that his method is "the *only* method by
which truth can possibly be attained in any department of the social
science."[2] This was a certainty taken to heart by one of the giants of
twentieth-century economic thinking, Gary Becker.

A protégé of Milton Friedman, and a longtime fixture in the University of Chicago economics department, Becker, in his 1976 opus
The Economic Approach to Human Behavior, claimed that "the economic approach provides a usefull framework for understanding *all*
human behavior."[3] Across a range of subjects, from conventional economics to immigration, prisons, racial discrimination, baseball, the
family, time and democracy, Becker has applied the tools of economic
thinking to the entire world. Think of him as the founding father of
Freakonomics. For his contributions to economics, Becker won the
Nobel Prize in Economics in 1992, and in 2007 George W. Bush
awarded him the Presidential Medal of Freedom, the highest civil-
ian honor bestowed by the United States. Becker explains that while
an undergraduate at Princeton, he tired of economics because "it

did not seem to deal with important social problems. I contemplated transferring to sociology, but found that subject too difficult."[4] Today, there is no field in the social sciences untouched by Becker's thinking, and in the early 1980s, he found himself with joint appointments in the departments of economics and sociology at the University of Chicago.

Becker's economic method involves three ideas: first, that everyone and everything is a maximizing animal. People, governments and corporations can all be thought of as *Homo economicus* pursuing, as best they can with the resources that they have, as much of a given thing as they can get. Second, *Homo economicus*'s behavior happens in a market of some sort. Third, Becker's method demands that *Homo economicus*'s preferences are the same across all societies and circumstances.[5] One of his earliest applications of this thinking was to the working of democracy. In a perfect democracy, "individuals endeavor to acquire political office through perfectly free competition for the votes of a broadly based electorate."[6] In other words, a perfect democracy should work like a perfect market, with voters instead of consumers, armed with votes instead of dollars. The trouble with this, as we shall see more forcefully in part two, is that it transforms the business of citizenship into one of constrained choice— democracy becomes an exercise in selection, like picking one of two kinds of soda, without ever probing deeper into why the status quo looks the way it does.

Becker's conservative analysis becomes even more controversial when he turns the tools of economics to the family. Since marriages are voluntary, people can be assumed to be maximizing their utility over the level they'd enjoy were they single, and because lots of people are doing it, we can assume a marriage market. Becker also suggests that there are reasons for marriage that transcend any particular human culture—no matter where you live, "persons in love can reduce the cost of frequent contact and of resource transfers between each other by sharing the same household."[7] With his three tenets of economic method nicely matched up, Becker sets to work. He demonstrates how, setting the wealth of prospective partners to one side, things like beauty, intelligence and education can generate utility, which explains "why, for example, less attractive or less intelligent persons are less likely to marry than are more attractive or more intelligent persons."[8] He footnotes that the statement about attractiveness isn't based on any statistical evidence, but feels able to ask, in a later publication, "Does our analysis justify the popular belief that more beautiful, charming, and talented women tend to marry wealthier and more successful men? . . . It does."[9]

Polygamy gets an analytical treatment too. Comparing it to monogamy, Becker shows on a supply-and-demand diagram how women are better off in a society where husbands can have many wives: Women who wouldn't make the cut as someone's first wife under monogamy might be able to get something for themselves as a second or third wife.[10] The most charitable explanation of this conclusion is Becker's pride in explanations derived from some very basic principles. As economist Barbara Bergmann notes, he rides roughshod over questions of power, tradition and identity, ignoring why it is that women in polygamous relationships are frequently worse off than those in monogamous ones. He ends up sounding like nothing so much as a "loyal Chicagoan [showing] once again that government restrictions on trade (in this case the laws against bigamy) reduce society's well-being."[11]

Government restrictions on trade have been in Becker's crosshairs more recently with his calls both for markets in organs—public welfare would increase if the rich were able to pay the poor for their kidneys—and for immigration, where rights to enter Europe and North America would best be distributed through auction, encouraging the right sort of immigrant, while at the same time swelling government coffers.

Becker's conclusions are, of course, deeply disturbing, yet they all tumble neatly from his small bundle of assumptions. Allowing *Homo economicus* to do as he wants, to give Ayn Rand–style freedom to let the market reign, will, by Becker's measurements, increase welfare. There are a number of problems, though. Let's set aside for the moment the questions around justice and politics that this approach begs, because Becker's project is shaky on its own terms. As behavioral economists are only too happy to point out, the foundation of his arguments around *Homo economicus*'s maximizing behavior is unsound, at least insofar as they apply to people. Dan Ariely's *Predictably Irrational*, for instance, counts the ways in which people aren't at all like the *Homo economicus* in Becker's world.

Beyond systematic human irrationality, Becker's assumption about preferences being the same across all societies just doesn't hold water. In many North American indigenous cultures, generosity is a central behavior in a broader social and economic system. One anecdotal account examined what happened when boys from white and Lakota communities received a pair of lollipops each. Both sets of boys put the first one straight in their mouths. The white boys put the second one in their pockets, while the Native American boys presented it to the nearest boy who didn't have one.[12] It's not surprising to see that culture can shape how resources are accumulated and distributed, and dictate the social priority of saving over sharing, but the experiment also reminds us that the opposite of consumption isn't thrift—it's generosity.

Other experiments have probed white North American society's cultural attitudes toward generosity a little more by playing the Public Goods Game. The game works like this: I give you (and many other people) a fistful of tokens, and tell you that you have to choose between two ways of investing them. You can invest some (or all) of them in my bank, in which case you'll get a guaranteed rate of a penny per token. Or you can invest some (or all) in a community bank. The community bank pays out to everyone, regardless of whether you invested in it, and the more that is put in the pot, the bigger the payout for everyone. It doesn't take many tokens in the pot for the payout to everyone to be bigger than a penny per token. The collectively rational outcome is for everyone to put 100 percent into the chest, but for any individual, the rational decision would be to hope that everyone else puts in 100 percent while you put in 0 percent—which means you get the collective payout *and* the penny per token from your investment in the individual bank account. When high school students in Wisconsin played the game, they didn't behave like *Homo economicus* and put in 0 percent—instead, they put in 42 percent. The experimenters varied everything from the payout schedule to the number of people in the group, and the amount that people put in remained roughly the same. They did it with a general group of college students, and the results were similar. With every possible permutation they could think of, there was only one time that the cooperation rate fell to 20 percent—and that when the game was played by first-year economics graduate students.[13]

Behavioral economics has a variation on this called the Ultimatum Game. You are given $100, and you divide it into two piles. You'll get to keep pile A, and I'll get to keep pile B. Once you've divided the bills, I can either accept whatever bills you stack in pile B, in which case you get pile A, or I can reject pile B, in which case neither of us gets anything. Now, while this may not be a game from which cherished childhood memories will ever be spun, it does tell us a little about the fabric of our society. What's the correct division of cash? Rationally, you'd keep as much, and give me as small an amount, as you could possibly get away with—a dollar, a cent, whatever the smallest increment is—because, again rationally, one cent is better to me than zero cents, and I'd be better off with something rather than nothing.

Most people playing the game, however, do not behave like this. They split it halfway or keep 60 percent and give away 40 percent. But in some cultures, the exchange works according to a different logic entirely. The residents of an island in eastern Indonesia, the Lamalera whale hunters, played the game with cigarettes instead of money, to avoid the appearance of gambling, and the player with the cigarettes on average kept 43 percent and gave away 57 percent. The researchers suggested that this was because the experiment reflected patterns of sharing and fairness in wider Lamalera society, where hunting whales is a cooperative village-level effort.[14] When a whale is killed, the rituals of fairly dividing it are always scrupulously followed.

In no cultures where these games have been played do people behave 100 percent selfishly, although the degree of cooperation varies widely. When the game was played in the jungles of southeastern Peru, where the Machiguenga practice seminomadic horticulture, they cooperated a great deal less, with the majority of people giving either 25 percent or 15 percent of the spoils and keeping the rest. Again, this behavior is attributed to a social structure that offered very little reward for cooperation.[15]

In general, the different outcomes in these games are linked to how society rewards cooperation, and one of the strongest predictors of cooperation was whether people engaged in market transactions, whether they bought and sold things with people beyond their families and villages. In other words, a good predictor of cooperating well in these sorts of games is having been involved in exchange and money in other contexts. This is an important clue. Exchange itself might not be the source of the problem in explaining our current economic crisis—the problem lies in the system that surrounds the act of exchange.

There's another reason why humans are bad at being *Homo economicus*—evolution. Recent experiments in neuroscience and primatology suggest that we're just not wired to be entirely selfish all the time, and that humans have evolved complex behaviors that include in-built desires for altruism and fairness as well as selfishness and avarice. One way of seeing this is with brain scans, which, despite some controversy, offer some suggestive preliminary findings[16] with an experiment in which people were given a series of choices about whether to accept money for themselves or suffer some monetary loss while giving to charity. Those who took the money lit up the part of their brains associated with food and sex, and those who gave the money away lit up an entirely different part of the brain—to do with attachment and bonding.[17]

This spoils the notion that altruism is just another form of selfishness in disguise. Since the parts of the brain involved are distinct, the process is at the very least physiologically different. Evolution suggests that altruism and a range of other nonselfish behaviors have some independent utility, that social relationships of mutual altruism help us to survive. Research with coyotes, for example, reveals that members of the pack who refuse to be a part of the social group are more likely to leave the pack, and face a 55 percent mortality rate, while those who stay face a 20 percent mortality rate.[18] Further proof that we're not hardwired egotists comes from our closest evolutionary cousins—primates. One of the pioneers of this area of research, Frans de Waal, has observed chimpanzees' interactions, trading in multiple "currencies" and exchanging grooming for food or other favors. The chimpanzees were well able to keep track of who had done what to whom, giving and taking fairly. To quote de Waal, "In humans, this psychological mechanism is known as 'gratitude,' and there is no reason to call it anything else in chimpanzees."[19] Gratitude isn't a characteristic of *Homo economicus*.

Gratitude isn't the only trait that primates share with us. They also have an innate sense of fairness. Tests with capuchin monkeys and chimpanzees involved giving tokens to two monkeys. One monkey exchanges the token for a high-value reward—a grape—while the other monkey, the experiment's subject, watches. Immediately afterward, the subject is given a less desirable reward for its token—a cucumber. If they were given the same thing as their partners, capuchin monkey subjects and chimpanzee subjects would behave as utility-maximizing agents, trading their tokens. But if they were treated unfairly, they often refused to complete the transaction, even if they'd have been better off.

Moreover, when the partner monkey was given things "free," without any trade, the subject capuchin monkeys (though not, interestingly, chimpanzees) were even more likely to walk away from the deal. So what does this show? That capuchin monkeys are happy to cooperate, but what seems to aggravate them is unfairness—either in rewards (the difference between grapes and cucumbers) or in behavior (no effort versus having to swap for a token). In tests with groups of chimps who had lived together the longest, they behaved most communally. The slower and possibly more deliberative the chimps were, the more they reacted to inequality.[20] In other words, the most basic childhood playground calls of "That's not fair!" are ones that we share with our closest animal relatives. This "inequity aversion," as it's called by researchers, can even be seen in dogs.[21]

Chimpanzees also punish one another for breaching trust. A chimp who betrays another can expect some sort of retaliation, from denial of food all the way up to a hefty smack in the face. The use of punishment to condemn uncooperative behavior is a fundamental building block of fairness, and a way that society is regulated among chimpanzees.

Humans have an advantage over chimpanzees because we have not only the possibility of punishment, but the quality of mercy too. A particularly striking set of experiments demonstrates this by asking you to put some money for me in an account. The sum grows, and you can then choose how much I should give back to you, threatening me with the option of a fine if I do not cooperate. When you don't threaten me with the fine, I tend to give more money than I would if there were the possibility of a fine.[22] So, having the ability to punish but choosing not to increases cooperation and trust.

What these experiments show is that while our genes may be selfish, we've evolved to transmit them in ways that need us to cooperate, socialize, build and maintain communities, love and share. Unlike Economic Man, people value mercy, fairness, trust, altruism and reciprocation for their own sakes. While *Homo economicus* has only an instrumental interest in these virtues, recent studies are beginning to show that our ability to appreciate the intrinsic value of generosity, sharing and selflessness is central to maximizing our well-being.

MAKING *HOMO ECONOMICUS* HAPPY

When this theory is applied to people, Becker argues that we become *Homo economicus* in a very specific way: Everyone is a producer of his or her own happiness. We obtain our own utility, to use his language, "through the productive activity of combining purchased market goods and services with some of the household's own time."[23] In other words, happiness is what happens when we take stuff, and add to it the time in which we use that stuff. But if the pursuit of happiness is what we're all after, and the economy is based on the assumption that we're greedily in the pursuit of it, can markets bring happiness?[24]

It's almost a cliché that most lottery winners report being less happy after winning their new millions than they were before, but we also know that not having money makes us unhappy. According to *This American Life* (one of the finest radio shows in the United States or anywhere else), dentists have seen a marked rise in broken teeth as a result of the recession—people are grinding their teeth at night, concerned about how they're going to pay the bills—but this evidence is, precisely, anecdotal. Recently, there has been a flood of research on happiness, much of it spawned in economics departments, investigating precisely how to get that warm inner glow that money often fails to provide.

The dismal science is taking happy pills, and discovering the truth of an almost universal cultural axiom—the *pursuit* of wealth doesn't create happiness. Although the path that consumer society lays out for happiness leads to the individual ownership of a house and new car, research increasingly points to the psychological harm associated with cupidity. A San Francisco Bay area psychiatrist observes that his patients have "bought the BMW, and they have the $3 million Mill Valley house. And they still wake up in the morning and say, 'I don't feel good about myself.' "[25] It's not just the bourgeoisie in Marin County who are afflicted. In one longitudinal study, 12,000 incoming freshmen from twenty-one select colleges in the United States took part in a survey in 1976 that included questions about their financial goals and life satisfaction in a number of areas. They were surveyed again in 1995. Those who placed more importance on money in 1976 were less satisfied in 1995.[26] Another survey, of 266 business students, found the same thing: The greater importance a person placed on money, the lower their reported level of well-being.[27] The greatest negative impacts were among those respondents whose motivation for earning money was to alleviate feelings of self-doubt.

At an international level, one of the most important pieces of research on money and happiness is called the Easterlin paradox, named after economist Richard Easterlin. In a 1974 article, he found that people with higher-than-average incomes reported being happier than their poorer counterparts. No big surprise there, but he also found that once a country had moved beyond a level of income where basic needs for housing, food, water and energy could be met, average happiness did not increase. The paradox, in other words, is that after a certain point, more money doesn't make us happier. Instead, we find ourselves on a hedonic treadmill, in which happiness is about matching our level of consumption with our peers, and when they do better and we don't, even if we are better off in absolute terms, we are less happy.

More recent data suggest that while it is possible for a nation to increase its average happiness, the cost of doing so is very high. After reaching the level of sufficient income to meet basic needs, happiness becomes geometrically linked to income. So to go from one to two units of happiness might take ten dollars, but after hitting the point at which our basic needs are met, to go from two to three units of happiness would take one hundred dollars, from three to four would take one thousand dollars, and so on.[28]

In the meantime, of course, happiness *within* the economy is dictated by the difference between people's expectations of relative income and their actual capacity to achieve it. Many people with BMWs and $3 million houses report that they are, in fact, happy, which is why those who are unhappy are encouraged to think of themselves as dysfunctional, and to seek psychotherapy. As Cornell economist Robert Frank argues, happiness achieved through the acquisition of yachts and Rolexes has profound social consequences, particularly when inequality is increasing. The gap between the richest and poorest in the United States has been growing steadily— between 1979 and 2005, posttax income for the top 1 percent increased by nearly 200 percent, while for the poorest fifth of the population, it went up by 6 percent.[29] More and more wealth is concentrated in the hands of a few, whose lifestyles are glorified by the media, which means that the expectations of the majority have become increasingly beyond their means.[30] We become less happy with goods that, ordinarily, we'd have been overjoyed with. Think about your television—chances are that five years ago you'd have been more than happy with it, but today, not so much. Nothing has changed about your TV, but confronted by hours of brazen and subliminal advertisements for flatter, bigger, brighter ones, all of a sudden, it seems clunky.

The inflation of what are known as "positional goods"—the kinds of goods that reflect your social status back to you and to society—is why rising inequality makes the majority of people less happy. Worse, this inequality is rising internationally,[31] which might explain the recent rise in crime in Bhutan—once the world's happiest nation. The steep dive in the country's gross national happiness, an index of how well its people are doing, independent of what they earn, coincided with the importation of satellite television by the new Oxford-educated king of Bhutan. Television's images of impossible lifestyles, body shapes, clothes and accessories have resulted in not only a deep resentment but a crime wave, as young people steal in order to afford the trinkets sold on Rupert Murdoch's Star Network.[32] TV presents a world unattainable to the majority of people both in the United States and Bhutan and, in seeking to recover their happiness, the youth have gone shoplifting.

At a national level, this suggests that both money and its big brother, gross domestic product (GDP), are poor measures of well-being and happiness.[33] Other indicators of social health and happiness not only exist, but are far more revealing. The Human Development Index published by the United Nations Development Programme bundles national income with data about health and education. The Gender Empowerment Measure, also from the United Nations, shows how women's rights are respected in different countries, and the extent of participation in political, social and economic life. The New Economics Foundation in the United Kingdom has published a rich set of data under the rubric of "national well-being" that looks at everything from personal feelings of happiness and vitality to supportive social relations. In European rankings, Denmark comes out on top almost every time. Britain comes thirteenth out of twenty-two, just ahead of France.[34]

These indices are attempts to capture the elusive notion of the good life, what the ancient Greeks called *eudaimonia*, in which happiness is linked to human flourishing, rather than cash. There is a branch of psychology that urges us to think of happiness as a by-product of something deeper—psychological well-being. The more psychological well-being we have, the more happiness we produce. Generosity and altruism are ways of building that repository of well-being, but they also have the benefit of creating happiness in the short run too. This hypothesis helps to explain a problem in the field of happiness studies right now—what happens when happiness is not acquired by receiving money, but by giving it away.[35] One experiment, performed with all sorts of controls, showed that

1. generosity doesn't directly lead to happiness, and
2. happiness doesn't cause generosity;
3. being rich doesn't cause generosity or happiness, but
4. psychological well-being is a source for both generosity and happiness.

There's a paradox here, one that John Stuart Mill understood well. To be happy, you need to forget to try to be happy:

> Those only are happy (I thought) who have their minds fixed on some object other than their own happiness, on the happiness of others, on the improvement of mankind, even on some art or pursuit, followed not as a means, but as itself an ideal end. Aiming thus at something else, they find happiness by the way.[36]

What Mill understood, and Becker seems not to, is the richer human experience that is destroyed if we try to live as *Homo economicus*, the bonds that rely on their *not* being treated as the fodder for markets and maximization. Becker's analysis and policy is a vector for Anton's blindness—yet it is pervasive, and it is so for a reason beyond its analytical tidiness. The applications of his method are not innocent—his parsimony is political. Invariably, it supports policies that favor the powerful, whether rationalizing the persistence of economic monopoly, patriarchy or trade in body parts. Were Becker merely an overenthusiastic advocate of a particular brand of analysis, it might be possible to enjoy the antics of an academic and his economic hammer, for whom the whole world is a nail. That the trace of his methods can be found so widely within social science, particularly those popular in the United States, suggests that he cannot so easily be dismissed. The French philosopher Michel Foucault, in his 1978–79 lectures at the Collège de France, took Becker very seriously indeed, arguing that he embodies pernicious and pervasive trends in modern market society.[37]

Far from being a crank, Becker is both a symptom and cause of the market society's new order. He is the herald of a fully neoliberal culture, one in which we internalize the virtues of the market, in which we behave as individual entrepreneurs of our own happiness, moving resources in markets and adding their time in order to create utility, thus consuming our way to happiness. The absurdity of Becker's conclusions on the family, immigration and medicine is a sign that current market society has not yet caught up with his theory. But give it time. We have seen how society's assent to where markets belong can change. The global life insurance industry today is worth over \$2 trillion,[38] but it was once a practice widely banned in Europe, and one which only overcame the moral stigma of "cash for death" after the 1840s in the United States.[39]

In advocating the spread of a world of markets and *Homo*

economicus, Becker contributes to the culture of market society in ways that serve the material interests of particular groups. Culture doesn't just hang in the air, but matters on the ground, in the world of flesh-and-blood people. Becker's views advance the interests of creatures far more akin to *Homo economicus*, and more at home within market society, than we are: corporations.

THREE

THE CORPORATION

> He who fights with monsters should take care lest he
> thereby become a monster. And if you gaze for long into
> an abyss, the abyss gazes also into you.
> —FRIEDRICH NIETZSCHE, *Beyond Good and Evil*

Every civilization has had traders and markets, but modern market
society has spawned the corporation, a novel human creation moved
by the search for profit, and which has in its short history come to
dominate our planet. In most countries, corporations are defined as
"legal people"—they enjoy the same kinds of rights and obligations
that normal humans do, even if they aren't made of flesh and blood.
In their fine documentary *The Corporation*, Mark Achbar, Jennifer
Abbott and Joel Bakan take modern law at its word and ask, "If the
corporation were a person, what sort of person would it be?" Using the
American Psychiatric Association's Diagnostic and Statistical Manual
of Mental Disorders (DSM-IV) to match behavior against a list of
symptoms, they find that corporations exhibit many of the characteristics that define psychopaths.[1] The American Psychiatric Association
classifies psychopaths and sociopaths under the general diagnosis of
"antisocial personality disorder," and to be diagnosed with the disorder, the patient needs to meet three out of these seven criteria:

1. Failure to conform to social norms with respect to lawful behaviors as indicated by repeatedly performing acts that are grounds for arrest
2. Deceitfulness, as indicated by repeated lying, use of aliases, or conning others for personal profit or pleasure
3. Impulsivity or failure to plan ahead
4. Irritability and aggressiveness, as indicated by repeated physical fights or assaults
5. Reckless disregard for safety of self or others
6. Consistent irresponsibility, as indicated by repeated failure to sustain consistent work behavior or honor financial obligations
7. Lack of remorse, as indicated by being indifferent to or rationalizing having hurt, mistreated, or stolen from another

The filmmakers find that corporations do indeed behave in these ways, breaking the law if they can, dissembling and hiding their behavior, sacrificing long-term welfare for short-term profit, being aggressively litigious, flouting health and safety codes, welching on payments to suppliers and workers and never once feeling a pang of remorse. In one case, to pick a serial offender, Monsanto poisoned an entire Alabama town and withheld the knowledge that it was doing so because it did not want, according to a confidential memo, to "lose a single dollar in business." The details, uncovered in a *Washington Post* report in 2002, are ghastly. For decades, Monsanto employees suppressed knowledge about what happened when they dumped toxic waste from their Anniston, Alabama, plant into local streams—the fish died within ten seconds, spurting blood and shedding skin. A representative from Monsanto's spinoff, Solutia, said it was unfair to judge the company's environmental performance in the 1970s by modern standards: "Did we do some things we wouldn't do today? Of course. But that's a little piece of a big story," he said.

"If you put it all in context, I think we've got nothing to be ashamed of."[2] While this stretches credulity just a little, it is entirely believable that this is rational, if psychotic, behavior for a company to undertake.

Corporations don't, however, have to break the law in order to do damage. The normal operation of market society means that there are everyday forms of "nothing to be ashamed of," and they come from the way profit-driven markets value the world. When companies make decisions about what they can produce and at what price, they are doing pretty much what *Homo economicus* is meant to do, acting as coldly rational beings, motivated exclusively by profit, in a world where the factors of production can be bought and sold in markets.

In order for profits to be high, corporations organize workers, raw materials, capital equipment and rents so that their costs are as low as possible. Let's take the hypothetical example of McDonald's, and follow the route it takes to calculate those costs. As an institution with a mission to return profits, it's keen to squeeze down what it pays for the things that go into making hamburgers, everything from beef to labor to rent to safety testing. The more it can drive down costs below those of its competitors, the more money it stands to make. If McDonald's is able to cause the emission of pollutants like CO_2 without having to pay for it, then the costs of the firm are not the same as the broader social cost. In modern economics, the term used for these social costs is "externalities." These are the costs that somehow slip through the net of prices. It was the early twentieth-century English economist Arthur Pigou who coined the idea that markets often miss the wider implications of their behavior because of a flaw in their very fabric—a fault that affects what is internal to prices and what is external.

To see externalities in action, let's return to the Big Mac's carbon footprint, to pick just one environmental impact among many. According to one estimate, the energy cost of the 550 million Big Macs sold in the United States every year is $297 million, producing a greenhouse gas footprint of 2.66 billion pounds of CO_2 equivalent.[3] In addition to the carbon in the footprint, we might want to add the broader environmental impact in terms of both water use and soil degradation, together with the hidden health costs of treating diet-related illness such as diabetes and heart disease.

While none of these costs are reflected in the drive-thru price of a Big Mac, they still have to be paid for by someone. It's just that they are paid not by the McDonald's Corporation but by society as a whole, when we pay the costs of environmental disasters, climate-change-related migration and higher health care costs. According to a report by the Centre for Science and the Environment in India, a burger grown from beef raised on clear-cut forest should really cost about two hundred dollars.[4]

That particular number may seem exorbitant, but when examined on a grand scale, the full costs of a four-dollar Big Mac may be even higher because, in addition to not paying their externalized costs, corporations often get a range of subsidies. Consumers in the United States are paying for cheap hamburgers directly through their tax dollars. The meat in McDonald's hamburgers is fattened on corn, the most highly subsidized crop in America. A report from Tufts University claims that the American beef industry saves some $562 million a year, on average, by fattening cattle on subsidized corn.[5] Total subsidies to corn topped $4.6 billion in 2006.[6]

When it comes to low wages, taxpayers also support America's favorite fast-food meal, through a "social subsidy." The average full-time fast-food worker makes just over $15,000 per year.[7] These poverty-line wages are supplemented by Medicare, food stamps, child nutrition, direct government payments, and other government services. The total estimated cost of state and federal payouts for Burger King employees alone is over $273 million a year.[8] Multiply that over all major fast-food outlets, and the government is shelling out well over a billion dollars a year to subsidize the industry's subpoverty wages. According to Phil Mattera from Good Jobs First in Washington, D.C., "Some of the big retailers and fast food companies simply won't provide adequate health care benefits for their employees. They have to turn somewhere, and if eligible they turn to state funded programs. We're seeing large companies that can afford it turning to these programs. . . . Companies like Wal-Mart have been known to encourage employees to sign up for taxpayer funded programs."[9]

Not all the social costs of cheap food are subsidies. One 1995 study of public health costs spent treating diet-related disease due to excessive meat consumption in the United States estimated the total cost at $30–60 billion a year.[10] Again, this is a global problem. In China, the public health costs of obesity and diet-related diseases far exceed those of diseases resulting from malnutrition.[11]

These direct and indirect social costs represent only a fraction of the dollar sum missing from the price of food. Antibiotics are becoming less effective due to widespread prophylactic use in the livestock industry. Pesticide contamination, nutrient runoff, and greenhouse gas emissions are compounding the environmental debt of industrialized agriculture. Voluntarily offsetting the 2.66 billion tons of carbon dioxide released in the production of Big Macs each year would cost between $7.3 and $35.6 million dollars.[12] One estimate by Chinese researchers concluded that for every private dollar spent on pesticides, the public will have to spend eighty cents to clean them up.[13] The "dead zone" in the Gulf of Mexico, largely due to agricultural nutrient runoff (in the form of nitrogen, phosphorous fertilizers and animal waste), is another example of environmental cost. Nutrient overload (called eutrophication) causes plants to grow excessively, choking navigable waterways with weeds. When the plants die, they rot, sucking the oxygen from the water and killing fisheries. One study estimated the cost of eutrophication in the

United Kingdom to be $105–160 million annually, with the direct cost of government clean-up programs from nutrient runoff at over $77 million.[14]

The two-hundred-dollar hamburger is, inevitably, an approximation. Accounting for the real environmental costs is a tricky business, because we do not know either the long-term environmental consequences or what the cost might be to future generations to clear up today's mess.[15] A University of Iowa study reviewed various valuation studies about the true cost of U.S. agriculture. By adding together the indirect costs to natural resources, wildlife, ecosystem biodiversity and human health, it estimated that the hidden price of U.S. agriculture lies between $5.7 and $16.9 billion a year. Impacts due to crop production are figured to be $4.9 to $16.1 billion per year, and livestock production in the range of $714 to $739 million more than the price that consumers pay at the checkout.[16] Another study estimated the external costs to agriculture in the U.K. at £3.7 billion a year.[17] While these types of studies leave plenty of room for interpretation, what is abundantly clear is that the market fails to account for all actual costs in the price we pay at the checkout counter.

Ecological debt is not just a theoretical exercise. The World Bank estimates that China's environmental costs add up to 8 percent of its GDP.[18] Again, agriculture provides striking examples of these costs. Farmers in northern China, where 95 percent of the nation's wheat is grown, have drawn down water resources so that their thirsty, chemical-intensive agricultural technologies will work. Overuse of water, and the resulting lower water tables (combined with unlimited use of grasslands for grazing, deforestation and climate change) is causing much of China to turn to desert. Some 18.1 percent of the country's formerly productive lands are now deserts and drifting sand.[19] Dust storms regularly sweep down from the north, blowing through China's industrial zones, picking up pollutants and becoming a miasma, enveloping cities from China to Japan. In 2001, part of a storm blew all the way into the United States, and was dense enough to linger over Denver, blocking views of the Rockies. The Chinese Research Department for Industry, Transportation and Trade estimates that desertification directly causes 54 billion yuan (US$7.89 billion) in losses each year due to the health, economic and environmental effects of sandstorms and water shortages.[20] The World Bank estimates the costs of desertification in China to be even higher—some $31 billion a year.[21]

The winter of 2008 was a particularly difficult one for China's arid north, with 43 percent of the winter wheat crop in danger of failing.[22] While this was not entirely due to the unsustainable use of water in agriculture, as Li Guangyong, a water conservation expert at the China Agricultural University in Beijing, points out, "There simply is not enough. And if reservoirs are emptying and wells drying up, it is because of the wasteful way in which Chinese farmers use water."[23] The low cost of wheat in both China and the rest of the world during the past several decades of intensified agricultural production in effect means that we have been running up a tab against future harvests. The same is true for a host of other commodities whose overproduction is based on a dwindling resource base. Indeed, water shortage is one of the major reasons why China and other countries are involved in land-grabbing in developing countries rich in rain and groundwater—particularly in Latin America and Africa.

China's failure to value water is one example of the failure of almost every country to value the natural world in the production of goods for the market. Ecosystem services such as pollination, water filtration, erosion control, soil fertility and regulation of water and climate systems are valuable, however, and it's possible to hazard a price on quite how much they're worth.[24] Returning to food, one New Zealand study estimated that the total economic value of ecosystem services in organic agriculture systems in New Zealand ranged from US$1,610 to US$19,420 per hectare annually, compared to conventional agricultural costs ranging from US$1,270 to US$14,570 per hectare annually. The value of ecosystem services in organic fields ranged from US$460 to US$5,240 per hectare annually versus US$50–1,240 in conventional fields.[25] In other words, farming systems that pay attention to sustainability put more back into the earth than systems using conventional industrial techniques—but they aren't rewarded for it. This is why food grown through industrial agriculture, which doesn't pay the full price of its ecological misbehavior, appears cheaper at the supermarket checkout.[26] What the hidden costs show is that this is not cheap food: It's *cheat* food. What is true for food is no less true for every other consumer item. Sustainably produced goods and services appear to cost more, because their cheaper equivalents are cutting corners in the short run but generating long-run costs that we'll all have to bear.

This systematic distortion in valuation is a direct consequence of profit-driven markets. Because they are looking to reduce costs, corporations are hardwired to wriggle out of paying social and environmental costs if they can possibly avoid it. This is not to say that the people who work in these organizations are vicious or cruel or callous. I recently debated Unilever's director of sustainable agriculture, Jan Kees Vis, by all accounts a decent, committed, thoughtful and caring man, trying to do right by the planet. He oversees many initiatives that benefit both the planet and his company—saving water, using less fossil fuel and so on. But as he admitted, the minute that he adopts a policy that benefits the environment but harms the company is the minute he will lose his job.

Corporations are *Homo economicus*. Quite rationally and without malice, they try to increase their profits by any means, legal and occasionally illegal. Corporations that don't follow this cardinal law of the jungle will go out of business, which means that whatever else a corporation makes, it'll invariably produce externalities.[27]

Everyone agrees that if we make a mess, we should clean it up. If prices really reflected environmental and social costs, then prices really *could* telegraph the relative abundance and scarcity of things. And if some goods produce positive social and environmental *benefits*—as agroecological farming does—and if that's reflected in prices, the market can successfully use prices to allocate resources to their most efficient use. This shouldn't be an optional "ethical consumer" choice for those who choose to buy products that don't pollute the planet. If products do generate costs and benefits, then those need to be reflected in the price in order for the economic logic of markets to work properly. Otherwise, this is corporate subsidy on a massive scale, and there's nothing free marketers claim to like less than a subsidy. You'd be forgiven for thinking that this ongoing bailout from nature and society to private enterprise is what puts the "free" in free market—despite its protests, corporate capitalism has yet to prove that it can operate without these kinds of subsidies.

When negative externalities are not paid for, the beneficiaries are in effect engaging in theft from those who bear the cost of their behavior. The language of theft implies a victim, and in a broad sense, everyone suffers from these externalities. Add up the health impacts from losing the ozone layer, the loss of fish stocks and ecosystem services provided by trees, the contamination of water by industrial agriculture and the adjustment to a world with more floods and drought because of climate change, and you end up with quite a tab. If humanity had to pay for the consequences of a degraded ecosystem, the bill could, according to one recent study, run to about $47 trillion. But the bill isn't split evenly. Another recent study estimated the environmental footprint—the hidden costs generated through consumption and production choices—of rich countries on poor ones. It included only six areas: ozone depletion, overfishing, deforestation, climate change, mangrove destruction and intensified agriculture. It will come as no surprise to learn that middle- and high-income countries pollute themselves, but they also outsource their pollution, costing poor countries more than $5 trillion in ecological damage. By contrast, the footprint of poor countries on rich ones is $0.68 trillion. The ecological debt of rich countries to poor ones dwarfs the entire third-world debt owed by poor countries to rich ones, which is only $1.8 trillion.[28]

This unevenness, the systematic tilt of costs from rich to poor, from powerful to disempowered, helps explain why these externalities are allowed to continue—because wealthier consumers share the spoils of the theft. If I buy a hamburger that should cost fifty times more than it does, I see a benefit, at least in the short run. Artificially low prices are the consumers' dividend from this system of profit taking, which has given us clothes that are cheaper to buy than clean and phones that are cheaper to replace than repair. It is through these "bargains" that we are conscripted into modern consumer capitalism. Of course, the circumstances under which I buy the hamburger, or anything else, matter a great deal. Consumers might well want to buy better, healthier, tastier food where the price really does reflect the full cost, but with many households earning less than a living wage, bargain hunting has become a form of social policy.[29]

It's important, then, not to lay the blame entirely at consumers' doors and to consider how we become consumers in the first place. We may have been seduced by the flood of cheap goods whose real costs are either deferred or paid by others, but this doesn't explain why we want the goods themselves. There's a subtle process at work here, a social construction in which we learn how to consume, and how to value our time, our happiness and each other. Corporations may be the creatures of modern market society, but in order for profits to flow, they need to conscript consumers to the market. Prices are part of the recruitment material. To see more clearly the frontier of power between consumer and producer, where supply meets demand, it's helpful to explore the limit case—to examine what happens when there's no label to see because the price is zero.

BEHIND THE SCENES AT A FREE LUNCH

Who, after all, doesn't like free stuff? Free samples, free games, free lunches, free phones, free TV—these are things from which we've all derived at least some satisfaction. Where could the harm possibly lie? Why, to use two of the English language's blandest clichés, is there no such thing as a free lunch, and why shouldn't one look a gift horse in the mouth? There's a systemic answer; that is, a consistent consequence of what happens when coolly rational corporations meet irrational human beings whose irrationality becomes even more pronounced when things are being given away for free in supermarkets and malls, on television and online. The tactic is always the same. The company has a business model that involves making a bet. It wagers that by offering you, the consumer, something for free, you'll be enticed back again into the store in the future, and that while you're picking up your free item, you will shell out for something that's a little pricier, consume a little more than you otherwise would, and nurture benign feelings about the particular brand paying for you.

Nothing wrong in that. You win because you get more stuff, and the company wins because it gets more cash. Looked at more closely, however, this free exchange is in fact an attempt to change your buying decisions and preferences. Economics deliberately turns a blind eye to the question of why people like what they like. Indeed, a common phrase in the profession is *De gustibus non est disputandum*— there's no accounting for taste—but corporations are constantly trying to adjust those tastes, and we ignore this at our peril. If someone tried to adjust your preferences for heroin by offering you free samples, you would likely refuse because you have a clear picture in your head of how drug addiction would change your preferences, and you know you don't want your preferences changed in that way. Clearly, the analogy isn't perfect—the exchange of free things may not be acutely addictive—but it does suggest that our choices are much less the product of rational contemplation, and much more subject to manipulation, than we might like to believe.

On February 3, 2009, the U.S. restaurant chain Denny's decided to give away a free breakfast of two pancakes, two eggs, two sausages and two pieces of bacon—for which it usually charges $6 (well, all right, $5.99).[30] The company bet that it could get coverage in every major newspaper, and develop a deeper customer base, by giving its food away for a day. So it did. Two million people came—some waited for an hour or more. The total cost to Denny's—including advertising at the Super Bowl, the ingredients to make breakfast and the labor to cook it—came to $5 million.[31] When asked whether it was worth it, the CEO of Denny's paused and, after factoring in the sales of high-margin products like soda, said, "We'll do better than break even."[32]

There's no such thing as a free breakfast, after all. Nor, indeed, is there such a thing as a free lunch. Here's Rudyard Kipling describing the nineteenth-century version of the free lunch in San Francisco in his *American Notes*:

> I was absolutely alone in this big city of white folk. By in-
> stinct I sought refreshment and came upon a bar-room
> full of bad Salon pictures in which men with hats on the
> backs of their heads were wolfing food from a counter. It
> was the institution of the "free lunch" I had struck. You
> paid for a drink and got as much as you wanted to eat. For
> something less than a rupee a day a man can feed him-
> self sumptuously in San Francisco, even though he be a

> bankrupt. Remember this if ever you are stranded in
> these parts.[33]

It's not terribly dissimilar to the Denny's breakfast, and the strategy of luring people in with food, and selling them immensely profitable beverages at the same time, has hardly changed. Again, the "free" turns out to be a gamble, in which our hunger for something for nothing is flipped back into a profit for the corporation.

So what would it look like to behave rationally in an exchange for free stuff? Economist Richard McKenzie describes how he bought his new computer in his book *Why Popcorn Costs So Much at the Movies*. The manufacturer offered him the option of getting a free printer, which he took. He knew that the manufacturer would make its money back on expensive cartridges, so when the printer ran out of ink, he did the rational thing—he threw it away.[34] Appalled? If it strikes us as wasteful to throw away a free printer, even if it's the rational thing to do, that's a sentiment we ought to hold on to. McKenzie is behaving like *Homo economicus*, and therefore beating the computer manufacturer at its own game, but the reason most of us are susceptible to these tricks is because we sense that there's something wrong with throwing free things away, not least because the free good must have cost *something*, and *someone* had to pay for it.

Consider this example: My cell phone company gives me a free handset, bristling with features, so I become a regular contract subscriber or buyer of pay-as-you-go minutes. I am pleased, not least because I can now navigate through the city without having to remember where I am, and I have the pleasure of palming the latest little gadget. In order for these features to work, I'll have to pay a little bit more, to buy either an app or bandwidth. Clearly, many people think it's worth it. Indeed, there's a cell phone arms race, in which increasingly swanky phones become socially necessary. These new phones come with new applications and uses that, again, become socially indispensible for the user, and permanent sources of revenue for the provider. In the United States in 2007, cell phone expenditure per customer reached six hundred dollars per year (surpassing that of a landline for the first time). That's a lot of cash, which gets divided out fairly unevenly.

In 2009, the cell phone company Nokia posted profits of €490 million, on €12.7 billion sales, with a dividend over 20 percent higher than in the previous year. To make its phones, as makers of electronic equipment the world over do, it uses minerals extracted from bloody conflict in the Congo, where 70 percent of the world's reserves of coltan are found. Coltan is the source of niobium and tantalum, used to make the capacitors at the heart of most portable electronic gadgetry. In patrolling access to these resources, military units in the Congo have raped, tortured, enslaved and killed. Women struggling to bring up children in the Congo have a life expectancy of forty-seven years, continue to suffer through the world's worst rape epidemic and earn just over half what men do—$191 per year.[35] This happens whether coltan prices are high or low, but with prices down at the moment, workers in the coltan mines now have to work much harder to be able to earn the same amount that they did in the boom years. These are the bloody externalities of electronics in general, but they look even darker when we are duped into believing we are getting something like a cell phone for free.

New Kinds of Free

The kinds of externalities associated with free things aren't always so visceral. Technology has changed the scale of free exchange and has also spawned a new range of free goods and services, each with their own hidden and subtle costs. *The New York Times* Web site offers me the chance to read the news for free, and it attracts millions more readers than those who actually pay for a two-dollar print copy. As a result, the *Times* is hemorrhaging cash. The story's even more dire for smaller newspapers. The revenue stream from classified advertisements has been captured by services like Craigslist, decimating the market for the local press. This, in turn, has costs.

As revenues fall, editors are reading the economic signals, scaling back their news coverage and firing journalists. It is invariably cheaper to recycle press releases and opinions than to pay for investigative journalism and public accountability. The biggest casualty here is the decline of local civic engagement that a newspaper provides—a community without the watchdog of a free press is a community without a commons.

This is the brave new world of free goods, offering the promise of future riches and the certainty of present sacrifice. In an influential essay available free online, Kevin Kelly, the cofounder of *Wired*, argues that while the Internet is one big copying machine, there is nonetheless money to be made, by providing personalized (free song, insert your kid's name for forty dollars), instant (get it at the library next week free, or online now for a fee), genuine (download the track free, but the signed CD will cost fifty dollars), live (read the Web page free, but hire the blogger to speak in person) and accessible (hunt around in a library, or save time and get it from us) versions of something that can't be copied.

These are the tactics of future digital free giveaways, and if the future is, as the pundits claim, bulging with free things, the past prepares us for what to expect. The giving away of things for free isn't new, after all. Consider the activity that takes up the largest slice of the day after work and sleep: watching TV. In the United Kingdom, people watch on average over two hours of it a day. In the United States, the figure is closer to four hours. In some countries, the owner of the TV might need to pay the national broadcaster or the cable company, and some service providers might be able to charge to watch special programming. In the main, though, plopping yourself in front of the small screen appears to be a free activity that doesn't incur costs.

On closer inspection, the price and the costs of programming can be wildly out of joint. Consider the world's largest TV event: the soccer World Cup. The 2010 final will be watched by 1.5 billion people. The government of South Africa has already spent US$2 billion on hosting the World Cup. In order to beautify the cities for the thousands of fans who will come to watch the games, the government is currently involved in "slum clearance," in which poor people are kicked out of cities in scenes strikingly evocative of the apartheid era. Shackdwellers are being removed to "alternative accommodation" in areas where there are no jobs, schools or health care facilities, and left to fend for themselves. These social costs, of course, will not be borne by the planet's World Cup Final viewers. The only price we'll pay is suffering through the halftime MasterCard and Coca-Cola ads.

Every advertisement also has a cost. When it comes to the World Cup, the advertisements on the screens will be for products that externalize the environmental and social costs of production (Sony's e-waste, Adidas's sweatshops), encourage debt (Visa), depend on fossil-fuel consumption that's destroying the planet (Emirates, Kia) or are just a cocktail of chemicals (Coke). This last example is particularly telling. Anne Becker observed the horrific consequences of introducing U.S. television images to Fijian adolescents, where she saw rates of eating disorders rocket from 0 to 12 percent within three years.[36] Girls in neighboring islands talk of the relative desirability of a Coke-shaped body over a Fanta-shaped one. Here is an accelerated version of a global problem, where the rapid introduction of modern consumer culture has had devastating effects, on boys as well as girls. In the United States, a recent study found that by banning junk-food advertising, the number of overweight children aged between three and eleven could be cut by a fifth, and the number of overweight adolescents by 14 percent.[37]

Externalities are partly a function of the size of corporations. Although they're taught as the exception in economics classes, monopolies and oligopolies like Google, Apple, Coke and Wal-Mart are the rule in the world of consumer products. One of the things that distinguishes a monopoly from a small business in a competitive market is that while a competitive business has to sell at the price the market dictates, monopolies are so powerful, they have a choice. They can fix either the price that they want to sell at, or fix the quantity they sell. But in the longer term, they can influence both how much they sell *and* how much you're prepared to pay for it.

In Southern Africa, a version of the free Linux computer operating system has been distributed by nongovernmental organizations (NGOs) to people with some of the lowest numbers of computers per person anywhere on earth. Seeing this as a threat to Windows' position as the dominant computing platform in sub-Saharan Africa, Microsoft has "sold" thousands of copies of Windows for a nominal fee of three dollars in many poor countries. In Namibia, Microsoft has even gone so far as to attempt to undercut an NGO that provides free Linux software by offering free copies of Windows *and* free computers to go with them.[38] While some school principals and teachers in Namibia suspect that Microsoft's long-term plan is to charge monopoly prices once the free Linux alternatives have been driven out of business, their limited budgets mean that they cannot resist such short-term bargains. The irony here, of course, is that free software is being killed by "free" software, but once Windows drives the competition out of the market, and pushes its vision of who gets to write, understand and modify the code, the price will go up, and people will be less free to choose.

This may not sound alarming, but there's reason for concern when this sort of tactic is used elsewhere in the Global South, with a very different product. There's nothing freer than mother's milk, but despite a vast body of research that proves definitively the superiority of breast-feeding over other forms of infant nutrition, baby-food companies have engaged in a systemic and protracted disinformation campaign to convince mothers to substitute infant formula for breast milk. One way to discourage breast-feeding has been the distribution of free infant formula by baby-food marketers. If you're a lactating mother, feeding free formula to your baby means stopping breast-feeding, which will cause you to stop lactating, making you dependent on the inferior substitute. Through this kind of marketing, baby-food companies have aggressively distributed free samples resulting in the deaths of up to 1.3 million babies, and millions of dollars of profit, annually.[39]

Again, the story follows a pattern. Mothers, particularly those on a low income, are seduced not only by short-term pecuniary benefits of "free," but by the misleading claims of infant-formula manufacturers, whose primary motivation is profit, not public health. Free becomes a way of creating consumers. In the case of baby-milk formula, it's a way for the makers of milk to manufacture a market for their product, and a way of fostering customer loyalty. Infant-formula manufacturers are behaving entirely rationally, and appear to be powerful enough to get away with it. As a result of public outcry in Europe and North America in the 1980s, the World Health Organization drew up the International Code of Marketing of Breast-Milk Substitutes, but it hasn't solved the problem. In a recent article, Annelies Allain and Yeong Joo Kean reported on the huge number of violations to the code of conduct, as well as the straightforward legal violations in selling contaminated product with incidents involving almost every major manufacturer of infant formula around the world.[40]

The baby-milk case is an extreme version of a wider phenomenon— that "free" can be a way of press-ganging us into behavior that we wouldn't otherwise choose had we been confronted with the full costs before we chose to pay nothing. Free becomes all the more seductive when our budgets arc tight, but this is why "free" also bursts the bubble of our pretense that we are rational economic agents, and conscripts us into the role of consumer. We may end up getting something that we appreciate, and even want—I'm writing this on free open-source software (and we'll come to discuss why that's different in a later chapter). "Free" might well open up new possibilities, but when it happens at the intersection of irrational people and for-profit corporations, particularly corporations with market power, there is invariably a hidden cost. The paradox of "free" corporate giveaways is how much they can enchain us.

Of course, promotional corporate strategies aren't the only way that free exchange happens. The French sociologist Marcel Mauss wrote *The Gift* to explore the complex social relations that surround the acts of giving and receiving. He concluded that, in sociology as in economics, there's rarely anything that comes free from expectations of reciprocity and respect. Under market society, the social bonds of exchange fall under the sign of profit. When it comes to free baby-milk powder, the rules and culture of exchange are written by corporations, those fictional "legal people" who seek profit wherever they can. For these entities, "free" is a bet, with odds and a degree of unpredictability, but one thing is certain. Whether something is free or costs $100 million, it will share the same features that arise from the profit-driven markets that make the goods possible in the first place. The blood on our cell phones suggests that there are wider externalities in the everyday cut and thrust of modern consumer capitalism, and those costs are ones that are generated through the normal daily operation of the way market society values the world.

It might seem as if the solution to this bloodshed lies in better ethics. There's a boomlet in talk about morality in markets, these days—from Harvard academic Michael Sandel's fine Reith Lectures[41] to the decidedly less convincing Lecce Framework of "Common Principles and Standards for Propriety, Integrity and Transparency" endorsed by the Group of Eight largest economies in July 2009. In official discussions, unethical usually means something that one should be ashamed of, but isn't actually illegal. The calls for capitalism to moderate its unethical behavior resemble the calls for corporate social responsibility of the 1990s, when the heads of several major companies promised not to destroy the environment or, if they had to, to do it as kindly as possible.

For a better understanding of the ethics of valuation, it's worth revisiting the original thinkers behind the free market, who had a robust sense of how prices, value and the wider economy worked. Before there were economists, students of market society were called "moral philosophers," and when they pondered the market, they were less concerned with the behavioral integrity of high finance or the interaction between consumer and producer, and more concerned with how value is bound up with indelible inequalities in power. Modern economics suffers from amnesia when it comes to what these philosophers had to say about value. The spirit of capitalism is jealous, and for it to thrive, different ways of thinking and valuing the world need to be smothered. But if the countermovement against profit-driven thinking is to be more than cosmetic, we'll need to start remembering some of that original moral philosophy.

(FOUR)

ON DIAMONDS AND WATER

> Capitalism is the astounding belief that the most wickedest of men will do the most wickedest of things for the greatest good of everyone.
> —JOHN MAYNARD KEYNES[1]

Over 1.4 million of Ayn Rand's books have been given away to American high schools by the institute that bears her name—the books are free to any teacher prepared to make their students suffer them. Her work is taught as a sort of Adam Smith Lite, an entry-level text in support of the free market that finds its most articulate and subtle formulations in the works of the great Scottish philosopher. This is unfair to Smith.

While Rand spun tedious rationalizations for selfish behavior, Smith was very far from a praise-singer for unfettered markets. The term with which his name is most singularly associated, "the invisible hand," appears just once in *The Wealth of Nations*. When it does, it isn't used to describe the beneficent effect of free markets at all. The invisible hand is the guiding force that makes Scottish investors behave parochially, preferring to put their money into the Scottish economy rather than investing abroad. By investing in their local economy, investors get a return, of course, but so does the society in which they invest and, because they live there, investors enjoy the economic stimulus too. This is the beneficial yet unintended consequence of investors' selfish motives, and it only comes about because of a preference for domestic over international investment. Not exactly the policy that people who quote Smith are usually in the business of advocating when they talk about the invisible hand.[2]

Smith was a far more subtle and complex thinker than his free-markets-rule caricature, holding sophisticated views on many of the issues that tax modern economics. His opinion on whether money could buy happiness, for instance, was that it couldn't: "In ease of body and peace of mind, all the different ranks of life are nearly upon a level."[3] He also thought that a primary animating principle behind economic activity was vanity. People worked in order to pay for things that held the esteem of one's peers. This keeping-up-with-the-Joneses, where everyone works ever harder to stay where they are in the eyes of their society, is today's "hedonic treadmill." But it is in his understanding of value that Smith and his descendents have most to teach us today.

In modern economics, students are often introduced to the mechanics of value through a classic comparison: Why are diamonds so expensive when they're so unnecessary, when something vital like water is so cheap? Here's what Smith had to say about water and diamonds in *The Wealth of Nations*:

> The word value . . . has two different meanings, and sometimes expresses the utility of some particular object, and sometimes the power of purchasing other goods which the possession of that object conveys. The one may be called "value in use"; the other, "value in exchange." The things which have the greatest value in use have frequently little or no value in exchange; and, on the contrary, those which have the greatest value in exchange have frequently

> little or no value in use. Nothing is more useful than wa-
> ter; but it will scarce purchase anything; scarce anything
> can be had in exchange for it. A diamond, on the con-
> trary, has scarce any value in use; but a very great quantity
> of other goods may frequently be had in exchange for it.[4]

In the economics classroom, today's undergraduates are taught that Smith's distinction between "use value" and "exchange value" caused him no end of trouble. Having two categories of value, one for when you use something and one for when you exchange it for something else, doesn't leave you any wiser about how valuable something is—no one talks about anything having a high use value but a low exchange value.

Undergraduates then learn that they are saved from confusion and puzzlement by a new breed of thinkers: nineteenth-century neoclassical economists—the British William Stanley Jevons, the Austrian Carl Menger and the Swiss Léon Walras—who, equipped with the latest in physics and mathematics, then solved the problem of value by understanding it as a question about prices. They did it by looking at the margin, at what happens when you add an extra unit of something to the market. They were able to show how and why prices look the way they do because water is relatively abundant and diamonds scarce.

The value of diamonds or anything else in neoclassical economics is a measure of what would be given up in order to obtain them. As the value of something is measured through exchange, you can't tell the value of something just by looking at it, or knowing how much it cost to make, or the good that it might do you. According to the neoclassicals, to find its value you have to trade it—that's the only way that our individual preferences can enter the public language of commerce.

This is how the paradox of something vital being cheap, but

something unnecessary being expensive, is explained. What is omitted in this version, however, is that no one seriously thought there *was* a paradox until the late nineteenth century. The diamond and water conundrum was popularized by a post–World War II textbook written by economist Paul Samuelson. The culture of free markets needed a bible, and Samuelson's 1948 *Economics* provided just the right sort of revisionist history.[5] It ignored the fact that Adam Smith understood very well why diamonds were more expensive than water. In his 1762 *Lectures on Jurisprudence*, he put it rather plainly:

> For these terms plenty and cheapness are in a manner synonymous, as cheapness is a necessary consequence of plenty. Thus we see that water, which is absolutely necessary for the support of mankind, by its abundance costs nothing but the uptaking, whereas diamonds and other jewels, of which one can hardly say what they serve for, give an immense price.[6]

In explaining the price, Smith points to relative scarcity, just like the neoclassical economists. The difference is not between their explanations of price, but in their concepts of usefulness—Jevons and the neoclassical economists have an abstract and quantitative utility, while Smith has a qualitative idea of value-in-use. To paraphrase Oscar Wilde, people today know the exchange value of everything and the use value of nothing. Smith's idea of use value is best understood not as an unsuccessful attempt to develop a theory of marginal utility so much as a technique for looking behind the scenes to explain why economic activity looked the way that it did at a more fundamental level. To separate out the superficial world from this deeper reality, Smith introduces a distinction between what we pay and a thing's "real price." For Smith to get from market price to the real one required time and effort:

The real price of every thing, what every thing really costs to the man who wants to acquire it, is the toil and trouble of acquiring it. What every thing is really worth to the man who has acquired it, and who wants to dispose of it or exchange it for something else, is the toil and trouble which it can save to himself, and which it can impose upon other people.[7]

Smith grappled with the links between value, labor and wages. In his view, the yardstick of the real value of everything was the trouble that went into making it:

Labour alone, therefore, never varying in its own value, is alone the ultimate and real standard by which the value of all commodities can at all times and places be estimated and compared. It is their real price; money is their nominal price only.[8]

He thought that the reason that some jobs were better paid was simply because some people were more willing to suffer the loss of nonmonetary goods. The reason a park keeper makes less than a stockbroker is because the broker doesn't get to spend the days walking in the woods. Smith thought that wages would tend toward equality in the long run, with minor discrepancies relating to the amount of time people could take for holidays and compensating for the unpleasantness of the job. By this calculus, people who work in sewers at night ought to be billionaires. For Smith, the fact that the world clearly didn't work like this signaled that something was wrong with the economy, something systemic, something that distorted what different groups of people received for their work.

These aren't the views typically associated with Smith, at least in modern lay thinking about him. Smith's fate was to end up as a crest on Reagan-era neckties, a legitimating figurehead for an untested experiment in neoliberal capitalism, but compared to Karl Marx, he got off comparatively lightly. Marx has had a far rougher ride, purged from the canon of economics as an insult to the purity of neoclassical thinking. You'd think that Marxist economists wouldn't be able to find a home anywhere in the academy, but they do exist, and— according to anecdotal evidence—many seem to have managed to find refuge not in the airless corridors of the economics department, but in business schools. With good reason. Although contemporary economic theory has little room for his thought, Marx has a great deal to say about contemporary economic practice.

Karl Marx agreed with Smith that time and effort were central to the production of goods, but he went one better, unpicking how that time and effort mattered through "the labor theory of value." Let's pretend that you are an ace short-order cook, and you can flip two hundred hamburgers an hour. I, a lapsed Hindu with beef issues, might be able to cook twenty in an hour. Does that mean that mine are ten times more valuable than yours? A simple labor theory of value would say yes, but Marx pointed out why the answer is clearly no. Very simply, yours is the normal industry rate of productivity, and I'm a laggard. The way Marx talks about this is through the idea of the "socially necessary" labor time—my hamburger flipping takes far longer than the socially necessary time, the time that's normal in an industry. The word "social" here implies that it's never "natural" but, rather, the outcome of a great deal of human invention, politics and power.[9]

This idea of socially necessary labor time opens the door to a central difference between Smith's and Marx's views on wages. Smith thought that, distortions aside, wages were a return on the amount of work that you do. For Marx, wages were the money you got for making your ability to work available for use by the capitalists. For a certain chunk of the day, the laborer works to earn enough money that might be exchanged to feed, house and clothe her family. But the laborer will work a whole day, because that is what her employer has paid for. This is the fulcrum of his theory of value, because the ability to work is a magic ingredient, one that can add use value to raw materials unlike anything else that capitalists can buy. Any value beyond that which it takes to replenish the laborer's ability to work goes to the person who hired her. Marx calls this the "surplus value," and this is the ultimate source of profit.[10]

From this little dance—in the exchange of work for money, and money for commodities—Marx pulls a description of capitalism. Capital isn't just money—a chest of banknotes isn't capital. Capital is the *process* of transforming money into commodities that can be sold for more than the wages paid to the workers and the costs of machines and materials, to make a profit.[11] The capital that is generated from this process has taken on a life of its own, as financial capital.[12]

As definitions go, it's not bad. It points to the constant process of growth and expansion that capitalism needs to sustain itself. It suggests why *Homo economicus* is the perpetually ravenous creature of such an economy. It also points to a central inequality in power, between those who control capital and those who have nothing to sell but their labor. In other words, the definition binds together ideas of power, ownership, work and—crucially—profit. These ideas prove useful in understanding not only the conundrum of value, but also how we might start to unlimit ourselves by restraining profit-driven markets.

It's not by labor alone that value is created. Another route through which profits might be expanded is by having to pay less to workers. The cheaper it is for workers to survive and reproduce, the better for profits. While it is beyond the means of any single capitalist to lower the price of labor power, it is something that they together can fight for collectively, as we shall see. To reproduce workers requires more than making babies: It's a long process of child-rearing, feeding, clothing, housing, educating, socializing and disciplining, and the costs of this are the source of perhaps the most fundamental misvaluation, worldwide—the market's treatment of women's work in the home. The daily work of rearing children, maintaining a household and engaging in civic work—the unpaid slabs of work that feminists have called "women's triple burden"—remains unpriced worldwide. Were all unpaid work to be remunerated, the sum was estimated in 1995 to be $16 trillion. Just to be clear, that's $16,000,000,000,000. Of that, $11 trillion represented women's unpaid work.[13] That's $15 trillion in 2007 dollars. Back in 1995, this was more than half of the world's total output. What's worse, this miscalculation isn't innocent. It's *because* this reproductive work has been naturalized as women's work, and because women's work is unpaid, that there can be such a large paid economy.[14] Because their work is uncounted, women appear to have "free" time, time that is used by development agencies to explain why women are able to "burden share," to pick up some of the slack where public services fail. This sexism spreads to the wage economy too—according to the International Labour Organization, women in most countries earn between 70 and 90 percent of what men earn for the same work, though in some places, particularly in Asia, that figure is lower.[15]

There's a final route through which profit might be created, one that doesn't involve labor: enclosure. Polanyi's observations about the creation of market society aren't mere historical curiosities. Geographer David Harvey has written about how the capitalist search for new resources to privatize generates its own maps of crises. When a national forest is sold for timber, biodiversity is put under patent or mineral rights are auctioned off, there's an enclosing, a privatizing of that resource that allows someone to profit from it at public expense.

Marx's discussion of the economy works by asking where it is that value comes from. He traces it back to labor, and then explores the dynamics of profit seeking in market society. It's a way of thinking about market society with great explanatory power, showing the origins of externalities in the rise of capitalism and in the social forces at play within our market society. It explains why corporate behavior consistently skirts the boundaries of ethics and legality—the corporation's need for profit drives it to rapacity and setting ethics firmly to one side—even if ultimately, Marx thought, the persistent quest for profit would lead to the end of capitalism itself.

Although today's economic crisis looks dire, Marx's predictions haven't come true quite yet.[16] Our current economic turbulence is a result of the way capital is invested, and the life that money takes on when it is not industrial capital, but finance capital.[17] Although Marx understood the importance of finance better than classical and neoclassical economists, his analyses come with a politics that are fundamentally incompatible with the ideology of today's market society—it's far easier to think about the crisis as the result of poor regulation or bad apples on Wall Street than to see it as emerging from a social system into which we have been folded. It is perhaps for this reason that in explaining today's recession, the theories of a much more recent economist, one who grew up amid the machinery of finance and whose thought presents only a moderate challenge to prevailing ideas about market society, have taken center stage: the twentieth-century British economist John Maynard Keynes.

THE SECRET LIFE OF FINANCIAL CAPITAL

Keynes began his economic career as an ardent disciple of neoclassical wisdom, spending much of the 1920s arguing its merits. The Great Depression spurred him into being one of its most insightful critics. It was to himself, as much as his peers, that he aimed one of the most frequently quoted parts of his *General Theory*:

> Practical men, who believe themselves to be quite exempt
> from any intellectual influences, are usually the slaves of
> some defunct economist. Madmen in authority, who hear

> voices in the air, are distilling their frenzy from some aca-
> demic scribbler of a few years back.[18]

Keynes addressed the question of why we have years when things go horribly wrong, like 2008 or 1929. He himself pointed out that the unemployment that accompanied the Great Depression couldn't really be explained by laborers obstinately refusing to work at low wages, as neoclassical theories implied.[19] It wasn't something that could be explained by supply and demand in the neoclassical sense at all. To answer the problem, Keynes turned conventional economics on its head by looking not at the behavior of individual firms, but at entrepreneurs' feelings about risk and uncertainty, and how they would ride the flows of capital.

Until his intervention, the economic mainstream made sense of how firms behaved, and where and how price, profit and wages were generated, using the tools of marginal utility analysis. These tools, which appeared to explain why supply and demand looked the way they did for individual goods and sectors, started to fall apart when talking about bigger trends in the economy. Keynes proposed that the way to make sense of things was to think about different levels of analysis. He broke with neoclassical thinking by observing that what might be rational for an individual acting in isolation might be bad for everyone as a whole. An example of this is "the paradox of thrift": In a recession, a reasonable thing for me to do is to start saving more than I did before, but if everyone does it, the aggregate level of demand in the economy falls because no one is buying things, meaning that the recession gets even worse, which means we save even more, and so on.

What Keynes observed, and what we've seen amply in the discussion of *Homo economicus*, is that the assumption of a predictable world and rational risk taking is unsound. People aren't rational, and the future is cloudy. If we knew for sure what the future would hold, then our irrationalities might be reined in with a little more circumspection. If we were perfectly rational, then we might plan an economy fully aware of the range of probable outcomes in that future. Since we are neither clairvoyant nor perfectly rational, we reach into the future a little more blindly and impulsively. This, for Keynes, is no bad thing. When he discusses the "animal spirits" that impel entrepreneurs to take decisions, he celebrates them because, in his words, "a large proportion of our positive activities depend on spontaneous optimism rather than on a mathematical expectation. . . . Most, probably, of our decisions to do something positive, the full consequences of which will be drawn out over many days to come, can only be taken as the result of animal spirits."[20] For Keynes, these spirits are the demons of innovation, and when they're bullish about the future, there's no end to what they can achieve. Optimistic animal spirits are the philosopher's stone of entrepreneurship, turning lead into gold.

Yet, precisely because the appraisal about the future is a gut-level response, the financing of the future also fluctuates according to these animal spirits. This is why, for instance, Keynes argues that "the rate of interest is a highly psychological phenomenon,"[21] because the interest rate is the price for money, the demand for which is slave to the individual psychologies of entrepreneurs. When entrepreneurs consider how to invest, they need to evaluate not their own opinion on the best return, but everyone else's opinion too. This is how Keynes describes the process:

> Professional investment may be likened to those newspaper competitions in which the competitors have to pick out the six prettiest faces from a hundred photographs, the prize being awarded to the competitor whose choice most nearly corresponds to the average preferences of the competitors as a whole; so that each competitor has to pick, not those faces which he himself finds prettiest, but those which he thinks likeliest to catch the fancy of the other competitors, all of

whom are looking at the problem from the same point of
view. It is not a case of choosing those which, to the best
of one's judgment, are really the prettiest, nor even those
which average opinion genuinely thinks the prettiest.[22]

Keynes found one nation particularly worthy of mention in this pursuit:

> Even outside the field of finance, Americans are apt to be
> unduly interested in discovering what average opinion
> believes average opinion to be; and this national weak-
> ness finds its nemesis in the stock market.[23]

Keynes was, among other things, a sociologist of the market, and his
understanding of collective psychology led him to his next insight—
that in times of depression, the personal virtue of saving could become the public vice of deflation. The solution, suggested Keynes, is
for the government to fill in for private enterprise until it gets its
nerve back, by stimulating demand *as a whole*.

The trickiest part of this to understand is that no matter what the
government does, as long as it spends, the economy will pick up.
Keynes suggested, rhetorically, that if they lacked the imagination for
anything more creative, governments could simply bury bottles of
money under tons of trash, and that this would help get the economy
going. It may sound bizarre, but it would certainly be worth someone's while to dig up free money. To find these banknotes would require workers. Those workers would need to pay for food and shelter
and everything else they needed to survive while they dug. The gro-
cers who fed them and the landlords who rented to the workers
would then have cash to spend, which they would use to buy other
goods, and so on. This is called the "multiplier effect," and it's the
added return that a government gets from spending its money in the

economy. The beneficial effects are greater among lower-income communities than high-income ones, because giving money to people who already have a lot of it won't make them spend more, whereas giving money to those who have none means that the cash will be spent immediately. This is why a tax cut for the rich is an absurd idea (according to one economist, making the Bush tax cuts permanent has a multiplier effect of 0.23), while one of the most effective ways for the U.S. government to stimulate the economy is through food stamps (with a multiplier effect of 1.73).[24]

It is his analysis of animal spirits and the possibilities of public spending that have made Keynes the economist of the moment. He shows why the free market needs governments to kick-start the economy, because there's something missing from the economy that money can't buy but that governments can substitute for—confidence. He also brings in a factor that the original political economists ignored—not only can people be motivated by the profit motive, but they can be irrational while doing it, and that irrationality can be magnified by finance capital.

To remedy this, Keynes saw a special role for government in economic management, fixing the collective mistakes that no one individual was able to address alone. It is under this banner that governments worldwide have made trillions of dollars available to the banking system, as well as promising "stimulus" to the economy, so that money can start once again to flow, so that employment might once again increase.

In our story so far, government has been lurking in the background. The main characters we've encountered in understanding value in market society have been consumers and corporations. Corporations are powerful—they constitute two-thirds of the 150 largest economic entities in the world—but it is governments that shape the terrain on which they operate, and it is time to see quite how they fit into market society.

FIVE

ANTI-ECONOMIC MAN

> We here highly resolve that these dead shall not have
> died in vain—that this nation, under God, shall have a
> new birth of freedom—and that government of the
> people, by the people, for the people, shall not perish from
> the earth.
> —ABRAHAM LINCOLN, *Gettysburg Address*

Although they lead a country founded on the revolutionary possibilities of government, recent U. S. presidents seem to have gone out
of their way to pour scorn on their office. Ronald Reagan believed
that the nine most terrifying words in the English language were
"I'm from the government and I'm here to help." Bill Clinton, in his
1996 State of the Union speech, announced that "the era of big
government is over." Alan Greenspan, of course, had ideological objections to the state, and Republicans have lately reformulated their
objections to big government—now that they're no longer the majority within it—with chants of "Socialism!" around the bailout or, if
the discussion turns to health care, "Nazism!"

In popular U.S. culture, a line runs from big government to the
fettering of free commerce and to totalitarianism, but only the most

fanatical libertarians argue that there should be no role for government at all. During the financial crisis, even Greenspan recognized the need for *some* role for government, finally catching up with the rest of the world: In poll after poll, citizens want their governments not only to fix economic problems, but also to be active in almost every domain.

In a 2008 survey covering 60 percent of the world and involving 50,000 people, 81 percent of people felt that governments should be in the business of preventing discrimination against women, 87 percent felt that governments should provide food to the hungry (the two countries with the lowest percentages being India at 70 percent and the United States at 74 percent), 92 percent wanted government-provided health care (again, with India and the United States being the least enthusiastic) and 91 percent wanted public education (with India at 64 percent, Egypt at 77 percent and then the United States at 83 percent).[1]

It isn't surprising that people feel it should fall to governments to provide health care and education. In theory at least, left to its own devices, the free market would settle on prices that would be higher than many could afford, and almost every culture finds distasteful the notion that poverty should exclude anyone from medical care or education. The task of correcting this underprovision falls to governments, which oversee the exchange as one not between consumer and producer, but between citizen and state. This distinction is important, because we expect governments to be "anticorporations," driven by quite different motivations from *Homo economicus*, using nonmarket means to fix market failure, recognizing value where the private sector sees none. So are our expectations being met?

Let's start with a health care story. Malaria kills more than one million people a year in Africa alone, according to the World Health Organization, and is responsible for a quarter of all young adult deaths there. The disease is spread by a parasite that jumps from humans to mosquitoes and back again, and as most of the people who contract the disease are poor, malaria has received relatively little research funding from the free market.

The treatments for malaria are fairly rudimentary, and in the absence of an effective cure, one way to prevent it is to stop the mosquito bites. A cheap way to do that is through bed nets treated with an insecticide that lasts from three to seven years, which cost between three and six dollars. They're 70 percent effective at preventing mosquitoes from biting. The World Health Organization recommends that they be given away free to mothers and children. Why? Because it's one of the cheapest ways of saving lives in some of the poorest areas of the world where health services are already desperately underfunded, and because it brings with it a positive externality. We came across the negative externality, observing the ecological and human footprints of pretty much any economic activity. Just as markets are bad at valuing social harm, they're also bad at valuing social benefits, "positive externalities." The value of these nets is much higher than their price, and if left to the market, fewer lives would be saved. To ensure that everyone gets a net, governments give them away for free. As we saw with the strategy of free for-profit goods, it encourages far more people to use a net than would be the case were there even a nominal fee.

It's easy to make similar arguments for other kinds of intervention, especially when there's a social benefit that's far greater than individual benefits. One of the reasons that childhood vaccination is widespread in every country that can afford to sustain such a program is because the public benefits of a population free of, say, polio, far outweigh the social costs of allowing the disease to run rampant or of making vaccination optional, or available only for those who choose to pay for it.

A similar case can be made for education—the public benefits of an educated population are greater than the private costs of educating children. Giving away education for free is, demonstrably, a good way of ensuring that every child is educated. It's also the route to reduced levels of crime, increased productivity and healthier and more engaged citizens. The British Department for International Development reports that the Rwandan government's efforts to ensure free primary education for 100 percent of Rwandan children in the aftermath of the violence that left 1.2 million children orphaned resulted in some of the highest enrollment rates, for boys and girls, in East Africa. Enrollment rates in Rwanda have increased from 73.3 percent to 94 percent, representing an additional 500,000 children.[2]

Sometimes even free is not enough—some of the most successful literacy programs are those that pay families to send their children to school. Subsidy programs in Brazil and Bangladesh provide families incentives (from cash to food) to keep their children in school. Positive effects include an increase in household income and caloric intake among the very poor, increase in enrollment and significant declines in dropout rates.[3] In many countries, free is not even an option: Primary education is considered so valuable, for society and for the future benefit of the children involved, that it is mandatory.

PUBLIC GOODS TURN SOUR

It seems, then, that governments and their institutions can indeed correct the failings of the market behaving in ways that maximize not profit, but the welfare of their citizens, and decommodifying the things that society deems valuable. Governments are able to shape the rules of the economic game and mobilize gigantic budgets in order to provide for citizens.

Governments do not, however, exist in a sphere separate from modern capitalism. The idea that corporations act as *Homo economicus* and governments as anti–*Homo economicus*, like matter and anti-matter, turns out to be a poor metaphor. When corporations and governments collide, there's no explosion of energy; instead, one conforms to the other.

As we have seen, education and health care are goods that have a higher social benefit than the individual private benefit to the person who receives them. In the economic literature, there's a class of goods that not only have a higher social than private benefit, but which by their very nature need nonmarket means to provide them; these are called "public goods." National defense is the quintessential public good: If you pay for national defense and I don't, you can't really stop me from enjoying the same defense. On top of that, your feeling safer doesn't stop me feeling safer too.[4]

Defense is one of the very few places where free marketers will acknowledge some role for government, but military spending is also a poster child for the kind of corruption that happens when public and private sectors collide. U.S. president and former general Dwight D. Eisenhower's final public words in office were a warning that we should remain vigilant against "the military-industrial complex." He added, "The potential for the disastrous rise of misplaced power exists and will persist. We must never let the weight of this combination endanger our liberties or democratic processes."

Eisenhower was right to be worried. He saw how the spirit of capitalism could hijack government, by using public money to line private pockets while using democratic institutions to camouflage the crime. The unpopular wars in Iraq and Afghanistan, together with dozens of ongoing counterinsurgencies and hundreds of "training" operations, reveal that the military-industrial complex is not subject to public control. Only now is it being mooted that private military contractors be held responsible for their actions in Iraq, and it looks unlikely that the architects and profiteers from this war will ever be held responsible for their actions, despite their being part of a governmental, and hence notionally democratic, enterprise. Firms like Xe, pronounced "Zee," but actually pronounced "Blackwater"— the infamous security company renamed itself in February 2009— have not only insinuated themselves into Iraq and Afghanistan,[5] but were even hired to patrol the streets after Hurricane Katrina.[6]

The vicious logic of privatized security consumes both the Global North and the Global South. In the midst of recessionary cutbacks, defense is one of the government line items that has continued to expand. In 2008 nearly $1.5 trillion dollars were spent on defense worldwide.[7] To borrow a trick from the brilliant essayist John Lanchester, if you were to count at a dollar per second, it'd take twelve days to count a million, thirty-one years to count a billion, and for a trillion, a thousand-fold more, it'd take six times all recorded history. Nick Turse points out that the figures declared by ministries or departments of defense tend to be lower than the grand totals across all government agencies: Adding up all defense spending in the public sector, the U.S. government alone plows over $1 trillion into its military.[8] Defense spending is increasing among a range of more and less democratically elected governments around the world (though none at the scale of the United States, which spends almost half of the planet's total). In France, domestic arms purchases are scheduled to double in 2009, while in the same year China's military budget is up 15 percent and India's is up 34 percent.[9] When the biggest crises facing the planet require education, training, health care and investment in sustainable energy and agriculture, governments are piling record sums into guns, not butter.

Is the merging of private interests and government in the provision of defense a symptom of a more widespread phenomenon? If it is, then it's harder to imagine that governments might effectively rein in profit-driven markets and that they might regulate the forces that seek to transform the world into a theater of profit. Keynes saw government as a tool that, when wielded intelligently, could help the market back on its feet—this is why his ideas are an addendum to, rather than a rewriting of, the rules of market society. But what if this tool is compromised? The first political economists worried about this a great deal. Once again, we need to raid the past for some help in understanding our current predicament.

ECONOMIC POWER AND THE GOVERNMENT

Classical economic theory suggests that the worst symptom of corporate power is the monopoly—a firm that so completely controls the market, it can call the shots on price. But what if there's something wrong with the corporation itself? Adam Smith noticed an inherent structural problem with certain kinds of corporations:

> The directors of such [joint-stock] companies, however, being the managers rather of other people's money than of their own, it cannot well be expected that they should watch over it with the same anxious vigilance with which the partners in a private copartnery frequently watch over their own. . . . Negligence and profusion, therefore, must always prevail, more or less, in the management of the affairs of such a company.[10]

Although the kinds of joint-stock companies in Smith's day were trading monopolies established by royal charter, very different from today's corporations, his criticism is still useful. Investors can be prone to speculation (Smith fulminated against the South Sea Bubble), and are more prone to irrational gambling when the money they play with isn't theirs. Economists understand this as an "agency" problem, where the people whose money is being managed, and the people doing the managing, face different incentives.

The problem of corporate power, however, runs far deeper than the divergent interests of stockholders and CEOs. In *The Wealth of Nations*, Smith argues that the economic world is divided into laborers, landlords and merchants. Laborers earn their money from the sweat of their brows, landlords from rents, and merchants from profit. In some ways, the interests of the first two groups are aligned with the social good—when the economy does well, rents and wages are high, and so both groups are happy. That said, Smith argues that landlords are a little too disconnected from the real world to understand how their interests align, and laborers work so hard that they have neither time nor education to understand how their interests are also those of society. Here's what he has to say about merchants, though:

> The interest of [those who live off profit], however . . . is always in some respects different from, and even opposite to, that of the public. To widen the market and to narrow the competition, is always the interest of the dealers. To widen the market may frequently be agreeable enough to the interest of the public; but to narrow the competition must always be against it, and can serve only to enable the dealers, by raising their profits above what they naturally would be, to levy, for their own benefit, an absurd tax upon the rest of their fellow-citizens. The proposal of any new law or regulation of commerce which comes from this order, ought always to be listened to with great precaution, and ought never to be adopted till after having been long and carefully examined, not only with the most scrupulous, but with the most suspicious attention. It comes from an order of men, whose interest is never

exactly the same with that of the public, who have generally an interest to deceive and even to oppress the public,
and who accordingly have, upon many occasions, both
deceived and oppressed it.[11]

Smith is pointing to a structural reason why the normal operations of
the economy might create a group of people who'd be able to hijack
it. When these "dealers" get their hands on the reins of the economy,
they are not to be trusted. For this reason, Smith saw a very strong
role for government, to do everything from punishing dishonesty to
regulating finance to providing education and public order.

But there's reason to think that corporations contaminate government. Karl Marx and Friedrich Engels saw the government as so
captured by the merchant class that its executive was merely "a committee for managing the common affairs of the whole bourgeoisie."[12]
This is, perhaps, to be expected from *The Communist Manifesto*, but
Marx and Engels weren't alone in their view. The twentieth-century
Algerian philosopher and psychiatrist Frantz Fanon also saw it as the
fate of newly independent countries' governments to succumb to
the "national bourgeoisie," who come to power on the back of a promise of democratic national development, and end up repeating, with
some variations, the policies of their former colonial masters.

That the interests of the wealthy should dominate governments
the world over is no accident—indeed, the governments under which
we live were expressly designed with this idea in mind. Alexander
Hamilton, the first U.S. treasury secretary, wrote in *Federalist* No. 35
that

mechanics and manufacturers will always be inclined,
with few exceptions, to give their votes to merchants, in
preference to persons of their own professions or trades. . . .
They know that the merchant is their natural patron and

> friend; and they are aware that however great the confi-
> dence they may justly feel in their own good sense, their
> interests can be more effectually promoted by the mer-
> chant than by themselves. . . . We must therefore con-
> sider merchants as the natural representatives of all these
> classes of the community.[13]

Hamilton wasn't alone in thinking that government was best left in the hands of people skilled in business. The idea that members of a certain class could represent the interests of society as a whole was widespread. In France, the nineteenth-century philosopher Auguste Comte favored bankers as the trustees of society. A quick look at the upper houses of legislatures around the world suggests where the balance of power lies—it's more than a little unusual to see a working-class member of a Senate or House of Lords. Upper houses are often justified as a way for calmer and wiser heads to prevail in govern-ment decision making, but what's the qualification that confers wis-dom? It appears to be this: owning a lot of property.

This explains, incidentally, why legislative upper houses are often called "millionaires' clubs." They're venues in which the wealthy can oversee and veto the demands of those lower on the social lad-der. It has to be said that the ladder doesn't go terribly far down—although in the United States, the gap between the two has been narrowing. Around half of U.S. senators are millionaires, compared to only a quarter in the House. The consequences of this for policy making are easy enough to see.

Imagine just for a moment that government had been, in its most important branches, taken over by industry and finance. In this hypo-thetical case, we would expect to see that reflected in the tax struc-ture, with the poor paying higher marginal rates of tax than the rich, and with corporations escaping taxes more effectively than people. In the United States, this has certainly been happening: Corporations paid less than a quarter of all federal income tax (with flesh-and-blood people paying the remaining 76 percent) and the Internal Revenue Service now audits millionaires at just half the rate they did even in 2007.[14] After conducting his own internal audit, Warren Buffett discovered that he pays a far smaller percentage of his income in taxes than the secretaries and clerks in his office. "There's class warfare, all right," Buffett said, "but it's my class, the rich class, that's making war, and we're winning."[15] Similar lucky breaks for the rich are to be found everywhere from antiworker employment regulation to carbon cap-and-trade systems, from environmental laws that place public resources in private hands to the bailout of the banks.[16]

The great French historian Fernand Braudel distilled this process of government capture by corporations and the rich, using a three-layer cake to show how the economy and the government really function together. At the bottom is the timeless work of survival, with which everyone struggles daily. Above that "comes the favoured terrain of the market economy, with its many horizontal communications between the different markets: here a degree of automatic coordination usually links supply, demand and prices. Then alongside, or rather above this layer, comes the zone of the antimarket, where the great predators roam and the law of the jungle operates. This—today as in the past, before and after the industrial revolution—is the real home of capitalism."[17] In other words, corporate capitalism runs anathema to proper free exchange. If you like decentralized markets and exchange based on needs, then contemporary capitalism isn't for you. So where, then, might one look for change?

WHENCE THE COUNTERMOVEMENT?

Governments don't float above market society—they're embedded in it, and the recent economic crisis demonstrated this amply. In one international survey, 63 percent of people thought that their governments were run in the service of "big interests" as opposed to the 30 percent who thought governments served the will of the people. In almost every country,[18] those polled wanted their governments to behave in ways that were more responsive to the people. An international survey of more than 29,000 people undertaken by the BBC revealed that two out of three respondents said that there was a need to transform the international and domestic economic systems.[19] The world is ready for change.

But here's the darker part of the story. The people under those governments, you and me, are *also* part of market society. There is no position from which, untainted by the world around it, some everlasting truth can guide us to a brighter future. Polanyi's second movement never simply reverses the expansion of the market—the Speenhamland laws were not a demand to return to feudalism. The second movement was made with the political resources that people had to hand—hence the idea of a *counter*movement. Polanyi wrote his book in the midst of the fight against fascism, and the economic collapse that had preceded it. He harbored no illusions about how societies could react to economic collapse: with exclusion and national chauvinism. And there's every danger that an unthinking desire for change could take us there again.

There can be "community failure" just as there is market failure, in which minorities risk persecution or worse. The recent rise of far-right parties around the world—from India to Europe to the United States—can also be understood as the second part of a double movement. In the United States, Louis R. Andrews, chair of the National Policy Institute—an advocacy group for white people—hoped to see "the Republican Party destroyed, so it can be reborn as a party representing the interests of white people, and not entrenched corporate elites."[20] Which, says Andrews, is why he voted for Obama.

If you're concerned with social change that isn't about a retreat into a politics of exclusion, but want to address how our supposedly democratic government has been captured by corporate interests, there's some hard thinking to do. Just as there is no Archimedean point from which prices might accurately reflect the world around us, there isn't some natural presocial position from which we can make politics happen. A recent and increasingly popular idea is that we ought to stop thinking of ourselves as consumers, and choose to be citizens. It's a laudable call, but when scrutinized, the idea of "citizen" turns out to be as all-encompassing and vapid as "change" or "hope." Some of the most repressive regimes in human history have rested on particular ideas of what to do with citizenship. Of course, citizenship isn't irredeemable simply because dictators have cowered behind it, but if you hear it as a call to action, the appropriate response should be, "What kind of citizen?"

Some have suggested that the foundation of a progressive politics can be found in the one thing that unites us as a species—our humanity. While there's an important egalitarian spirit here, this insight by itself doesn't generate unambiguous political principles. Observing that we're all humans isn't by itself a political fact—it's just a biological one. In order to derive a politics around our common humanity, you need to specify what that means. Once again, this is ground well trodden by two very different founding thinkers of Western political thought: Thomas Hobbes and Jean-Jacques Rousseau.

THE PROBLEM WITH ARTIFICIAL PEOPLE

Hobbes's *Leviathan* has in its early chapters a long and detailed list of human nature's attributes. Among the key traits are competition, pride and the desire for glory. These are the assumptions from which he proceeds, like a geometer, to build his model of people and society. The outcome isn't pretty. One of his concerns can be parsed out as a conflict over resources: "If any two men desire the same thing, which nevertheless they cannot both enjoy, they become enemies." Desire and the enmity that it provokes can, however, be reigned in by the existence of a "Power to keep them all in awe," some authority more capable and bigger than any individual's natural inclinations. Without this power,

> there is no place for Industry; because the fruit thereof is uncertain: and consequently no Culture of the Earth; no Navigation, nor use of the commodities that may be imported by Sea; no commodious Building; no Instruments of moving, and removing such things as require much force; no Knowledge of the face of the Earth; no account of Time; no Arts; no Letters; no Society; and which is worst of all, continuall feare, and danger of violent death; And the life of man, solitary, poore, nasty, brutish, and short.[21]

This is why, for Hobbes, the state of nature was a state of war. War could, however, be prevented by the Leviathan, the government that would keep people's antisocial behavior in check. Hobbes thought that by joining together and using their reason to create an artificial person, government, humanity could impose upon itself the virtues of restraint and cooperation that people would, in a state of nature, lack.

Jean-Jacques Rousseau turned this on its head. Although he shared with Hobbes the view that people were generally unsociable, he disagreed that humans were inherently machines of infinite want. It was possible, he argued, for people to feel that they've got "enough."

Being sated is something that people can learn—and it is after they have managed to control their instincts and impulses in the best interests of themselves and society that they are truly free. This process, for Rousseau, was the fount of liberty—precisely the opposite of Greenspan's vision. Rousseau also went on to argue that "artificial people" were, in fact, precisely possessed of the characteristics that Hobbes saw in the state of nature. Entities like corporations and governments were nasty and brutish. Worse, because they didn't have to eat or sleep, and could never die, artificial people were more worrisome because they could never have enough.

Rousseau wasn't the first to worry about insatiable nonhuman creatures living among us. Almost every cultural tradition has cautionary tales of similar beings with appetites run riot. In what is now called western Canada and the United States, indigenous cultures told of Weendigoes.[22] A giant, hungry spirit, a Weendigo had lips that were bloody from its constantly gnashing jaws, and its hunger became deeper with every drop of human blood it drank. Weendigoes were cannibals, people whose desires had so entirely become the core of their being that they were prepared to eat others in order to survive. Weendigo tales were told as a reminder that unbridled consumption in harvest months meant less food for everyone in leaner seasons, which meant that eating more than your fair share today was effectively a kind of cannibalism inflicted on the rest of the tribe in the future. Basil Johnston, an Ojibwe scholar, argues that Weendigoes are alive and well. Few people in North America have seen giant spirits, but many more people have seen their modern incarnation, giant creatures with few interests beyond the satisfaction of their immediate appetites, even if this prevents tomorrow's hunger from being met. The modern Weendigo, Johnston suggests, is the multinational corporation.

Other cultures also have icons of insatiable and constantly suffering beasts. Thai and Japanese Buddhists tell of hungry ghosts, once covetous people who when they die become ghosts with mouths as small as the finest needle's eye and who are cursed with perpetual hunger. These mythic people weren't blind to the world—they merely saw it through the optic of their own desires, desires that outweighed any care they might have had to the damage they caused. Like Asia and the Americas, Europe also has an example of a creature like this, and when Marx wrote about capitalism's progeny, he drew on it directly. For him, capitalism bred vampires.

Rousseau helps make sense of these insatiable artificial people—*Homo economicus*, corporations and governments. He saw the artificial people that we allow in market society as a potential problem, but he didn't simply demand the abolition of government or economic organizations. Institutions, organizations and governments will always be with us, and are vital because they help socialize us into achieving more collectively than we might as solitary individuals. These artificial people can be dangerous when their appetites run unchecked, and if they've been captured, then the part of us that depends on them to see the wider world has been captured too. The kind of citizen we are depends on the institutions around us, and vice versa. Artificial people are never neutral.

This leaves us unmoored. There's no timeless politics that we can conjure from human nature to generate a countermovement to the self-regulating market, no hallowed place from which to launch a political response. Instead, we have to start from where we are, with the politics we have to hand. T. S. Eliot put it well: "Success is relative: it is what we can make of the mess we have made of things."[23] To understand the mess, we need to think about where markets do and don't belong, and return once again to the creation of modern market society. Markets were born as twins, conjoined to their own forms of government, but in order that modern market society might thrive in the five hundred years since its birth, other forms of economics and government have been smothered. There has been a very long battle to control and value the basic materials needed both to sustain life, and to thrive.

There were organizations before what we call the modern state, and there'll be organizations after it. Some of them were, and will be, more democratic than those we have right now. Those that thrive will have figured out how to make governments manage "free" goods in ways that are both sustainable and equitable. Insofar as tomorrow's governments succeed, they will owe a debt to yesterday's politics of the public domain, to older ways of valuing and sharing the world, which were once more thoughtfully called "the commons."

The commons is, slowly, beginning to be more widely remembered as a way to govern our world. The 2009 Sveriges Riksbank Prize in Economic Science in Memory of Alfred Nobel[24] was awarded, in part, to U.S. economist Elinor Ostrom for her work in studying the commons. The best way to understand what's at stake in her work is to look at the urgent politics of value that attend the commons today.[25] In so doing, we'll see that a democracy with fewer free lunches can be one that, paradoxically, has much more genuine liberty.

SIX

WE ARE ALL COMMONERS

It is more reasonable to suppose a thing to have been
invented by those to whom it would be of service, than
by those whom it must have harmed.
—JEAN-JACQUES ROUSSEAU, *Discourse on Inequality*

The first three times I heard the word "commons," I had no idea what
it meant. Hearing the phrase "House of Commons" in a media report
from the British Parliament, I guessed that to be a part of the "Commons" meant being rich, white and aggressively drunk. The next
time, it appeared in the context of a British children's television series
in the 1970s—*The Wombles*, a group of furry creatures who practiced
the dark arts of recycling on Wimbledon Common. A common was a
place I imagined to be littered with exciting things that were removed
by the Wombles to be reused in their burrow. The third time was on
a holiday in New York, where my family was told that if we wanted
to have the full American experience, we needed to head to Wood-
bury Common, one of the larger shopping complexes outside New
York City, so that we could shop like real Americans. (I got a sweater
with an American flag on it.) Commons, I thought, was American
English for "shopping center." What I never quite understood was

that "common" could be not only a place, but a verb to describe how to value and share the world around us.

Although it is often associated with Britain and its colonies, the commons as place and process can be found in societies from Central America to South Asia and, most recently, cyberspace. A commons is a resource, most often land, and refers both to the territory and to the ways people allocate the goods that come from that land. The commons provided food, fuel, water and medicinal plants for those who used it—it was the poorest people's life-support system. This was why the commons in England was ground zero in the great transformation. To value something involves both identifying it and setting up rules through which it can be used by society, and the rules of commoning were fundamentally incompatible with capitalism. By turning public land into private property, not only did land become a commodity, but the rural poor were cut off from their only means of survival, and forced to sell the only thing they had left— their labor. From the enclosure of the commons were born two new kinds of payment—rent and wages.

This history, however, is far removed from the understanding of "commons" that circulates today. Look to the *Oxford English Dictionary*, for instance, and you'll read that a common is "the undivided land belonging to the members of a local community as a whole. Hence, often, the patch of unenclosed or 'waste' land which remains to represent that."[1] The entire history of enclosure and rural dispossession has been collapsed by the lexicographers into the word "hence." The dictionary, however, merely reflects contemporary thought, making space for a more modern interpretation of how the commons became waste; today, the idea of a commons is most often associated with its dereliction, with its "tragedy."

The term "tragedy of the commons" was coined by microbiologist Garrett Hardin in a 1968 *Science* article, in which he asks what happens when individuals compete for a scarce resource.[2] The principal character, in fact the only character, in Hardin's tragedy is one we've met before—*Homo economicus*. Hardin argued that when faced with a shared resource, people will be overrun by their own selfish desires to consume it, even if they know that they're destroying it in the process. So, propelled by animal urges of self-satisfaction, in a world of scarcity, people will end up destroying the thing that they depend on for survival. Hobbes couldn't have said it better. Hardin's views weren't, however, based on any experimental or observed evidence, and they ignored the history of the enclosure of the commons. Despite this disconnection from the past, his essay became one of the most widely cited think-pieces in the twentieth century.

In many ways, Hardin's world looks a lot like our own, as we destroy it at a pace made more frantic by the recession. If you're looking for a tragedy, you can find it everywhere from the scrambling coltan-mining communities in the Congo to the increasingly desperate actions of farmers applying inorganic fertilizer to the soil to replace the fertility that their monoculture has destroyed. Hardin's is also a perspective that resonates with a particular breed of environmentalist. The Friends of the Earth saw their concerns reflected in his work—in 1972, he was inducted into their Environmental Hall of Fame.[3]

Scratch the surface, though, and Hardin's arguments blame the victim. The question isn't whether we are in dire environmental straits—we are very clearly in trouble. Every indicator in the Millennium Ecosystem Assessment, an exercise involving 1,360 scientists over five years in an international effort to measure humanity's impact on the natural world, shows that we're destroying the planet. The issue is a question of motive. The logical structure of the tragedy of the commons rests on a foundational model of the world in which people are, for whatever reason, prepared to override their own better judgment in service of their selfish natures. It's a world that resembles the one painted by the first professional economist, Thomas

Malthus, in his *Essay on the Principle of Population*. Malthus argued that any population would, tragically, always exceed the resource base available to feed it. It's not hard to see how the tragedy of the commons could apply here—poor people driven by their urges to procreate (even though they know the consequences) make more babies than there is food to feed them and this, according to the theory, explains why there is hunger in the world.

It's not surprising that Hardin was a strong advocate of population control. He is not alone in thinking that the way to solve environmental degradation, hunger and climate change lies in preventing the poor from reproducing, but it's a view that misunderstands the problem. The reason people go hungry today has *nothing at all* to do with a gap between the amount of food in the world and the number of people who are hungry. There's more than enough food on earth today to feed the world one and a half times over. The reason people go hungry is because of the way we distribute food through the market, as private property, and the people who starve are simply too poor to be able to afford it. If there were fewer people in the world but the way we distributed food remained the same, the poor would *still* go hungry. This isn't to say that women shouldn't be in charge of their own fertility—on the contrary, the single best route to reducing fertility rates in developing countries, bar none, is girls' education, and one of the victims of the fee-for-service model of education is that women and girls have been prevented from attending school.[4]

This is intimately connected to why Hardin's tragedy is misleading. For Malthusians, modern and classical, the reason we're headed to hell in a handbasket is that people are rapacious and untamable, creatures of passion and impulse. Those drives will lead us inexorably to consume endlessly, but we've seen that people aren't always like that, while corporations *are* always like that—the profit motive makes them so—which offers a way for us to understand the deeper tragedy of the commons.

Fisheries are perhaps the most cited example of the tragedy of the commons.[5] The argument is that every little fisherman is driven to catch as much as he possibly can, knowingly driving his fishery, and his livelihood, toward collapse. Many of the world's fisheries are in sharp decline—one article in the journal *Science* predicts the collapse of global ocean fisheries by 2048[6]—but writing off fisheries' decline as the tragedy of the commons is misleading. There have been fisherfolk for millennia, and the modest growth of fishing communities can't explain the destruction of the oceans. In many instances the commons are not being overrun, but taken over. A report by the international development NGO ActionAid provides a striking example.

Pakistan's six-hundred-mile coastline is blessed with marine riches—squid, mackerel, shrimp, tuna and scores of other fish have supported over 180,000 small-scale fisherfolk, like Abdul Majeed Motani, for centuries. Motani fishes with a crew of ten other villagers in his small wooden boat. He and his fellow villagers have seen their catches drop off dramatically in the past decade. The Pakistani Fisherfolk Forum (PFF), a local fishermen's group, reports a 70 to 80 percent decline in the local fisheries, and with it, growing hunger, indebtedness and poverty in villages across the Arabian coast.[7] So why, after centuries of sustainable use by local fisherfolk, have the seas been emptied?

Locals report that the decline began when Pakistan's military government, eager to step up the nation's export earnings, relaxed restrictions on foreign-owned industrial trawlers. Pakistan first opened its waters to foreign boats in 1982, but in 2001, it rewrote a rule that kept foreign boats at least thirty-five miles off the coast. Now only the largest foreign-owned trawlers are supposed to stay thirty-five miles back, while smaller foreign-owned trawlers are permitted between thirteen and thirty-five miles off the coast. The closest twelve miles inland is supposedly reserved for locals. The government officially licensed twenty-one transnational trawlers and twenty-three midsize trawlers in 2007,[8] but local fisherfolk have identified over one hundred foreign-owned vessels trawling Pakistan's coast each year. Many of them are joint-owned ventures, reflagged as "local" boats, which openly fish the twelve-mile local zone. Local fisherfolk complain that the government flouts these rules, turning a blind eye to abuses in order to keep the graft economy turning over.

Unlike the locals, industrial trawlers can scour the oceans day and night, with nets stretching three kilometers out to sea, dredging up everything in their path. According to the PFF, only 10 percent of the trawlers' catch has any value on the international market, and the other 90 percent is thrown away. It sounds high, but internationally, even factoring in some of the best-regulated global fisheries, bycatch makes up some 40 percent of all marine catches.[9]

Once again, women disproportionately bear the burden from reduced catches. Net and basket making and local fish drying and marketing, traditionally women's work, is no longer in high demand. According to the ActionAid report, women are being driven to work in local textile factories or industrial shrimp-processing plants, where many complain of hazardous working conditions.

The Pakistani proverb "When all else fails, the sea will provide" remains partly true. Even though fisheries are on a sharp decline, they continue to provide—but who they provide for is changing.[10] Pakistan's marine commons aren't being overrun by rapacious local fisherfolk. They have been enclosed by transnational business interests, facilitated by the government. These interests are in no danger of destroying their own livelihoods. Free international markets mean that when Pakistan's fisheries collapses, the industrial trawlers will simply move to more lucrative and profitable waters. Pakistan's traditional fishing families, however, are not so free. No richer waters await them.

The story in Pakistan is one with wider resonance, and a longer history. Looking at the twentieth century's great environmental disasters, one doesn't see people run amok. The environmental tragedies from the Dust Bowl to the mass extinctions of rain forest and ocean are the result of the behavior of corporations, of capitalist agriculture and forestry and fishing. The Dust Bowl happened because while individuals knew full well the value of the topsoil, their induction into capitalist agriculture turned them into exploiters of the very land on which their survival depended, transforming their connection to the world around them into one solely of short-term profit.

Commoning involves a web of social relations designed to keep our baser urges in check, fostering different ways of valuing our world, and of relating to others. We can see the destructive effects of enclosure not only in the scars left on the natural environment, but also within the most intimate of social relations around gender. When the way society valued work was transformed, the socially acceptable roles for men and women also changed. Those who wouldn't accept the new order were targeted, and in certain parts of the world that persecution continues today. The term for this hasn't changed, though—it's still called "witch hunting."

FENCING OFF THE COMMONS

In 2009, the pope visited Africa, where he managed to generate controversy, first by announcing that condoms aggravate the problems of HIV/AIDS and then by observing that Africans were "living in fear of spirits, of malign and threatening powers. In their bewilderment they end up even condemning street children and the elderly as alleged sorcerers."[11] This is a sort of caricature of Africa as a savage and superstitious place waiting for, depending on your faith, either the word of Christ or of free enterprise to be more forcefully spread so it can be fully developed. There is, of course, a link between the two—the spread of Christianity in Africa as in the Americas, and to a lesser extent Asia, was accompanied by the arrival of armed colonial forces in search of riches.

In a recent series of thorough and provocative articles, historian and social scientist Silvia Federici has suggested that the resurgence of witchcraft in Africa at a time of land grabbing and privatization isn't an accident.[12] The same coincidence could be seen in the great witch hunts that scoured Europe from the fifteenth to the seventeenth centuries. The number of Europeans who died as a result of the witch trials is impossible to know. In Savoy, a hotbed of witch hunting, the trial documents were hung from the neck of the convicted woman and burned along with her. Conservative estimates put the death toll across Europe at between forty thousand and sixty thousand.[13] The majority of those killed were women. Federici argues that their persecution coincided with a drastic change in their place in society.

She shows how the politics behind witch hunts concerns a new vision of the world, where women who insisted on their rights to value land, to their freedom to common, had no place.[14] It was in their defense of commoning that women were killed as witches. Enclosure wasn't, then, just about fencing off patches of land—it was also a way of foreclosing a set of political processes, and replacing them with novel ones in which women's participation was circumscribed in new ways. While not all witch hunts were in response to some attempt to protect a particular common, they are always signs of deeper political struggles. It is not by chance that we use the term "witch hunt" as a metaphor for a mass hysteria that distracts us from bigger political machinations.[15]

To understand the commons today, it's worth starting in feudal England—the birthplace of modern capitalism—by looking at the Magna Carta's twin charter, the Charter of the Forest. Although largely forgotten today, the Charter of the Forest guaranteed the ability of commoners to access pasture for their animals, to till land, to collect wood, harvest honey, use medicinal plants, forage and so on. Peter Linebaugh, who has done more than any other contemporary historian to recover the history of this charter, observes in *The Magna Carta Manifesto* that a commons right guaranteed freedoms in perpetuity over local resources for everyone.[16] This did not mean that everyone could take as much as they wanted. To have a commons isn't to license a free-for-all, as Hardin suggests, and it is not what happened historically. The precise shape of commoning was negotiated in a particular place and time, dependent on the ecology and the community. Common rights evolved over time, shaped by the relative power of those around the table, as well as the changing geography of the physical commons itself. The commons was, in other words, both a place and a "process of freedom," in which people fought for the right to shape the terms on which they could share the commons.

It's important not to romanticize the idea. Commoning did not take place in some protodemocratic Eden where everyone got a fair and equal say. The commons were an ongoing battlefield between lords and their serfs, but it was one in which the poor had won some victories, and had managed to stake a claim to public space in defiance of those who oppressed them. The Magna Carta itself represented a line in the sand, a negotiated end to the rapacity of King John of England who, in order to bankroll both a crusade and a war in France, had committed all manner of crimes. He taxed barons, stole forests, took children hostage and even sold his first wife, Isabella of Gloucester, to the Earl of Essex for twenty thousand marks.[17] The barons rebelled. In 1215, they marched into London, where they were met with open gates, a mark of the City's approval. They confronted the king, and negotiated hard. The Magna Carta certainly included demands made by the barons, merchants and the well-to-do in London, but it also included a strong set of protections of common rights, providing common access to the food, fuel, freedom and fruits of the forest provided for common people, returning to the public the natural resources that King John had taken for himself. This is the commons that historians have pointed to in rejection of Hardin's arguments. Contrary to the prediction, people figured out how to manage and maintain access to a scarce resource, despite the desire of kings and nobles to privatize it. If one's looking to affix the word "tragedy" to the commons, the nightmare did not begin with the creation of the commons, but with the process of its destruction, the process under which it was taken under private ownership.

Sometimes piecemeal, sometimes sweeping (as with Henry VIII's 1536 dissolution of monasteries), enclosure was the process by which land was once again taken out of public hands. Surveyors would use their chains, known as the devil's guts, to rope off areas of common land and formally assign title to a single individual. Not only fields, but forest and water were similarly enclosed—with lords preventing access to ponds and streams well stocked with fish, and forests teeming with game that had provided the poor with meat. By 1500, 45 percent of cultivable land in England had been enclosed, and took on a new logic—not only to provide private land for individual landlords, but also to drive up the price of rent for those landlords.[18]

Needless to say, this theft was deeply unpopular and provided the backdrop for rebellions ranging from small-scale acts of insubordination (the Lord of Arundel lost one hundred swans in a night—the killing of game was a warning to the rich) to the 1381 Peasants' Revolt, to the Diggers in the mid-1600s and beyond. The protests and resistance were always crushed, and because enclosure had seized the peasants' only means of survival, they had only two choices: to work for their new landlords, or to try their luck in the cities. Adam Smith lamented the violence being done to the commons by the spread of private property, though by the time he made his remarks, the process was already over: "The wood of the forest, the grass of the field, and all the natural fruits of the earth, which, when land was in common, cost the labourer only the trouble of gathering them . . . [he must now] pay the license to gather them; and must give up to the landlord a portion of what his labour either collects or produces."[19] It was these displaced peasants who, within a generation, were to become the proletarion backbone of the Industrial Revolution.

The world was being enclosed well beyond England, of course. By the time capitalism was firmly entrenched in Europe, colonists were killing and commodifying overseas. "Savage" was colonialism's magic word—it not only opened the door to the Aladdin's cave of land from Ireland to Australia, but was also used in the sorcery of turning bodies into things that could be bought and sold, in the Middle Passage enslavement of over ten million Africans. In the Americas, 75 million died in the century after colonization,[20] and although straightforward killing was a tool of enclosure, the colonists also had a set of arguments and rationales with which to explain their actions as those of civilized people. The justifications for enclosure were provided by none other than John Locke, the man who today is considered one of the godfathers of liberalism. His argument that the natural rights of man were "life, liberty and estate"[21] appears, with one slight change, in the American Declaration of Independence.

As secretary of the Board of Trade and Plantations, and in his role as secretary to the Lords and Proprietors of the Carolinas, Locke was intellectually and financially invested in finding a reason to increase the acreage under his company's ownership. His justification for turning "unowned" land into private holdings had two parts. First, because everyone owns their labor, improving land with that labor means you own it. If you've worked on land, that's yours to keep, but anything that appears not to be used properly was considered fair game for enclosure. Second, land can be taken out of the commons if there is "enough and as good" left for everyone else.

Although the reasons that the English wanted to scoop up property in the Americas were utterly selfish, the justification for property and ownership yields an important clue about how a different market system might work. Private property requires society to approve of it being taken out of common hands. Property is, in other words, social—there's nothing natural about the way some people are allowed to exclude others from land, for instance. Indeed, it was the rescinding of rights to share common resources that radicalized a young German thinker who had recently left the academy, and was working as a journalist. His political opinions ran to an optimistic liberalism—think of him as a nineteenth-century *Wired* reader—a man who thought that with a free press and functioning parliament, the future would be bright. Two events would change his opinion. The first was when he witnessed the debates in the local parliament over customary wood-gathering rights in Rhineland forests, which made him realize the centrality of questions of property to politics. The second was the ease with which the Prussian censorship closed down his paper. It was these events that nudged the young Karl Marx toward thinking about the centrality of property in politics and society.

One doesn't need to be a Marxist to see how property is social. To take one example, consider how governments deal with broadcast spectrum. The airwaves are owned by the government, and the right to broadcast on a particular frequency is sold to media companies subject to their fulfilling certain social purposes. If broadcasters transmit material that's considered lewd or inappropriate, they will be fined, and if they continue to violate those sanctions, their right to use that bit of spectrum can be taken back. The laws that govern how animals can be treated provide another example.[22] Most countries have laws that permit animals to be owned as property, but there are nonetheless restrictions—cruelty to cats and dogs is prohibited in most countries. Under the "social function" doctrine in a number of Latin American countries' constitutions, there are similar provisions when it comes to other private property. Land, for example, can be privately owned as long as it's being put to use, but the moment it is left derelict, or if the land is owned purely for speculative purposes, ownership rights to the land are forfeit, and it becomes available to anyone who will put it to greater use. Property rights, in other words, can be far more flexible and elastic than we currently imagine them.

When the social role of the land was decided by the standards of the colonial British, however, things didn't work out well for native North Americans. Although their hunting techniques were in harmony with the environment, and often improved it, they couldn't prove this to the people who took their land. When white people came along, they saw rich and fertile land that appeared to be occupied by Native Americans only for a short period of time every year—they didn't see how the land was part of a wider system of sustainable nomadic grazing. Among some tribes, however, there *was* permanent agriculture, with large areas of land under cultivation, using sophisticated agroecological methods of maintaining soil fertility and ecological integrity—one example is the intercropping of corn, beans and squash (the Three Sisters of Native American agriculture). Within these tribes, as in much of the Global South today, it was women's work to tend to the growing of food for domestic consumption while the men went out hunting. The English couldn't comprehend that agriculture was exclusively managed by women whose English counterparts had been confined to domestic, noncommercial duties. So the colonists described the women's activity not as agriculture, but as gardening; and then they expropriated their land.

Along the Pacific coast in North America, indigenous economies came under different forms of attack. An institution central to many cultures was "potlatch." It was a ceremony in celebration of a guest or event—each society had its own specific set of rules and customs. The common denominator, and the one that most exercised the white government, was that a potlatch involved the mass redistribution of wealth in which the giving away of things was a sign of rank. In the eyes of the U.S. and Canadian governments, without the morally improving virtues of frugality and prudence, Native Americans would be condemned to perpetual backwardness. Potlatch was described as "[the] parent of numerous vices which eat out the heart of the people. . . . [It] is not possible that Indians can acquire property or can become industrious with any good result, while under the influence of this mania."[23] So, from 1885 to 1951, the Canadian government declared it illegal, levying a punishment of between two and six months in jail.

These nasty little stories have contemporary variants: Governments and corporations are still enclosing forests, fisheries and agricultural land because, allegedly, the indigenous people on the land are incapable of managing it for the common good, or because the indigenous people simply don't count. Locke's legacy can be seen in the international legal standard of *terra nullius* (land belonging to no one), which was used to vacate the rights of indigenous people from the United States to Australia. It remains a live issue, with the same legal doctrine being haggled over from the West Bank to the South China Sea, and wherever "marginal land" is licensed over the objections of marginal people.[24] Which returns us to the rise in witch hunts in Africa today.

The boundaries of African countries look as if they were drawn with a ruler because that is precisely what happened in Berlin in 1884. The Berlin Conference brought together the great European powers, who bickered and trucked over who should get what in Africa, setting off a ruinous chain of events that today leaves the continent desperately impoverished, militarized and degraded. In the early twenty-first century, the continent finds itself once more in the crosshairs of the world's great powers. This time, though, there's no formal conference at which the spoils are decided. Instead, the

United States, Europe, the Middle East, China, India and other Asian countries are staking claims through various means, such as private sector contracts, mercenaries, armed bases (the United States recently unveiled AFRICOM, its unified command post, which, because of its unpopularity among Africans, is currently based in Frankfurt), development deals and "aid." All of these are attempts to control and channel resource wealth, biodiversity, food supplies and land.

As with the enclosures in Europe, the deepening of market society has meant a transformation of gender roles as traditional ways of managing resources are uprooted. Figures are hard to come by, but in the 1990s, according to one conservative estimate based on published figures, 22,000 people were killed for witchcraft.[25] It's no accident that violence against women, couched in accusations of witchcraft, has been particularly intense in and around areas where resources are being expropriated for tourism. In Zambia, witches have frequently been found on land destined for game reserves, and on breeding grounds for animals destined for "canned hunts," in which rich tourists celebrate the wonder of Africa's Big Five—the lion, elephant, buffalo, rhino and leopard—by killing one of each.[26] In Nigeria, women in the Iguobazuwa forest reserve were displaced from their land when the government sold the forest to the Michelin tire company. Michelin set about turning the forest into a rubber plantation, destroying the subsistence farms that women had been using to feed their communities.[27] Mabel Ubara, one of the women affected, reported that "two years after my husband's death, I started farming. . . . Michelin came with his evil bulldozer and destroyed everything I had planted. I was crying. . . . I was trying to stop them; they threatened to bulldoze me with their caterpillar if I don't allow them."[28]

Reports of landgrabs do not, however, appear in the newspapers alongside the stories of African witch hunts—so it's not surprising

that from afar the killings of women appear mysterious and barba-
rous. Outside Africa, we're encouraged to understand this as an inex-
plicable symptom of the Heart of Darkness. Yet it is nothing less
than the death throes of one form of society at the hands of another.
This is not to suggest that there isn't an ecological crisis, in Africa as
elsewhere, or that these traditional systems were absolutely just and
desirable, but in their transformation into modern market society,
the voices most silenced are those of Africans themselves.

In addition to the loss of life, there's a cultural loss that attends
this kind of destruction, the disappearance of knowledge about
sustainably managing natural resources for the local community.
Preserving this knowledge about how to value natural resources can
mean the difference between sustainability and extinction. Let's return to the quintessential "tragedy of the commons," the fisheries.
There is no one-size-fits-all solution, especially when it comes to
near-shore, artisanal fisheries. But in asserting their collective political and economic rights, the Pakistani fishermen's groups may
have the key to protecting their fisheries. A case study of traditional
fisheries in Chile suggests that giving communities the rights to the
commons *as a commons* can be highly successful. Chile banned industrial trawlers in the 1960s so that its artisanal fishing sector would
be sheltered from competition with destructive transnational operations. After a quota system failed, the government began to work
with fishermen's organizations up and down the coast. Together,
they came up with a system of TURFs—or territorial use rights in
fisheries. Fishing villages and fishers' organizations were awarded
collective rights over specific traditional fishing grounds that they'd
known and fished for generations. Enforcement was devolved to
local fisher people's unions. It worked: The fisheries recovered.
The TURFs were modeled on the historical fishing grounds of local
fisherfolk, essentially granting present-day collective rights to what

in previous centuries had already belonged to the local community.[29]

The Chilean experience is, however, an exception to the rule.
Generally, commons systems aren't being supported in the twenty-
first century—they're being dismantled. As they disappear, we lose
millennia of accumulated knowledge about how to manage scarce
resources sustainably, both in terms of the harvesting technology
to keep the resources abundant and also the social systems necessary to ensure that no one takes more than his or her fair share.
These systems of knowledge are displaced by the guiding motives
of profit-driven markets. This isn't to say that the existing systems
are perfect—they're not—but they do seem to have offered ways in
which societies have survived, and thrived, with a mechanism for
setting the value of resources different from that exercised by the
profit-driven market. As British activist and writer George Monbiot
has noted, the European Union's "transferable quota" system of fishing rights has resulted in millions of tons of fish being thrown away,
88 percent of fisheries being overexploited and the cost to the public
being far greater than the value of the catches.[30]

The enclosure of the commons has destroyed the rich networks
of knowledge that once helped guide the way we valued the world.
Polanyi's transformation is, however, never total and never complete—
there are always practices, ideas and experiences that persist, and
offer tools with which we might begin to think of new ways of valuing
beyond profit-driven markets. Now that the ecological and economic
crises created by the first of Polanyi's two movements have become
so acute, it seems reasonable to ask where the second movement is.
Why hasn't society started to automagically heal itself from the violence of profit-driven markets? The answer heard all too often on the
left is that things aren't quite bad enough, and that it will take im-
mense tragedy to mobilize enough sentiment to spur political change.

The trouble with this argument is that things are fairly bad already; the number of people going hungry in 2009, for instance, is projected to be in excess of one billion—a planetary record. A second response to the question of why Polanyi's double movement hasn't happened is that the original countermovement protagonists aren't around anymore. The Speenhamland laws were spearheaded by a failing sliver of the landed aristocracy, and there aren't too many of those people left. But perhaps the most satisfying answer is that, in fact, there *is* a countermovement—indeed, there are many countermovements, progressive and reactionary, inclusive and exclusive. It's just not widely reported, as, especially in the case of progressive examples, the people leading such movements are the poor, the dispossessed, the marginalized, the people on whose shoulders the externalities of the rich often fall, the world's least free people who are discovering that they are The Change They've Been Waiting For. In the next part, we'll look at how, exactly, they've tried to rebalance market society and how they're trying to transform the way value is set, not by returning to the commons, but by reinventing it.

PART TWO

It's one thing to know that everyone has a seat at the lunch counter, but how do we figure out how everyone can pay for the meal?

    —BARACK OBAMA, *Speech at the National Association*
        for the Advancement of Colored People's Fight
        for Freedom Fund Dinner, 2005

SEVEN

THE COUNTERMOVEMENT AND THE RIGHT TO HAVE RIGHTS

Live free or die!
—*State motto of New Hampshire*

Give me liberty or give me death!
—PATRICK HENRY, *arguing for rebellion against the British*

There's a poetry of choice, freedom and death that weaves through political rhetoric in the United States, past and present. It's a language of frontiers and revolution, but its grammar fits the way capitalism sets the terms of value. At its heart beats the idea that private property and profit-driven markets provide one thing that no other system can: liberty. Commoning involves other people putting limits on what resources you can exploit, how much you can accumulate, how things will be shared. The free market has none of those constraints. Within it, you're free to buy, sell, consume or produce whatever you like. With a walletful of cash and a pinch of entrepreneurial spirit, the world lies at your feet. There is no system more attuned to this version of liberty than capitalism. This soft power of the market, its ability to suggest liberty as part of exchange, is one of its most attractive elements.

When the Obama bailout plan mooted salary caps on bankers receiving public money, howls could be heard throughout corporate America—from the inhabitants of C-suites to the fresh-faced graduates who wanted one day to claim those corner offices for themselves. Without the liberty to be entrepreneurial and to receive adequate reward, they bleated, talent would leave the business. Given that it was such unleashed "talent" that had allowed the economic crisis to bloom, few tears were shed for their loss of freedom beyond the world of banking. But were they right, at least in theory? Does capitalism provide the most freedom?

The late Oxford philosopher Jerry Cohen concieved a thought experiment that helps us to understand how money works, and the way that it intersects with the liberty offered by free markets. When the market rations goods on the basis of money, he argued, there's reason to quarrel with the idea that markets make freedom. Imagine that we live in a world where we have little tickets distributed at random. On these tickets are rights—the right to go visit your sick mother, the right to cross a particular road, the right to live somewhere, the right to eat a steak, the right to treatment for a disease and so on. You don't *have* to do what's written on any given ticket—they simply limit the extent of your freedoms. If you try to do something for which you do not have a ticket, the law intervenes. The tickets map out the degree to which you are free (or not free) to do something—they are a complete accounting of your liberties. The more tickets you have, the freer you are.

So here's the twist: Money is just like these tickets. What, after all, does money offer in a market society if not the ability to buy liberty, to afford health care, decent food, housing, the security of not working in retirement, insurance against accident or unemployment? Those without money are as unfree as those without tickets. Without cash in a market society, you're free to do nothing, to have very little and to die young. In other words, under capitalism, *money is the right to have rights*.

The deepest irony is that the spread of the empire of prices is said to be compatible with freedom. Yet the freedoms that the free market offers are illusions. For the poor, the price of decent food, of health care, of Social Security, of housing are all substantially beyond reach. The gap between what people earn and the cost of their freedoms means that, for more and more Americans, freedom is just another word for nothing they can afford. This tension is becoming much more acute with the current global recession. In Sacramento, the capital of California, new tent cities have sprung up. Hundreds of people live there, and there are reports of fifty new arrivals every day. In developing countries, of course, the situation has long been dire, and the global recession is pushing millions more into poverty, but in both cases, this poverty has deepened under a system that offered progress, prosperity and development for the poorest, and has delivered its opposite—a yawning inequality gap, less happiness and a dogged persistence of diseases and afflictions to which we have long known the cures.

In the land of the free, the market delivers few choices to those who cannot afford them. In the U.S. health care system, for example, the value of life is famously defined by the market. Michael Moore's film *Sicko* shows the U.S. health care industry's profit-driven approach at its nadir, with stories of patients asked by their insurance company to choose which of their fingers they'd like to save—a middle finger costing sixty thousand dollars, or the index finger for a much more reasonable twelve thousand dollars. Less well known is quite how inequitable the health industry's effects are, and how much the things we have the least choice over—our race, our sex, the wealth of the family we're born into—shape our destinies.

If we wanted to find a number that captures the inequities of freedom in America, the data on maternal mortality rates, the rates at which women die in or soon after childbirth, make grim reading. The figure in the United States is 11 per 100,000 births. In the United Kingdom, 8 women die per 100,000 births. In Slovakia, the figure is 6.[1] In the United States, expenditure on health care is over $6,000 per person. In Slovakia, it's $565.[2]

Worse, since 1995, maternal mortality rates for every minority group have gone up. With better medical technology, increased average income and more billionaires than ever before in America, *more* women are dying in childbirth, with African American women experiencing rates almost five times higher than white people. If the African American population in the United States were a separate country, they'd be ranked below Uzbekistan, which has a maternal mortality rate of 24 per 100,000, and where the average income per person is $840 per year. In the United States, one corollary of free market liberty is dying young.

The U.S. story can't be told without incriminating the various cultural, political and economic pressures that have kept the country away from single-payer health care, yet America's failure to provide women's health care is also part of a global story. In 2000, when world leaders met to discuss how to improve their social policies, they announced the Millennium Development Goals, a set of targets intended to address the most egregious inequities and social injustices. Few of the goals look like they'll be met by 2015, and that of lowering maternal mortality rates will certainly not. In 1990, 576,000 women died worldwide from pregnancy or complications due to childbirth. The goal is to reduce that figure by 75 percent, to 144,000 by 2015. In 2005 the rate was 536,000—a 7 percent reduction.[3]

The Millennium Development Goals were controversial. Critics saw the goals as a diluted version of the rights enshrined in the Universal Declaration of Human Rights.[4] The Declaration was meant to be a new social pact, reining in every government, committing it to guarantees of the right to life, property, employment, health and education, among other freedoms. Defenders of the Millennium Development Goals appealed to realism, arguing that because governments had made and failed to keep promises in the past, these more modest goals could eventually be met, because they were within every government's grasp. Rights on paper are all well and good, ran the argument, but governmental goals were an excellent second-best.

Under this model, rights are what governments give, not what citizens take. Governments seem to have given a great deal, though. The Universal Declaration of Human Rights, humanity's most widely translated document, seems a remarkable achievement today. It is hard to imagine twenty-first-century governments seriously committing themselves to the redistributive and progressive domestic policy that human rights demand. But in the early 1940s, when Polanyi was completing *The Great Transformation* and the declaration was first conceived, the ongoing horrors of World War II were at the forefront of everyone's minds, as were the conditions that gave rise to it—the Depression of the 1930s, and its murderous political consequences in Europe. There was also a popular appetite for active and redistributive government, due in no small part to the power and militancy of workers' movements around the world. In 1942, President Roosevelt could call for a "supertax" rate of 100 percent on income above $110,000 (in 2007 dollars, that's $1.4 million) and Congress could settle on a compromise that required a tax of 94 percent on all income above $200,000 ($2.5 million today) and still be consonant with public opinion.[5] The rights that came from these politics guaranteed everything from the right to free speech and political organizing to the right to food and paid holidays from work.

Unsurprisingly, after the initial flush of enthusiasm for human rights (and after its championing by people such as Eleanor Roosevelt, who headed the UN Commission on Human Rights) the U.S., UK and Russian governments tried to backpedal. They were worried about what "rights" would mean to groups deprived of them within their own borders. In 1947, the United States had a taste of this when W. E. B. DuBois presented a petition to the United Nations from the National Association for the Advancement of Colored People (NAACP) titled *An Appeal to the World: A Statement on the Denial of Human Rights to Minorities in the Case of Citizens of Negro Descent in the United States of America and an Appeal to the United Nations for Redress*. The civil rights movement had found an opening in the government's defenses.

In the closing months of the war, governments anticipated this, and in October 1944 the United Kingdom, the United States, China and Russia drafted a document for postwar governance in which there was no mention of human rights.[6] The backpedalers were, however, met with an international storm of protest, from British colonies and from domestic public opinion in the United States, demanding a more forthright commitment to human rights. Roosevelt himself had done much to foment this backlash—after a meeting with activists asking him to support human rights, the president said, "Okay, you've convinced me. Now go on out and bring pressure on me!"[7]

In the end, a compromise was reached—while the language of individual rights was strident, the enforcement mechanisms would be left to individual countries to decide. So, on December 10, 1948, the Universal Declaration of Human Rights was signed in Paris. It took several more years, and a lot more negotiation, before the international community could agree on two treaties that would oblige its signatories to provide rights, rather than merely declare that the rights existed. Just like the Magna Carta's guaranteeing civil rights, and the Charter of the Forest providing some basic guarantee of common social and economic rights, there were two treaties—the

International Covenant on Civil and Political Rights and the International Covenant on Economic, Social and Cultural Rights. Together, the declaration and the two covenants made up the International Bill of Human Rights. When they were finally adopted in 1966, they were intended as a definitive line beyond which neither governments nor corporations should cross.

The story hasn't, however, ended happily. Particularly in the Global South, governments have encouraged their citizens to wait for rights to be delivered while the government addresses the concerns of each citizen in turn.[8] The command to be patient implies that in time we will, one by one, reach the Promised Land. History suggests, however, that asking for patience serves an altogether different purpose. It's a way of demobilizing popular demands, and of letting governments wriggle out of providing anything at all, while suggesting that the cardinal duty of being a citizen is to wait with an outstretched hand. In other words, rights can be understood as a bedtime story, in which the future ends happily ever after, if only we allow the profit-driven markets to continue their reign undisturbed, and agree that the most fundamental right of all is that of individuals to private property.

As W. E. B DuBois and the civil rights movement have shown, however, the way to make governments deliver rights is not to wait, but to demand. This understanding of rights has broken free of attempts to define it merely as the future dividend of present patience. Today, the language of rights has been reappropriated by oppressed and marginalized groups looking to reclaim some of the power that market society has taken from them. From women's movements to the demands of indigenous people, it is a mark of the success of rights talk that there are millions of people promoting democratic social change in the name of rights, despite calls from their governments for patience until they can find the political will to enact change.

ON "POLITICAL WILL"

If "savage" was the magic word for colonialists, "political will" is the
fairy dust of today's democracy. When change fails to happen, it is
for want of "political will," a sort of magic powder that stirs the powerful to action (even if that action ends up being merely "rinse and
repeat"). What contemporary ideas of "political will" betray, more
than anything, is our own ambivalence about government. The public at large have more than enough political will for health care, for
education, for reduced spending on weapons, or for the environment.
It's just that, all too often, the abundant will of government representatives is shaped by a corporate agenda, rather than a popular one. In
Italy, one of the best-selling books of recent years is *La Casta* (The
Caste), a political exposé by senior journalists Sergio Rizzo and
Gian Antonio Stella that portrays the political establishment as a
club of more or less well-meaning kleptocrats. When government
really is a caste apart, it seems there's little that can be done to bring
them back to earth except, as history suggests, through widespread
civic engagement. Curiously, in one of the more cited studies of
what makes bureaucracies work for the people, Robert Putnam's
Making Democracy Work, a key factor in Italy has been the presence
of the Communist Party.

While the Italian Communist Party may seem a rather unlikely
and remote source of hope, its 1970s foot soldiers knew something
that has largely been forgotten in Western democracies—that the passivity of the majority is what allows the powerful to rule. It is in this
insight that we can find the rocket fuel for Polanyi's double movement.
The second part of the double movement, where society reclaims
power from the market, happens through *demand*, not gift. In a sense,
this was the promise of the Obama election campaign. The slogans of
"No more politics as usual" resonated, as well it should, with disenfranchised people around the world, not just in the United States.

There is, however, a difference between rousing campaign rallies and widespread democracy. The Obama administration is, for instance, firing up the campaign machinery that first got him elected, to push his agenda on education, health care and climate change. One of the characteristics of the new campaign meetings is the lack of time for questioning the substance of these policies—there's just one enemy: "politics as usual"—and just one solution: the president's new politics. The proper name for this is populism. The cult pact between leader and led isn't, however, a sign of reinvigorated democracy—it's the last desperate substitute for it. For democracy to flourish, we need our own moment of admission that our economic system has failed us. Just as Greenspan lost his faith in an economic organizing principle, we also need to take a long hard look not only at the free market but at the political system that supports it. It's in reclaiming the idea that we're able to think for ourselves and that we're ready for politics, rather than outsourcing it like so much else, that we will be able to reclaim both democracy and our economy.

This seems a tall order, but there's an organization, about which I've written before,[9] that understands the relationship between rights, democracy and action very well indeed: the international peasant movement La Via Campesina. Founded in 1993 by a number of American and European farmers' groups, they have grown, by some estimates, to a movement with over 150 million members in sixty-nine countries, all of them peasants, farmers, farmworkers or landless people wanting to grow food. One of those original organizers is now the president of Bolivia—Evo Morales. Although constituted in the early 1990s, their member organizations have been going for considerably longer. The creation story of La Via Campesina is an object lesson in how democracy works, and how to make rights happen. There's an irony here: The people least able to value the land—the word "peasant" in English is laced with spit and contempt—offer through their politics a way of saving the planet.

La Via Campesina concentrate much of their effort on democratizing both the public and private sectors—their target is market society. They measure their success by the fact that governments around the world, from Mali to Nepal to Bolivia, are adopting their visions for change. The movement actively lobbies local and national governments, and has already made considerable progress at the United Nations.

La Via Campesina's politics did not arrive by magic, but as a result of confrontations with both governments and the private sector. Theirs is an experience of the double movement in microcosm. Through the 1980s, the World Bank was busy bringing the market to the Global South. With messianic zeal, economists trained in the gospel of the Chicago School spread the news of unfettered free markets, by hook and by crook.[10] They brought with them their tactics of enclosure—not only the old-school seizure of public land, but also new forms of commodification involving culture and knowledge, as demonstrated in the "biopiracy" of the intellectual property in seeds.[11] At the stroke of a pen, the genetic information in seeds that had been bred by generations of peasants became a new El Dorado for transnational seed companies, intellectual property ripe for the taking. This replaying of the great transformation was driven by unaccountable experts, who destroyed local forms of knowledge and governance in order that their own might take root. The consequences of these actions, particularly in agriculture, were disastrous. The World Bank's own Independent Evaluation Group in 2007 wrote that the Bank's performance in Africa was, in the main, a catastrophe. The invisible hand was meant to allocate resources better than governments, but when governments were swept away, the invisible hand was nowhere to be seen.[12]

Of course, this didn't happen without a fight, and we didn't have to wait until 2007 for an indictment. In countries where the free market was to be enforced, there were riots and protests—at least 146 such mass actions happened around the world between 1976 and 1982. People living through the consequences of these policies knew full well the changes that they brought—from hikes in the price of bread and fuel to cuts in Social Security benefits—and were unequivocal in their protests. These were the initial consequences of the first part of the double movement. International critics charged that the World Bank wasn't listening to the needs of the poor, that its policies of state shrinking, exchange-rate floating and market promoting were very far from what poor people wanted. The Bank responded to its critics by setting up "consultations" with civil society in the countries in which it operated, hiring a largely ineffective "Human Development Unit," and starting to counter its human toll with some social spending.

For this to happen, the Bank needed to "consult" with people, and as most of those affected by their actions wanted the Bank to get the hell out, there was a problem. So it advertised for organizations with a rural constituency with which it might powwow in a friendly, not-paying-too-much-attention kind of way. By calling for organizations willing to consult with the Bank, an army of nongovernmental organizations with designs on employment within the Bank was created, with third-world brokers offering their legitimating services in exchange for a tax-free per diem, a ticket to Washington, D.C., and a shot at the big consulting contracts. The World Bank was engaging in a sort of democracy puppet show.[13]

It was against this backdrop that a group of membership-based peasant movements—the people most affected by the Bank's policy, together with supportive NGOs and foundations—got together to talk about what should happen instead. With the experience of being told what was best for them still fresh in their minds, they created a federation in which this sort of domination couldn't and wouldn't happen. Particularly in a group where some movements claim tens of millions of members, while others had only hundreds, the smaller movements fought for, and won, a great deal of autonomy. La Via Campesina settled on an internal structure where no organization can tell another what to do, but where decisions are arrived at through an extensive, and lengthy, process of grassroots consultation. This meticulously democratic process was shaped by a suspicion of governments and development experts who had, for so long, told them how to live their lives.

By confronting the destruction of the commons and the creation of a fake democracy in its stead, La Via Campesina has faced the challenge of modern market society. Their response wasn't just institutional, but philosophical. The vision that they developed as part of their countermovement is called "food sovereignty," and of its many definitions, the basic one is this:

> Food sovereignty is the peoples', Countries' or State Unions' RIGHT to define their agricultural and food policy.

It doesn't look like much, but it's dynamite. Although there are some specific accompaniments to food sovereignty, such as women's rights and a demand for freedom from interference by the EU and United States, the call for food sovereignty itself is pretty light on *exactly* what should happen. It isn't a call for a specific set of rights so much as a call to be able to set the terms of value—and they want to exercise these rights over the stuff that they need to survive: land, water, seed and culture. They want to have the right to decide what their rights should be. Sound familiar?

ON THE RIGHT TO HAVE RIGHTS

Members of La Via Campesina are not the first to come up with the idea of "a right to have rights." Hannah Arendt used the idea to describe the plight of those without a nation: Jewish refugees in the interwar years. In her *Origins of Totalitarianism*, she makes this observation: "People deprived of human rights . . . are deprived, not of the right to freedom, but of the right to action, not of the right to think whatever they please, but of the right to opinion. . . . We became aware of the existence of a right to have rights . . . only when millions of people emerged who had lost and could not regain these rights because of the new global political situation."[14]

We might think that these rights are at best some sort of moral force, to be appealed to when all else has failed, but in La Via Campesina, rights have very concrete consequences. But first they had a lot of meetings and debate. Talk of a "people's right to have rights" isn't a program of action—it's what precedes concrete demands; it is a statement of will.[15]

In a series of iterations of the definition, successive La Via Campesina meetings have made it very clear that they are not proposing to abolish markets or world trade entirely; they just want it to happen without domination. They want a social control of markets, to reclaim some value from what free markets destroy. The trouble with this iterative process is that more and more people flock into the tent, and as the tent enlarges to accommodate them, it can sag in the middle and begin to collapse. In a later definition, it rather looked as if the whole "let's get everyone around the table and hash it out" went too far. A 2007 definition wanted to bring "producers, distributors and consumers" of food under one roof—but doing this would put the very people in conflict on the same side of the negotiating table.

This sounds fairly damning, but it's part of a process of figuring

out what the movement actually wants. It's a collective version of
E. M. Forster's question "How can I know what I think till I see what
I say?"[16] There's no guarantee, as personal experience teaches us
all, that the first thing out of one's mouth is necessarily the most
sensible—ideas need exposure to the world to become effective. One
of the rights that movements are fighting for is the right to make
and learn from their own mistakes, rather than suffer someone
else's—and it works. Newer definitions of food sovereignty are, happily, more coherent.

At their conference in Maputo, Mozambique, in 2008, La Via
Campesina came up with a new slogan and a series of strategies
around food sovereignty in which they're explicitly targeting transnational corporations, in a move that focuses and unifies its various branches. The new slogan is the most revealing, because it
puts society's most pervasive inequality of power front and center—
"Food sovereignty is about an end to all forms of violence against
women."

Here is a statement from the world's poorest people, those whose
main constituents, peasants, are synonymous with the most un-
schooled and ignorant. Yet their latest declaration shows an understanding of hunger as the most recent manifestation of millennia of
exploitation, and of the distortion of relationships around how value
is set. They diagnose the problem of hunger and poverty not as a
shortage of food but as a lack of power, which is why the idea of all
forms of violence against women is fundamental. Beyond the physical violence of beating, rape or assault that one in three women will
be subject to in her lifetime,[17] hunger is a form of violence, one that
affects women disproportionately. Of the people going hungry in
the world today, 60 percent are women or girls. It's a story that takes
place in rich countries as well as poor ones, where mothers skip meals
so that their children can eat. When a woman cannot sell her food
in the market because the subsidized alternative from the European

Union or the United States is cheaper, that's a kind of violence. When a family cannot afford to send their daughters to school because they need their labor at home, that too is a form of violence. The migrations that climate change have already started are a form of violence too.[18]

La Via Campesina's path is promising. If there is to be enfranchisement, then everyone has to be able to shape their rights. There's no obvious or natural way for this to go. That's why there are so many definitions of food sovereignty and also why there are so many ways in which to claim it. Although similar stories might be told almost anywhere, here is an example from the United States. It's a story from the southern tip of Florida, in Immokalee, where members of La Via Campesina are organizing their countermovement in response to the spread of a capitalism that not only turned land and work into commodities, but turned workers themselves into private property.

AMERICAN APARTHEID

When I took my guided tour around the town, Immokalee felt familiar. "Immokalee" means "my home" in Seminole. The trailers in which tomato pickers slept reminded me of other homes, in South African townships—the densely packed low-income houses built by the government to keep the supply of black labor close, but not too close, to the cities where their work was required. But the apartheid-era township houses seemed better than those in the American South.

In Immokalee, housing stock is owned by a handful of local slumlords who rule over an archipelago of run-down and unsanitary houses. I visited a trailer in which eight people slept and lived in poverty, queuing to use the bathroom every morning, and the stove top every night. For this, they paid forty dollars a week. If they wanted an air conditioner, they paid twenty dollars a week more. In one case, workers wanting to wash a day's worth of pesticides off their skin were charged five dollars to hose down outside. Some workers found it cheaper and more effective to wash their hands in bleach.

It's not only the inhumane living conditions that resemble South African apartheid. Immokalee is in Collier County, where the largest city, Naples, is (a second or third) home to Bill Gates, Steven Spielberg and Donald Trump. Average family income is over $100,000. The walls are high, the golf courses lush and well-patrolled, the police assiduous in escorting the indigent out of sight. Immokalee lies on the other side of the county, and is the source of some the state's largest profits.

Florida produces 90 percent of the U.S. winter tomato supply, and it appears to be a lucrative business. Quite how lucrative is hard to say, because corporations like Pacific Tomato Growers, Six L's Packing Company, and DiMare Fresh are private family-owned businesses, so the companies aren't publicly listed. When the workers on their tomato farms formed the Coalition of Immokalee Workers (CIW) to fight for change, this ownership structure mattered a great deal to them. The private family-owned businesses are not accountable to shareholders, so they don't care if they are shamed publicly. This is why the CIW has targeted companies like McDonald's and Taco Bell, which buy the tomatoes from the growers, and which are more concerned with their brand reputations.

Work for tomato pickers is irregular, dependent on the weather, and merciless. A talented picker who is lucky enough to work in a field that hasn't yet been picked (they're picked up to four times, and on the fourth sweep, there's pitifully little left on the vine) can fill 150 buckets a day. Workers lift up to 2.4 tons of tomatoes per day, sold in the stores for about $5,000, and for which they might be paid

$67 for twelve hours' work. This is a rate of forty-five cents per thirty-two-pound bucket of green tomatoes, and it has increased only five cents in the past thirty years—if the piece rate had only kept pace with inflation, it would today be $1.02 per bucket. The only reason the five-cent increase happened was due to a month-long hunger strike by six members of the CIW.[19]

Nely Rodriguez, an organizer with the coalition, describes the disproportionate burden that women bear. "Women in the fields work as hard as men and many times earn less because we might not pick as fast or be chosen every day to work. Because of our low wages, we live in overcrowded trailers and bad conditions, we have to raise our families in these places. And we have to sacrifice time with our children to try to give them a better life."

As if the living conditions and wages aren't abysmal enough, some workers are literally modern-day slaves. Since 1997, with the help of the CIW, over one thousand people have been freed from slavery by Florida law enforcement officers, and the labor brokers who enslaved them have been prosecuted under the same laws that were written in the wake of abolition.[20] In the most recent case, twelve slaves escaped from the back of a truck where they'd been held captive.[21]

Whites living under apartheid in South Africa practiced a special sort of self-deception, believing that there were two worlds, separated for the benefit of all and hermetically sealed from one another. The high walls served a psychological purpose, reinforcing the deniability and ignorance fostered by remove. Yet, when it suited those in power, the two worlds could be made to meet, one parasitic upon the other. In South Africa, that bridge was the use of black workers to generate wealth by providing industrial, agricultural and domestic labor. A similar story might be told in Florida.

Most of the time, no thought is paid by the tomato growers to the treatment of their workers, who are kept hidden from sight and mind, like stepchildren in the basement. Occasionally, however, these inequities come to some sort of public light. While Congress was in recess during the Christmas of 2008, the Florida Tomato Growers Exchange—whose president and vice president were Larry Lipman and Billy Heller, Jr., representing Six L's and Pacific, respectively—approached the government for a $100 billion bailout. This, apparently, was in the public interest.

It was due to democratic socialist Senator Bernie Sanders that the bailout was blocked, reports Katrina vanden Heuvel. Sanders's press secretary, without singling out any individual growers, said that the senator "had a problem with a government bailout for folks who wink at slavery and can't figure out a way to let other people pay their pickers a penny a pound more for their back-breaking labor."[22]

The reason Sanders took such an aggressive position was because of the CIW, which had joined up with students and church groups, carried out aggressive congressional lobbying, demonstrated by handcuffing themselves like the slaves in the fields to the Florida Capitol building in Tallahassee, and boycotted brands linked to farmworker exploitation. From its inception in 1993, the coalition has grown into a powerful voice for workers, with major victories including deals with the world's four largest restaurant companies (McDonald's, Yum! Brands, Burger King and Subway). In 2003, they won the Robert F. Kennedy Human Rights Award. Lucas Benitez, one of the organizers, explained why talk of rights is central to their movement:

> Rights are not new to us. We didn't get off the boat and find ourselves in the land of rights. We come from countries like Mexico, Haiti and Guatemala, where we have been using this language of rights many years in our own struggles. And here in America, we are not asking for

anything that isn't already a right. When there are cases of modern-day slavery here, the people who are rounded up aren't just those without papers. A 2001 slavery case, for instance, involved African Americans who were recruited in homeless shelters and rehab centers to work in the tomato fields, but then were sold cocaine and crack from a "company store" that kept them always in debt. They were US citizens. What we're asking for is the right to a fair wage, for just pay for work done, for the right not to be robbed, for the right to organize, which has always been denied to farmworkers. Aren't these civil rights? Sadly, the US public thinks rights are respected here, which is why they don't know how to ask for them.

Benitez explained to me how they were organizing to make those rights real, using the words of abolitionist and former slave Frederick Douglass: "Power concedes nothing without demand. We have been excluded from organizing, but these are our rights, so we have to fight. We're not asking for a CEO's pay—we're just asking for our dignity." The CIW is a nonviolent organization, but as Benitez explained, it cannot avoid conflict. "Conflict is everywhere. In a marriage, there's always conflict. Conflict isn't bad—it's natural." The trick is to figure out how to manage it, and in doing so to make it a constructive process. This means perfecting the art of deliberation, as the right to shape tactics is the first prerogative of democratic organizing. "We're not children," said Benitez. "We are people, we are workers. We know how to think, and how to see about our own development. We don't need some professor to do it for us."

It was through public deliberation that the CIW developed their most successful tactics. The decision to boycott Taco Bell came from an ordinary meeting of ten CIW members where someone suggested that, since no one had heard of Pacific or Six L's, they should target the corporations farther up the food chain. At a labor meeting after the campaign was announced, a teamster approached Benitez and told him, "You're nuts." Four years later, the CIW scored their first victory, when Taco Bell agreed to their demands for a penny-per-pound increase in piece rates. Subway, Burger King and McDonald's have followed suit.

The tomato growers in Immokalee are part of a tradition. "I once heard a grower say that it began with African slaves, then they were free but were turned into sharecroppers, and now we've got Mexicans," said Gerardo Reyes, another CIW member, told me. "We're just as disposable as slaves in the past. But that's why one of our slogans is this: 'Yo No Soy Tractor.' I'm not a tractor. And in the struggle against these companies, our biggest weapon was our reality." Silvia Perez, another organizer with the coalition, agrees: "Seeing us as human beings will be the first step to changing things." All that the coalition wanted was that they, and their work, be valued properly, and that they be treated as human beings capable of politics. In order to do that, they needed to move against the forces that had transformed them into disposable vessels of labor, and priced their work so low that they could simply be used and discarded like last year's cell phone. So they organized, and became a countermovement.

The story doesn't end there. The tomato industry has pushed back with its own voluntary code—SAFE (Socially Accountable Farm Employers), a relaxed set of recommendations written far from the eyes of farmworkers. The code urges compliance with all existing laws, which include ones that deny farmworkers the right to organize, and the right to overtime pay. Both Six L's and Pacific, the two companies reported to have employed labor brokers who in turn hired the slave crews that were the subject of the latest federal prosecution in Immokalee, were certified under SAFE. These kinds of voluntary codes are what are given in order to prevent the coalition from demanding the very things, such as wages, to which they have a right.

The tomato pickers have rejected the SAFE code—as they had no hand in crafting it, why should they accept it? Instead, they've been mobilizing at every level, from the local to the national, to get the changes they always wanted. Although they've lobbied state and local governments, they haven't simply approached the governments as supplicants, waiting for the donation of rights. The coalition has challenged the complex web of private and public institutions that make up market society, taking on individual labor brokers and multinational corporations, and spreading a culture of respect for rights. One measure of their success was that in her first speech, the Obama administration's newly appointed secretary of labor, Hilda Solis, pledged to support the coalition. Yet the coalition's counter-movement has not placed the federal government at the heart of their mobilization. It is far more sweeping, and because of their success, the federal government has been dragged along.

Ultimately, a penny per pound of tomatoes might seem trivial in the transformation of market society. But in the way that they have tried to set the value of their work, the tools, politics and social bonds that the coalition has created offer a platform for wider change, change that can be seen not only in the fields of Florida but in the world's great cities, where the idea of "a right to have rights" is also being used to reshape urban space, and reclaim the terrain on which our city lives, work and existence are valued.

(EIGHT)

DEMOCRACY IN THE CITY

The main work of a social movement is to put the rich in
their place.
—SHAMITA NAIDOO, *activist with the Abahlali
baseMjondolo shackdwellers' movement*

Beginning in 2007, many of the world's major cities were venues for
organizing and protest around hunger during a global resurgence of
what were popularly referred to in the press as "food riots." Unfortu-
nately, the media missed the bigger story. Throughout the first half
of 2008, reporters routinely filed food-riot stories from dozens of
countries—from Haiti to Egypt to Madagascar to Italy. Their reporting usually involved pointing to tires smoldering in the road, and the
information that just hours ago an angry mob had rampaged through
the streets crazed with hunger and smashing windows. The repre-
sentation of the protests as fueled by nothing more than mute or in-
articulate pangs of hunger was both insidious and widespread. The
head of the United Nations' food program, Josette Sheeran, talked
of the food crisis as "a silent tsunami which knows no borders sweeping the world." Except it wasn't silent. People were very clear about
what they wanted: The reason they were protesting was because every
other attempt to make themselves heard had been ignored.

In Haiti, successive waves of World Bank/IMF structural-adjustment loans, together with the requirement that local farmers had to compete with U.S. rice farmers, have decimated the local rice industry, making the country entirely dependent on imports. When the price of rice went up by 30 percent in a single day, yet more people went hungry. Protesters responded not simply by demanding food—they came with a political agenda, calling for the restitution of Jean-Bertrand Aristide, the president deposed by George W. Bush in 2004. In Italy, the pasta protests simultaneously demanded cheaper wheat and indicted the Prodi government for its many failures. In every case, the rebellions were also an expression of a deeper anger at the politics surrounding food that had resulted in high prices and low incomes.[1]

These uprisings tend to happen when people understand both how they've been wronged in the social of the order of things, and that they have no other way of being heard. One of the most successful series of food rebellions in world history took place in the United States at the end of World War I, when there was a food-price spike similar to the one we saw in the late 2000s. The people charged with putting food on the family table were women. In 1917, despite the rhetoric of their country being the land of opportunity and freedom, women experienced neither. They were unable to afford food and were denied the vote, so, having no other way to hold the government accountable, they took to the streets. The women who protested in New York, Philadelphia and Boston weren't a mob—they were well organized, often immigrants and members of women's socialist leagues, and they knew how to wield political power.

In a Madison Square Garden protest, comprised mainly of immigrant women, one speaker roused her audience to follow her to the Waldorf Astoria, where the governor was reportedly dining. One thousand poor women stormed the hotel, demanding that the politician act to curb the price rises. Ultimately, the food rebellions were

Source: The Independent, *March 12, 1917*

successful. The government was forced into action, providing relief
from immediate hunger. More significantly, however, these protests
were also a demand for political franchise: In the United States,
working-class women fought for the right to vote, and as a result of
protests like these, the Nineteenth Amendment to the Constitution
was passed by the end of the decade.

This twentieth-century urban food rebellion hints at what the
right to have rights might look like in twenty-first-century cities. In
New York, protesters brought markets for their daily needs back un-

der their control by explicitly challenging the political order. These are ideas that French intellectual Henri Lefebvre tackled in his 1968 book *The Right to the City*, in which he called for an inclusive and transformative political reimagining of how, and for whom, cities might work. More recently, a cluster of NGOs, parliamentarians, activists and citizens have taken Lefebvre's vision rather more literally than he intended, producing in 2002 a charter of rights to the city, available to everyone who lives in any urban space. The Right to the City charter includes everything from the right to work to access to drinking water and toilets.[2] As we've seen with human rights, however, drawing up a charter is the easy part—without a city that's prepared to listen, the charter may as well be toilet paper. But just as in rural areas, where peasants, farmworkers and the landless have mobilized to make their rights real, in the city the demand for rights has come from tenants of low-income housing, shackdwellers, informal settlers, slum and pavement dwellers. Insisting that we can make demands because we live in the city, just like everyone else, is a call for equality and a call for participation in the control of the city, even if we don't own it.

Earlier, I compared Immokalee to apartheid South Africa, but my first visit to South Africa was in 2004, fourteen years after Mandela was released from jail. While the postapartheid government had overseen an end to the brutal system of racial exploitation and to the indignities of the Bantustans and an increase in entitlements for ordinary citizens, the transition from an apartheid economy to a modern neoliberal one has not delivered the freedom it promised. Despite the government having replaced the predations of apartheid with one of the most inclusive and progressive constitutions on earth, neoliberal capitalism has stalled the rights of ordinary people in South Africa. The country's Human Development Index, a composite indicator of wealth, health and education, has been falling consistently since 1995—dropping from 58 in the 1990 world rankings to 121 by 2005, somewhere below Palestine.

Free market transfers of land have resulted in less than 5 percent of the land moving from white to black ownership. The government has pushed an economic model of "black economic empowerment" by preferentially awarding contracts to businesses owned or run by black entrepreneurs. These contracts have been won by the most connected and wealthiest black entrepreneurs, but the wealth has yet to trickle down to the poorest. As Archbishop Desmond Tutu observed:

> What is black empowerment when it seems to benefit not the vast majority but a small elite that tends to be recycled? Are we not building up much resentment that we may rue later? It will not do to say people did not complain when whites were enriched. When were the old regime our standards? And remember some of the most influential values spoke about, "The people shall share." We were involved in the struggle because we believed we would evolve a new kind of society. A caring, a compassionate society. At the moment many, too many, of our people live in gruelling demeaning, dehumanising poverty.[3]

Tutu earned himself a telling-off from then-president Thabo Mbeki, but he isn't the only one who has noticed the incongruities. In a country that is now, at least on paper, free, the promises of freedom are betrayed every day. Even as South Africa prepares to host the world's largest sporting event, soccer's 2010 World Cup, the poor are being evicted from the cities in ways that recall apartheid-era tactics. Under apartheid, the poor in cities were sent to township houses of approximately 580 square feet. Today, when they're evicted, they're lucky to find themselves in houses with 390 square feet, many miles from their work, schools and communities. In Durban, what began as a protest against the failings of a local councilor grew into a national movement of thirty thousand shackdwellers. The organization, Abahlali baseMjondolo (Zulu for "people who live in shacks"), has fought hard for the first right to the city—the right to stay put.[4]

Worldwide, around one billion people live in shacks and informal settlements, on land that they occupy but do not own.[5] One way to lift them out of poverty is simply this: Give them title to their land. This idea is the brainchild of Peruvian economist Hernando de Soto, author of *The Mystery of Capital* and founder of the Institute for Liberty and Democracy, praised by establishment figures such as Alan Greenspan, George H. W. Bush and Bill Clinton. De Soto's mystery is that while people in developing countries have houses, like their counterparts in successful capitalist countries, they are not able to turn them into resources with which to invest. De Soto suggests that they are occupying around $10 trillion worth of land, and the challenge is to reanimate their "dead capital" into the "live capital" that has brought prosperity to rich countries by administering a strong bolt of property rights. It's Frankenstein's economics.

Giving the poor title to land they already occupy sounds unimpeachable. De Soto hails it as a way of unleashing everyone's inner entrepreneur, and there's some ambiguous evidence that land titles do create entrepreneurial expectations about market society. In Argentina, researchers surveyed urban areas where some shackdwellers were given land titles and others were not. Those given land titles, the "lucky" group, were more likely to trust others than their untitled counterparts.[6] Curiously, "lucky" shackdwellers also thought that "you can succeed on your own" at rates 30 percent higher than "unlucky" ones, despite the fact that land titles had been handed out, rather than earned. Those who received land titles started to hold more individualistic and materialistic beliefs than their untitled counterparts, despite the fact that both the lucky and the unlucky groups earned about the same amount. De Soto sees this as an educational benefit: "Property makes capital 'mind friendly,'" he says.

Ultimately, what matters is whether getting land titles actually helps lift people out of poverty, and here's where De Soto's arguments fall down. He never shows us the data on which his science is based—appropriately enough, it remains a mystery. In peer-reviewed studies of his claims, in Egypt, Nicaragua and even De Soto's native Peru,[7] a pattern emerges: After the poor are given land, things fall apart. Land titling turns dead capital into live capital, but because the rules under which it is managed were written by the powerful, the poor often find themselves divested of their assets far sooner than they'd hoped. As with Gary Becker's philosophies, De Soto's push for markets favors the powerful. Transforming land has not meant greater wealth and freedom—it has meant that the poor have something that they can hock in a distress sale, which has led to the concentration of land in the hands of the rich, and higher rents for the poor. So De Soto is right in one sense—land titles encouraged entrepreneurship—but it's not necessarily the poor who benefit, because unless the underlying inequalities in power are addressed, there seems to be little benefit for the people in whose name the transformation was carried out.

In his defense, De Soto regards land titling as merely a platform for other changes, especially in government, so that bureaucracy is scaled back and enterprise might flourish. But the evidence seems to be that property rights work only *after* governments are democratic and limits on the unfair concentration of property are put in place, not the other way around. The chant of "Property rights first, and all else will follow," doesn't just put the cart before the horse—it turns out to be a way to camouflage a grand theft. This is something that the shackdwellers in South Africa have learned the hard way.

The residents of a group of shack settlements in Durban petitioned their local councilor for the right to legally settle some public land. The councilor was a machine politician who used to be in the National Party, and then gradually drifted with the political winds to end up in the ruling African National Congress. He promised the earth but then sold the land rights to a local developer. The shackdwellers then appealed to the city's officials, to no avail. They appealed to the provincial government and, finally, to the national government, where they were again ignored.

They refused to give up, and instead developed new ways of representing their demands. They insisted on the ability to think for themselves.[8] To quote one activist, Mdu Hlongwa, they were "professors of their own suffering," who would not be bubbled out of their rights by the chatter of development experts who "talk about us, not with us." One of the earliest banners from the movement insisted on the shackdwellers' humanity and intelligence—it read THE UNIVERSITY OF ABAHLALI BASEMJONDOLO.

The politics of the shackdwellers are hammered out in regular meetings. In a meeting pictured on the following page, Moses Mncwango is studying a municipal council report on the shacks by candlelight. These are documents in which the government assesses the number, employment and future prospects of shackdwellers. The professors of their own suffering studied the report submitted to them by the government, and were unimpressed. At the meeting, they discussed strategies that would allow them to insist on their right to the city, on their value as human beings—and their responses have ranged from protests to community-wide celebrations of "Un-Freedom Day," in counterpoint to official celebrations of the first postapartheid elections on April 27, 1994. The shackdwellers have

*Moses Mncwango studies council documents by candlelight,
November 23, 2005, in the Pemary Ridge meeting hall, Durban,
South Africa.[9] Source: Author's photo*

experienced the wrath of the state, with members imprisoned and beaten, and with protests illegally halted by the police, but they have also tasted victory. When I lived in Durban, the police were a constant source of worry. They harassed shackdwellers, routinely abused the residents of the settlements, refused to hear their complaints, illegally prevented protests and generally treated shackdwellers as less than human. More and more, the police have stopped their intimidation and have even, occasionally, been seen defending the rights of shackdwellers against those who would expropriate them. The shackdwellers' worth in the eyes of the police has risen, through protest, reflection and collective action.

S'bu Zikode, a former petrol-station attendant (a job from which he was fired because of his activism) and former president of Abahlali baseMjondolo, is clear about the bigger victories that his movement has won. "I don't just mean victories in court, or evictions that have been stopped, or water and electricity connected. I am talking about seeing comrades becoming confident, being happy for knowing their power, knowing their rights in this world. Seeing comrades gaining a bit of respect, seeing people who have never counted being able to engage at the level at which the struggle is now fought. Young comrades are debating ministers on the radio and TV!"[10]

The power of these meetings, and their place in promoting the kind of humanity and equality that marked the greatest ambitions of the antiapartheid struggle, were made clear in June 2008. With winter's fuel costs hitting hard, a wave of violence swept through many poor communities in a spate of xenophobic attacks in South Africa[11] — dozens of South Africans and foreigners were killed and thousands displaced in what most Western news sources characterized as a Malthusian struggle for scarce resources. In the shacks organized by Abahlali baseMjondolo, however, not a single violent incident was reported. No matter what your nationality, if you're living in the shacks, you're of the shacks:[12] a truly inclusive idea of citizenship.

THE LIVING POLITICS OF THE CITY

What Abahlali baseMjondolo is doing is creating a kind of living politics, one that's open to everybody, rich or poor, lettered or un-schooled. Again, S'bu Zikode defines this eloquently:

> A living politics is not a politics that requires a formal ed-ucation—a living politics is a politics that is easily under-stood because it arises from our daily lives and the daily challenges we face. It is a politics that every ordinary per-son can understand. It is a politics that knows that we have no water but that in fact we all deserve water. It is a politics that everyone must have electricity because it is required by our lives. That understanding—that there are no toilets but that in fact there should be toilets—is a liv-ing politics. It is not complicated; it does not require big books to find the information. It doesn't have a hidden agenda—it is a politics of living that is just founded only on the nature of living. Every person can understand these kinds of demands and every person has to recognise that these demands are legitimate.

They demand to be a part of the city's politics in the same way that they are *already* integral to its society and economy. For poor resi-dents of any city, the first substantive right to the city is the right to stay put. This is an acute issue for many cities' poorest residents, espe-cially now that evictions and foreclosures stand at record highs. Some groups have realized that their demand to stay put can also become a tactic. Home foreclosures in Philadelphia are being fought, for ex-ample, by groups such as ACORN[13]—the Association of Community Organizations for Reform Now—who recruit "Home Defenders," com-munity members who stay with families under threat of eviction, and who peacefully prevent the police from evicting them from their homes. The demand and the tactics are similar to those practiced by La Via Campesina as they resist their eviction from rural life by asserting the right to participate and build a community, despite the apparent "economic madness" of doing so. In order to have "a right to have rights," you first have to be allowed to sit at the table.

OPPORTUNITY COST AND THE SHAPE OF THE CITY

With the right to participate guaranteed, the next step is to shape the local politics of value. To better understand what this means, it's helpful to know one of the foundational ideas in modern economics: the notion of "opportunity cost." When we weigh up the alternatives of spending ten dollars on the cinema, or ten dollars on dinner, or saving the same ten dollars as part of a bigger spend at some point in the future, we're calculating opportunity cost. Economists, it must be said, have a hard time with opportunity cost. Before explaining how exactly it operates, here's a question that two professors posed their colleagues at the 2005 Allied Social Sciences Association:

> You've won a free ticket to see an Eric Clapton concert (which has no resale value). Bob Dylan is performing on the same night and is your next-best alternative activity. Tickets to see Dylan cost $40. On any given day, you would be willing to pay up to $50 to see Dylan. Assume there are no other costs of seeing either performer. Based on this information, what is the opportunity cost of seeing Eric Clapton?
>
> A. $0   C. $40
> B. $10   D. $50

Nearly two-thirds of the respondents had taught an introductory economics course and only 21 percent got the right answer—a little worse than picking it at random. The right answer is ten dollars, because if you go to see Clapton, you don't get to see Dylan. What's Dylan worth to you—what's his benefit to you? Fifty dollars. What does it cost to see Dylan? Forty dollars. The net benefit forgone is ten dollars—the correct answer. You might think that you need to know how much you'd have been prepared to pay for the Clapton ticket, but it's not relevant to the question of opportunity cost. It's easier to understand this when it's phrased as a "cost-benefit" calculation. So the researchers tried the test again, asking, "Based on this information, what is the minimum amount (in dollars) you would have to value seeing Eric Clapton for you to choose his concert?" The answer, again, is ten dollars, and more people got it right when the question was phrased in everyday language.

Let's not dwell on the fact that only 20 percent of Ph.D. students in economics got the right answer, statistically the same level as undergraduates who had never taken an economics course.[14] The key issue here is the difference between the market price and what the Dylan ticket is truly worth to you. If, heaven forbid, you don't have a soft spot for Dylan, if wild horses couldn't drag you to see Dylan, the cost-benefit analysis would look very different. So it is with everything else.

When it comes to choices over bigger blocks of resources, the opportunity cost becomes less clear. Consider the case of toxic waste. Such waste is usually generated through industrial processes that don't have to pay the full cost of pollution. If industry did have to pay, there'd certainly be a great deal less pollution. But what is to be done with the waste when it's created? Larry Summers, the director of President Obama's National Economic Council, once followed market signals to their logical conclusion in answering this question. In a leaked memo, written during his tenure at the World Bank, Summers asked, "Just between you and me, shouldn't the World Bank be encouraging MORE migration of the dirty industries to the LDCs [Less Developed Countries]?" His logic, impeccable by economic standards, was that poor people value environmental harm less than rich people, and so toxic waste could more efficiently be disposed of in Africa. For insight such as this, Summers was soon after promoted to Clinton's Treasury, and is now the architect of the United States' economic policy. *The Economist* magazine observed that "the language is crass, even for an internal memo . . . [but] on the economics, his points are hard to answer."[15] And all because the dollar amount that Africans would pay to avoid being killed by pollutants is less than that paid by people in North America. This is Gary Becker's word made flesh.

Let's take the example of dumping toxic waste in Africa a little further, because it isn't an abstract case; it has been happening for decades. It costs corporations in Europe $1,000 to dispose of every ton of hazardous waste—in Somalia the same waste can disappear for $2.50. After the 2005 Asian tsunami, barrels of toxic waste that had long been dumped offshore finally washed up on the Somali coastline. The waste caused a range of symptoms that looked like radiation poisoning, but the suffering of local populations was not addressed by the international community. Chronic illness caused by toxic waste is now cited by pirates as a motivating factor for their hijacking of passing ships off the Somali coast.[16]

Summers couldn't have predicted this chain of consequences, which might have made his calculus look a little different, but it shows how the idea of opportunity cost might help. Choosing how to use resources has consequences with which we all live, and in which we all have a stake. There is no *single* opportunity cost—the examples taught in classrooms assume a common economic language of money, but Larry Summers's opinion as to how to handle the toxic waste is going to be very different to that of a woman in a Somali fishing village who has to live with the consequences. That woman values her children no less than a German or American, and wants them to grow up healthy just as much as her richer counterparts— but because she's poorer, her love is worth less in the calculus of costs and benefits facing the corporations dumping their waste (and the policy makers who support them). Opportunity cost when it comes to public policy is something that needs to be defined and debated collectively. When opportunity cost is a matter of debate between the European corporations that dump toxic waste and the Somali villagers who live with the consequences, the assessment is not a technical exercise, but a political one that requires democracy, not experts.

Economics is about choices. But it's never said who gets to make them. Markets are a way of making a choice about that choice: By choosing to value the world through markets, we choose the principle of "The more money you have, the more you can get." This, however, is not a very democratic way of distributing public funds. Although modern politics often appears to be run along the lines of "one dollar, one vote," some municipalities have discovered that there are other ways of dividing their common resources.

Porto Alegre in Brazil has a celebrated "participatory budget" process, where citizens gather in forums to decide how funds will be spent in their neighborhoods—what the priorities are, and which groups will receive government money first. Similar experiments in Kerala, India, have been incredibly successful—civic participation is up, but so are levels of satisfaction with government services and responsiveness. This is what happens when people stop being consumers in the market and become the authors of their lives, political subjects who both preside over resources and develop democratic ways of sharing them.

PARTICIPATORY BUDGETING

Porto Alegre is a town of almost 3 million people where, in 1988, the Workers' Party (Partido dos Trabalhadores, the party of the current Brazilian president Lula) came to power. Under their government, and as a result of pressure from networks of neighborhood associations in the municipality, participatory budgeting was introduced in the late 1990s. It's a policy now implemented in over three hundred cities worldwide.[17] The move allowed citizens to have a great deal more say in what their municipal government did. In neighborhood discussions, the opportunity cost of the city is discovered through debate. It's the quintessential nonmarket mechanism through which value is set—a concrete expression of their participants' right to the city.

Participatory budgeting involves a series of assemblies in each of the city's sixteen districts, combining representative and direct democracy. The discussions about how the budget will be spent happen in a range of places, from smaller informal neighborhood meetings to annual district conferences. The debates center on how to allocate resources in local government budgets, whether to spend money on housing, sanitation, roads, health care or education.[18] Regular annual assemblies take place in March in each district, and the previous year's projects are reviewed. Neighborhoods and organized groups select delegates for subsequent proceedings, who then attend further assemblies to learn about the criteria and the costs involved in city projects. Communities then allocate resources through voting and debate. In this way, the people administer an annual budget for construction and services of over US$200 million.

Central to the success of participatory budgeting is the level of citizen engagement. The number of people involved has grown from 900 in the first year to over 30,000 in the early 2000s.[19] The process seems to have had some fairly positive outcomes—by 2004,

99.5 percent of Porto Alegre's population was connected to the water network, and 83 percent to sewage; participatory budgeting had seen a tripling of the numbers of children in municipal schools. An attraction of the process is that political participation leads to concrete outcomes—people see results. For this reason, it has fans from across the political spectrum—it's admired by the World Bank for its greater transparency and more efficient investment climate, and by citizens groups for its redistributive power and the direct democracy that it builds.

Fans of participatory budgeting can find support for their positions from institutional and behavioral economics, where experiments show that people cooperate best in situations where they themselves can adapt and change the rules of the game.[20] The process of talking about these issues, and the choices that citizens make about what gets built first, where and for whom, encourage a kind of engagement rare in most democracies.

There's also a built-in margin of error in participatory budgeting systems. Because the decisions made today will affect people in the future, there are self-imposed limits in the budget cycle to make sure that future generations are cushioned from today's possible mistakes. Fixed spending like debt servicing and pensions is not subject to participatory budgeting, and money is always set aside so that past and future debts do not fall on the shoulders of subsequent generations.

Central to participatory budgeting's success is citizens' engagement. Indeed, without it, participatory budgeting wouldn't exist, because it's a form of government that wasn't given—it was taken. According to one activist:

> It wasn't just the mayor's office that started participatory budgeting on its own, out of good will, because it had an ideological commitment to popular participation. It was

the independent popular movement too. This region, Gloria, for example, already had an independent People's Council in existence before the participatory budgeting came into existence. So for us the participatory budgeting started as a sub-committee of the Gloria People's Council. It was this autonomous popular movement that initiated [it] in Porto Alegre, which resulted in the Workers' Party being re-elected for four consecutive mandates.[21]

But such budgeting isn't tied to one party. About half of the current participatory budgeting cities in Brazil, including Porto Alegre now, do not have Workers' Party mayors, but it is through this active local politics that Brazil's citizens have been able to be a part of the process in deciding what is valuable and what is not. In doing so, they have changed the political geography of the city. It's not just the richest or most ambitious person making decisions for community, or some technocrat who may or may not have to live with the consequences. It is the opposite of apartheid: Everyone works together to reclaim some autonomy from the market, nudging forward a countermovement by setting value democratically. Think of it as modern commoning.

Of course, there are problems. While the process helps to build community, it also depends on community, and no community is perfect. If you hate your neighbor, or if you'd rather not think of your neighbor as part of your community at all, then it'll be harder to budget with her than if everyone gets along. Participatory budgeting has been criticized for excluding the very poor, and for attracting single-issue participation, after which some people stop attending altogether. These problems of genuinely democratic organizing and budgeting are significant, but fixable. Organizing efforts with excluded groups need to be supported by a system of individual and collective rights, which can prevent the rise of a kind of democratic tyranny. Beyond changes in process, there are also more profound ways to tackle exclusion—by addressing the material bases of inequality within communities. The most successful national democracies—whether you look at indicators ranging from life expectancy to women's participation in society, happiness or any other metric—tend to be those in which there is more equality. What is true at a national level is also true at the local level. The paradox, then, is that in creating a democracy in which everyone can participate, it's helpful to have a society that's relatively equal and democratic to start off with. This is, of course, enshrined in the joke about the wandering traveler who asks the fool how best to get to the city. The fool replies: "I wouldn't start from here if I were you."

Given that here is where we find ourselves, we muddle through as best we can. One strength of an approach that relies on local democracy is that it contains its own in-built mechanisms for climbing learning curves. Learning happens through mistakes, as one United States–based organization working on the rights to the city discovered. The United States is home to an increasing number of organizations that bring citizens and immigrants together, and one of the oldest is Tenants and Workers United (TWU), based a short drive from the White House, in Alexandria, Virginia. There, in 1986, African Americans and a largely Salvadoran refugee community came together to fight one thousand evictions by slumlords in the Arlandria section. Starting with a group of mainly African American activists, the Tenants and Workers Support Committee convened, and built one of the most active and vibrant community rights movements in the country.

It was a learning experience from the outset, which means, to quote Jon Liss, the organization's executive director, "There were mistakes made every day." This is the process through which the organization has learned lessons ranging from "If you think it'd be good to have an urban farm, you should probably learn what poison oak looks like" to "Don't let lawyers make concessions without telling you." To take a concrete example, members of the organization designed, developed, fought for and won a living-wage ordinance. As part of that process, unionized ironworkers learned the tactics and strategy of campaigning door-to-door—a kind of mobilizing that most workplace-based unions don't ever have to worry about. By the same token, undocumented people have successfully campaigned for the right to vote in school-board elections, so learning what it is to be a part of government, rather than being hunted by it. While the results of these campaigns are important, the process is vital. According to Dan Moshenberg, an organizer with TWU and an English professor at George Washington University: "The geography of the city unfolds in the fight for the right to it."

It's a process that works, albeit imperfectly. According to a range of indicators, participatory government builds better communities.[22] On the way, mistakes will inevitably be made, by the people who will most directly bear the consequences, but this is an improvement on the way development institutions, governments and corporations currently work. Bureaucrats making mistakes shrug off accountability for their actions, and even those voted out of office can be assured of a pleasant afterlife in the private sector from which they were charged with protecting us—Bush, Cheney, Rumsfeld and Wolfowitz are enjoying comfortable retirements.

There's a learning curve in every kind of social action, a social scientific discovery of the world by struggling for it. This is true in every context I've come across, from the smallest shack settlements to the largest country on earth—China. For outsiders, it's still difficult to piece together an accurate picture of what is happening in China behind the official façade, but it's possible to get an imperfect picture. The right to strike was removed from the Chinese constitution in 1982 because there was no need for workers to strike if they owned the means of production, but, depending on which source you believe, there were between 50,000 and 100,000 "mass incidents" in 2006—the government's euphemism for worker unrest involving more than 100 people. By 2009, according to one source, there were 58,000 incidents in the first three months of the year.[23]

A key source of information about China is Han Dongfang, the man who founded the Beijing Autonomous Workers' Federation. After being detained and harshly interrogated, and losing a lung to the tuberculosis he contracted from his cell mates, he now lives in exile in Hong Kong, where he runs a radio station and Web site reporting on workers' rights. In one interview, Han explained how he ended up creating the first independent trade union during the Tiananmen Square uprising:

> The reason the workers came out onto the streets was to provide moral support for the students, like a big brother, but there was nothing in particular they wanted for themselves. When we asked factory workers, they said they wanted the government to treat the students better—and nothing more. Even when we got organized and drafted our charter, we wrote in a very general way; there was nothing as concrete as benefits, salaries, working hours or collective bargaining, though we did mention factory democracy, if I remember correctly. Politically and socially, we had never had the chance to be ourselves, as individuals or even as working-class people; we had not been able to base our thinking on what we needed. We were trying to make a leap, but it was our first leap, and we didn't know how.[24]

Workers are generally not free to organize independently of the government-controlled All-China Federation of Trade Unions

(ACFTU). Up to the end of 2008, the ACFTU had achieved some positive results for workers by, for example, unionizing Wal-Mart. The union's efforts meant that workers enjoyed a wage increase of 8 percent.[25] In the United States, by contrast, Wal-Mart is not unionized.

The recession has dampened the Chinese government's enthusiasm for workers' rights, just as workers, particularly recently unemployed workers, are finding their voices amplified. The recent rise in worker militancy is also supported by a range of labor-rights NGOs. In one case, an NGO called the Yirenping Center provided support to those fired on the basis of their hepatitis B status (there are 130 million hepatitis B carriers in China). Nokia and Coca-Cola are among those against whom accusations have been made, and while the companies deny the allegations, some reports suggest that 80 percent of multinationals discriminate on the basis of hepatitis B status.[26] In addition to this kind of legal support, new communications technologies have made it easier for workers to broadcast the abuses that they suffer, and text-messaging has made it possible for them to evade the censorship that the state might otherwise impose.

These Chinese workers are fighting for something very similar to workers in Immokalee—the right to remain, the right to be treated fairly, the right to have a voice, the right to control things they do not own; in short, the right to have a politics that they are denied under the Chinese communist government, no less than shackdwellers are denied a right to politics under South African capitalism.[27] That politics necessarily involves taking on inequalities in power. This happens not only through direct confrontation, but through a constructive project of genuine social science, in which ordinary people conduct experiments on how to organize, imagine and build social relations in new ways.

If this sounds too abstract, or painfully anachronistic, it may be reassuring to know that in meetings held online involving millions of participants, activists are addressing these questions with very real results. The free software movement is, to use a widely bandied slogan, "Free as in speech, not as in beer." In other words, while the software is usually given away, the "freedom" in free software is that the product is yours to change and share, just as you'd like—the free is free like liberty. This is rather different to getting a version of software gratis, which you're legally prevented by, say, Apple or Microsoft from teasing apart, reading and learning from. With free software's model of cooperation and decentralization, millions of people are now sharing their expertise and insight in developing everything from browsers to medical information systems.

This is how Mike Linksvayer, vice president of Creative Commons, described it to me: "We're voluntarily re-creating an intellectual commons, trying to get back the intangible goods enclosed in the past century." Trained in economics, Linksvayer is able to make arguments about the efficiency of common ownership compared with private ownership. That said, the more compelling arguments aren't about efficiency— after all, says Linksvayer, "There may be software that is most efficiently written in prison camp." What is indisputable is that the process involves more liberty, and that individual authors have more autonomy when questions of private property are suspended or, to use a better word, hacked.[28]

It's one thing to be able to share resources that can be copied and distributed virtually for free, but the real world isn't like that. The break between the real world and cyberspace can, however, prove to be an advantage. In the time it takes to negotiate who does the dishes in a commune in the real world, the digital world can develop, implement and fix prototype ways of governing. "It would take generations to do that with human society," says Linksvayer. In the free software movement, in barely twenty years, democratic and decentralized forms of government have evolved and spread. The skills haven't been taught anywhere, but have been learned by doing and asking.

Perhaps the best-known example is Wikipedia, which recruits by working well. It isn't perfect, but the processes of peer review and collective rule making to which contributions subscribe is part of the reason for its success. Beyond the ability of being able to look up practically anything online, Wikipedia and the free software movement provide something far subtler—a way of socializing and being together that encourages us to share. It's an educative experience of which Rousseau, I think, would have been an enthusiast, not least because of its potential application to the real world.

There are reasons to think that the spirit of the commons that works on Wikipedia can affect the real world. The world of computers generates its own externalities—information technology is responsible for 2 percent of greenhouse gas global emissions, about the same as the airline industry. British newspapers reported that two Google searches are responsible for the same contribution to greenhouse gases as boiling a kettle for a cup of coffee, which means that the world's daily Googling is the equivalent of ninety-one around-the-world plane rides. Google disputed the claim, saying its figures were far lower—but since Google's IT infrastructure is a trade secret, we'll just have to trust them. The argument from the free software movement is that this needs to be transparent, and open. If the search world operated on more open principles, those people who wanted to write more efficient code would be able to contribute. Right now, the only option is to petition Google to use less energy.

Questions raised by the free software movement bring us back to the heart of private property, and the notion that property could serve a social role. There's nothing *natural* about ownership—it's the result of a negotiation, and modern social change has always questioned the boundaries of public and private ownership. The Lockean idea that working on something confers ownership is just another social expectation—but it's one that is malleable. When no one expects to own a collective project, then private property has been suspended, and something far more open put in its place, dependent for its survival on the restraint and collaboration of its creators. From food rebellions to free software, social movements are at the cutting edge of practical politics and economics, trying to create new ways to control the world without owning it.

The stakes in their success couldn't be higher. To see why, we need to return to discuss food sovereignty and climate change. With over a billion people now hungry, and science pointing to far higher rates of climate change than originally forecast, understanding how to value the world around us without sticking prices on it may be the key to our survival as a species, if it is not already too late.

NINE

BACK TO FOOD SOVEREIGNTY

I am at two with nature.
—WOODY ALLEN

OWNING AIR

South African shackdwellers, participatory budget councils and the free software movement can all be understood as part of Polanyi's double movement—responding to the transformation of the world into property and the destruction of ways of managing shared resources. But there's a problem. While Polanyi had an idea of the mechanics of how society might protect itself from the market, there isn't a comparable mechanism for the planet. As the slogan goes, "Mother Nature doesn't do bailouts." Any number of indicators show what we as a species have already done to the planet, with the lion's share of that damage caused by people living, as I do, in rich countries. The best scientific knowledge available argues that, as a matter of survival, we need to reduce the level of CO_2 equivalent in the atmosphere down to 350 parts per million—we're at 390 now, and rising by 2 parts per year.

Governments around the world are coming to understand that

greenhouse gas pollution needs regulation, a realization that is long overdue. It's clear that what the planet needs is a combination of profound structural investment in the Global North to wean their citizens off their resource gluttony (if everyone were to pollute as much as the average United States or Canadian citizen, we'd need nine Earths to absorb the emissions), as well as huge investment in the Global South to make non-fossil-fuel energy available to the poor. The problem lies in how, and in whose interest, the rules governing this regulation will work. Current thinking in government policy circles tackling climate change is to let the market figure it out. In other words, after recognizing the atmosphere as a public good, it seems that governments now want to privatize it, by creating a "cap-and-trade" system, where pollution levels are fixed (the "cap"), but where some polluters will be allowed to buy "pollution permits" from others to ease the burden of transition to a lower-carbon economy (the "trade"). By creating a price for carbon, a high one if need be, the market will sort it all out. At least, that's the hope.

Any policy that has been touted as heavily as cap and trade deserves our skepticism, not least because it shares DNA with, and emerged from the same deregulation of, the financial instruments that spawned some of the more exotic (and now toxic) financial products of the 2000s. In the middle of a financial meltdown, it would be lunacy to make the same mistakes again. Yet that appears to be exactly what's happening.

Before discussing the scheme itself, it's worth noting the moral objections to a market-based approach that effectively turns the atmosphere into something that you can foul for a fee. It's a way, as Woody Allen suggests, of being "at two with nature"—both depending on it, and destroying it. Under pollution trading the United States can, for instance, continue its addiction to oil while upgrading polluting factories in India and China. Observing that this is effectively a license for the United States to continue its unsustainable behavior, some activists have created a parody Web site called CheatNeutral .com, on which people can offset their marital infidelities by relying on the absorptive power of people who are more constitutionally suited to monogamy.

There is, nonetheless, something appealing about the idea that polluters should pay for the damage they cause. If one accepts that polluters should foot the bill for their behavior, the question becomes, What should they pay? Given that climate change is a form of pollution, it seems reasonable enough that it should carry a cost. What pollution trading seems to do is create a mechanism for generating that price. So what's wrong with that?

Larry Lohmann, one of the leading thinkers on climate change, and a researcher at the United Kingdom–based Corner House, gave me an answer that dismantles the question. "The 'polluter pays' principle is useful in certain contexts, when prices can be set in considered and democratic ways and when prices have some effect on the problem." The trouble is that before prices can make a difference to climate change, a great deal of groundwork needs to be laid— alternative forms of energy need funding, regulation needs to be up and running, transfers from rich to poor need to be unequivocal and binding. And, of course, democratic mechanisms need to be in place. "All of that is prior to talk about carbon pricing," says Lohmann. "Until then, it's all very interesting, but a secondary concern."

And a poor mechanism for change too. If the only lever to control climate change is the price of carbon, everything relies on the price mechanism actually working. The idea that a high carbon price will, in and of itself, fix climate change simply doesn't hold water. The oil crisis in the 1970s didn't shift the planet away from fossil fuel. Even the astronomical oil prices in 2008 have done little to lay the foundations for a sustainable economy. Advocates of cap-and-trade systems suggest that it has a good track record, crediting it with reducing sulfur emissions in the United States in the 1990s. A closer examination,

Lohmann suggests, shows that it was not the "trade" that reduced the sulfur, but the cap; not the market, but the hand of regulation.[1]

If it's the cap that did the work before, it's worth asking what the "trade" part of cap and trade does today. The CEO of a utility with many coal-fired power plants is unlikely to look kindly on a carbon price. If the policy is passed with any sort of teeth, it could cost him his job. So, he'll fight hard to get the government to cut him some slack, to give free permits to pollute because the cost of adjusting would otherwise put him out of business. In five European countries, windfall profits from these sorts of exemptions are estimated to reach $112 billion by 2012. Polluters are allowed to "offset" their pollution by buying carbon credits from companies and organizations that reduce their carbon output so that the polluter doesn't have to. The trouble is that this carbon-reducing behavior is ripe for fraud. About 30 percent, the largest proportion of offset credits, come from the destruction of trifluoromethane—HFC-23, a by-product of manufacturing refrigerator gases. In fact, refrigerator gas manufacturers make more by selling emissions permits than they do by selling their own refrigerant gas. Has this set the Global South on the path to better technology and development? On the contrary, it encourages firms in the Global South to use outdated manufacturing technologies. Simply buying updated equipment for the seventeen manufacturers in the Global South who produce these gases would cost €100 million—the money they earn from trading on the emissions is €4.7 *billion*. There are similar stories about the greenhouse gases produced by nylon manufacturing and the fertilizer industries. In short, this "polluter pays" system turns out to be a "polluter earns" system.

The winners from cap and trade aren't only to be found in Asia's clouds of smog. Lohmann quotes Peter Atherton, Citigroup's head of European Utility Research, on his balance sheet on the European

Emission Trading Scheme: "All generation-based utilities: winners. Coal and nuclear generators: Biggest winners. Hedge funds and energy traders: even bigger winners. Losers?? Herm . . . consumers! . . . Have policy goals been achieved? Prices up. Emissions up. Profits up. . . . So, not really." Atherton is right that although industrial polluters do very well under the scheme in Europe, bankers have done even better. This is why Goldman Sachs, as Matt Taibbi reports, is so very concerned to get in on the action—because what cap and trade does is to effectively take the right to collect pollution taxes away from government and place it in the hands of the private sector.[2]

Behind the idea of a carbon price is the assumption that the market will price it properly, even though the market has proven itself very bad at assessing the risk of unlikely but devastating events. Remember the failure of the Efficient Markets Hypothesis? Exactly the same articles of faith underwrite carbon trading. We've already seen how corporations are able to co-opt government, and they are doing it again with the Obama cap-and-trade system, by persuading the government to give away 85 percent of emissions permits *for free*. With climate change the stakes are incalculably higher than the trillion-dollar meltdown, and it seems unwise to use the same tools that have hewn this recession to solve the most pressing problem facing the planet. Yet so blind are we to alternative ways of valuing the world around us that this market-based larceny is the only answer to climate change that we can see.

Gwyn Prins and Steve Rayner write in an influential *Nature* article that

> climate change is not amenable to an elegant solution
> because it is not a discrete problem. It is better understood
> as a symptom of a particular development path and its
> globally interlaced supply-system of fossil energy. Together

they form a complex nexus of mutually reinforcing, inter-
twined patterns of human behaviour, physical materials
and the resulting technology. It is impossible to change
such complex systems in desired ways by focusing on just
one thing.[3]

What we need is a range of policies, designed not to price carbon,
but to stabilize greenhouse gases at below 350 parts per million.
Everything we know about the kinds of animals humans are can
help us in coming up with solutions. We know that while we can be
selfish, we can also value fairness; we're capable of cooperation and
altruism and can demand justice and democracy.

It is also important to start paying off the ecological debt that rich
countries owe poor ones, and today governments in the Global
North and South urgently need to break our addiction to oil. In this,
markets will serve us poorly. Commons need rules and regulations—
and the ones that have most effect are ones that the majority of
people have had a hand in devising. The idea of a commons, of using ideas of regulation, punishment, shame and justice as well as
money, opens the door to understanding how to put a price on climate change. Larry Lohmann points out that the "climate problem
isn't a new problem—it's a continuation of old problems." Creating
the infrastructure for the energy gluttony of the rich has already im-
posed tremendous costs on the poor, costs that affected communities are already shouldering. So, suggests Lohmann, "if you want a
system for valuing climate, let's start with what we've already got.
People don't have any problem with valuing land and destruction
that has already taken place. That's only one example. The first step
is to connect the climate problem with things that people already
know how to value."

There will be many steps, and no magic bullet—climate change,
if we are successful in fighting it, will be killed by a thousand cuts.

The cuts will come from different sectors, and will be guided by the best science, in the public interest. They will involve regulation, changing cultural attitudes toward the use of fossil fuels, individual restraint and the public funding of clean energy and green jobs. And this brings us back to one of those sectors, the one we started with: food.

AN EDIBLE REVOLUTION

Thinking about food brings together the common valuation of land and water, the need for responsive institutions, the rights of individuals and the politics of genuine democracy. Last year, a report by over four hundred leading scientists, led by Robert Watson, the World Bank's chief scientist, asked how we're going to feed the world in 2050, when there will be 9 billion of us. Their study, *Agriculture at a Crossroads*, concluded that we'll need to shift away from the current industrial system of agriculture because it doesn't adequately value natural resources. In the future we won't have the vast amounts of water or fertilizers that capitalist industrial agriculture requires, and the climate will be far more variable than it is now. In this story, peasant farmers are both victims and saviors. Because they are poorer, farmers are more vulnerable to the shocks of climate change, even though small-scale farms themselves are ecologically less vulnerable to hazard; and, according to data from one of the longest-running farm-scale studies, sustainable organic farming could sequester up to 40 percent of current CO_2 emissions.[4]

For us to follow the report's advice, and forestall resource wars, we'll need new, decentralized planning and locally adapted ways of commoning resources. In practice, this means engaging in democracy across a number of different institutional levels—the decisions about how to share water will need to be conducted over the geography of a watershed. Decisions about how we grow and distribute food should come from a different, possibly municipal, geography. The way that these decisions interact with climate change will need to be coordinated globally. When the world's top scientists addressed global hunger, they came up with the same kinds of solutions that the world's poorest people had—local, ecologically sensitive solutions that respect local knowledge, democracy and autonomy.

It would be foolish to sugarcoat the challenges that lie ahead, both personal and political, if we are to feed the world. In a world with 9 billion people, we'll need to cut back on meat. If meat's to be eaten at all (and I'm not sure it should be), the global allowance will be 25 kilograms of meat and 50 kilograms of dairy per person per year—any more, and the climate will suffer. According to Tara Garnett of the Food Climate Research Network, that means, at most, two sausages, one small chicken piece and a small pork chop a week, and milk for cereal and tea. Suppressing the Western diet's lust for flesh will be hard to do—it'll mean taking on all manner of food-processing and retail interests, as well as our own habits—but we will need to get used to paying the price for our two-hundred-dollar hamburgers, and ensuring that everyone can make similar consumption choices. We'll also need to make *time* for politics, which involves changes that will affect everything from watching TV to reducing the extremely long working hours that we have come to accept as normal.

What will be lost in old expectations will be more than balanced by new ones. In an economy geared to greener jobs, agroecological food production will generate more employment than conventional farms, producing more on less land. In one study, merely shifting 20 percent of farmland to organic (as opposed to fully agroecological) production in the United Kingdom would create 73,200 jobs. Local consumption is also a stimulus, to both climate and economy. In an Iowa study, a 10 percent increase in local food purchases would cut state emissions by over 3,500 tons a year. In Japan, a similar study found that eating locally grown food would involve the equivalent of a 20 percent energy savings per household. Local food initiatives have also been found effective in fighting malnutrition in poor urban areas, which saves millions of dollars in future social and health care costs.[5] There's reason for hope here.

While national governments have been dragging their feet over food sovereignty and climate change, ordinary people have been seizing the reins of government to create local change. Municipal food-policy councils, which find ways of committing local government to systemic ways of fighting hunger, and "transition towns," which lay the foundations for post-fossil-fuel urban life, can be found from Toronto to El Manzano in Chile to Fujino in Japan.[6]

These examples point to a deeper principle: In order for sustainable policies to take off, the artificial people—public and private—that we have allowed to dominate our world will need to be remade, as will our ideas about what constitutes property. This is already starting to happen. Ecuador has adopted a constitution that grants nature "the right to exist, persist, maintain and regenerate its vital cycles, structure, functions and its processes in evolution." The granting of a right on paper doesn't necessarily lead to its being granted in practice, of course, although the government has taken on the oil giant Chevron for destroying a patch of jungle the size of Delaware in a case where, *The Wall Street Journal* reports, Chevron "expects to be on the losing end."[7] In the Ecuadoran case, much of this power is concentrated in the hands of the central government, which is still pressing ahead with other extractive industries and is, through its own state-run and pollution-generating enterprises, guilty of violating these rights. There's nothing simple about using the machinery of governments against corporations, of setting one artificial person against another, in order to push back what can and cannot be turned into property, but the fight is happening even in the seat of contemporary capitalism—the United States.

DETHRONING *HOMO ECONOMICUS*

Thomas Linzey, the Pennsylvania lawyer who helped to draft the Ecuadoran constitution, is also active in the United States, with the Community Environmental Legal Defense Fund (CELDF). Initially founded to help campaign against single-issue environmental problems, the CELDF found itself fighting a wider range of battles, mainly against state-level legislation that prevented communities from protecting themselves against environmental harm. In one case, communities were opposed to factory hog farms, but the industry was granted a dispensation that meant that the waste from these farms avoided heavy regulation, and the state only required that the effluent be tested every three months for *E coli* and heavy metals. The waste was lethal. In 1995, two young men, Daniel Pennock and Tony Behun, both died from coming into contact with the waste. The CELDF's democracy school—where students learn organizing techniques to tackle corporate power directly—is named for Pennock. The school curriculum includes a history of the ways that corporations have managed to trump communities' rights to create their own democracies.

One case on the course syllabus involved voters in Vermont who in 1994 demanded to know whether their milk contained recombinant bovine growth hormone. Banned in Canada, Australia, New Zealand and parts of the EU, the hormone is widely used in the United States. Federal courts struck down the Vermont labeling law, saying that it violated the corporations' right "not to speak." This is just one of any number of laws in the food industry that follow from the right of corporations to be treated as "legal people." The net result, as Linzey observed in a 2003 interview, is that "the only thing that environmental law regulates is environmentalists."[8] Which is why he was instrumental in getting corporate personhood revoked in Clarion County, Pennsylvania. Linzey's organization has recently been involved in one of the most remarkable local democratic moves. When Nestlé wanted to tap the aquifer of a small town in Maine for its Poland Spring brand of bottled water, residents used the CELDF's tools to mount a campaign to save their water, declaring their sovereignty over their resources. There's no reason to believe that local is foolproof, or even that local is necessarily more enlightened, benign or sustainable than national government, but these small acts are a kind of community-driven escapology, slowly freeing us from the fetters placed on democratic society by the market.

And this points to perhaps the greatest prize in pursuing food sovereignty: the liberty it brings. In the Medak district of the Indian state of Andhra Pradesh, the poorest Dalits (so-called untouchable, but literally "oppressed" people) are in desperate straits. In a population nearing 3 million, one in a hundred people is in bonded labor, a form of debt servitude that turns people from humans into chattels. Virtually all of them come from a "scheduled tribe or caste," nearly 70 percent of which are children. India has been independent and democratic for sixty years, but the roots of democracy have had to curl through centuries of feudalism and religious bigotry.[9] Those most vulnerable to exploitation within Dalit communities are women, and it has been from their ranks that a remarkable experiment in community organizing has flourished.

The experiment, called the Deccan Development Society, began in 1979 and rapidly grew into a series of 75 *sanghams*, village-level associations of poor women, most of whom are Dalits.[10] Bina Agarwal, an academic studying the Deccan Development Society, notes that as India urbanizes, the business of feeding the cities is increasingly women's work—58 percent of Indian men work in agriculture compared to 78 percent of women. Worldwide, statistics also show a dramatic increase in the ratio of women to men in agriculture.[11] For over a decade, the roughly five thousand women who comprise the society have experimented with new, and old, ways of growing and distributing food. They manage and run their own market, in which they buy and sell goods that they produce and consume. By cutting out the middlemen who tend to scalp both producers and consumers, the Deccan Development Society has made food available at much lower prices than comparable merchants, and because the produce is organic, they have managed to attract a flock of urban middle-class consumers.

The society has also pioneered land-leasing schemes. For the most part, the women who form part of the *sanghams* used to be employed doing the back-breaking labor of weeding. By forming collectives, they have been able to rent land collectively from the landlords. The landlords are happy to rent out some of their tired land—they know that after four years under the agroecological systems the *sanghams* use, the land will be returned in far better shape.

Renting may seem an unlikely revolutionary activity, but the magic comes less from the monthly payment of rent than from the process of women's organizing. The women from one *sangham* say, "There was a time when we were afraid even to speak, but now, with much help from the Sangham, we are discovering our own strengths, and also our own voice. We feel strong enough to handle any challenge." This strength matters when landlords try to insist on the "old way" of doing things. One *sangham* had been sharecropping, splitting the produce on the land fifty/fifty with the landlord. One day, the landlord refused to give the women their 50 percent, so the women retaliated by bringing their bullock cart into the fields and stealing the irrigation equipment. The landlord took them to the Panchayat, the local village assembly, which decided that the landlord should get his pump back, as long as he gave the women what was theirs. Again, this isn't a moment of radical equality or revolution—but it's a transformative step toward it. The women were able to reclaim their power by playing with the boundaries of private property, not only by stealing the landlord's water pumps, but also by insisting on their right to have access to land so that they might farm in the first place. Rukmini Rao of the Deccan Development Society, quoted by Gayatri Menon in her pathbreaking analysis, observes that "if each woman was to farm individually, the odds are against her. By bringing women together, you are stacking the odds in their favour because you are bringing together different skills, ideas, experiences and resources."[12]

The resources that the women of the society have under their stewardship include culture and biodiversity. Part of the process of reclaiming their dignity has been to store, and develop, varieties of seeds that have been displaced by the arrival of "modern agriculture."[13] As stewards of biodiversity, the *sanghams'* push for food sovereignty means that they've created community gene banks, from which a wide variety of traditional seeds can be freely borrowed. These varieties are far more robust than the varieties of wheat and rice that are grown commercially elsewhere, and require less water and fossil fuel in order to grow. Climate change is expected to hit India hard, with temperature increases of 3–5° C., and with one of the country's principal water sources—the Himalayan glacier melt that feeds Asia's rice basins—expected to disappear by 2035. At a recent expert meeting convened by Jeffrey Sachs, director of the Earth Institute at Columbia University, Sachs argued for genetically modified climate-change-ready crops. What he seemed rather unprepared to hear was that there *aren't* genes for climate change. There might be genes to resist a particular disease, but there are no genes to resist the half-dozen symptoms of human-generated greenhouse gases. Any serious agronomist or geneticist knows that while the one-gene-one-triat idea was once fashionable, it's hard to maintain it today. Farming systems that capture carbon through rich soil fertility, and spread risk among a range of species that have been bred over centuries to thrive in a particular geographical region, provide a model for the kind of system we will need in a world of climate change, and that's precisely what the Deccan Development Society has pioneered, prompting one national Indian newspaper to declare in a headline that WOMEN FARMERS [ARE] SET TO BEAT CLIMATE CHANGE.[14]

What the women of the Deccan Development Society understand is that knowledge for sustainable change can't come from one source. It has to come from many. That's why the knowledge coming from the *sanghams* isn't limited to a single seed, or a single set of patents or even a single agronomic system. It spans a range of agricultural techniques in the community gene banks. Agricultural sustainability doesn't depend on agritechnology. To believe it does is to put the emphasis on the wrong bit of "agriculture." What sustainability depends on isn't agri- so much as *culture*. And that's why the women in the *sanghams* are producing other kinds of culture and knowledge using twenty-first-century media.

One of the convenors of the Deccan Development Society, P. V. Satheesh, believes that video provides a kind of literacy. The video produced by the women of the DDS is both literate and sophisticated in ways that put Hollywood to shame. The camera angles they prefer are low, looking up at their work. They don't like the "Patel-angle," the view of landowners looking down on them. (While in Britain the name "Patel" has all the distinguishing connotations of "Smith" or "Jones," in the fields of Andhra Pradesh where land is owned by Patels, it has all the force of "Madoff" or "Gekko" or "Stalin.") In all the social movements I've studied across the world, every one appreciates the importance of maintaining, curating, developing and celebrating not only the physical resources but their culture, understanding both the material and the cultural worlds as bodies on whose shoulders everyone stands, and which everyone is free to use, share and build upon.

The possibilities of this sort of commons are liberating.

The problems caused by the mismatch between prices and values do not stem from a lack of skilled practitioners, but from the deep failure of the market to value our world properly. McKinsey, the management consultancy, has a maxim that it imparts to its junior trainees—"Everything can be measured, and what gets measured gets managed."[15] The increased mismanagement of the planet's resources is almost inevitable when profit-driven markets set the terms of value. It is possible to quantify some of the hidden costs behind prices, and this should happen, but the overall solution to the misallocation of society's resources is not to start slapping prices on everything. There are some things that can't be captured by a single number, but still need management, and the only way that can happen fairly is through democratic politics. The answer to the market's valuing of the world at naught is not a democracy run by experts, but the democratization of expertise and resources.

TEN

ANTON'S BLINDNESS

Nothing will come of nothing: speak again.
—WILLIAM SHAKESPEARE, *King Lear*

There are two novels that can transform a bookish fourteen-year-old's life: *The Lord of the Rings* and *Atlas Shrugged*. One is a childish daydream that can lead to an emotionally stunted, socially crippled adulthood in which large chunks of the day are spent inventing ways to make real life more like a fantasy novel. The other is a book about orcs.

The trouble is that the fellow travelers of *Atlas Shrugged* have been helming government for decades. As of 2008, their attempt to make the world into some imagined paradise of prices and egotism has come unstuck. Millions suffered the consequences during the course of the attempt, millions more when the experiment exploded, and possibly billions will suffer if our way of dealing with the combined economic, social and environmental crises simply repeats the mistakes of the past.

Over the past thirty years, the accelerating pace of enclosure, and the increasing scale of the theft, have brought our planet to the edge of destruction. Internationally, environmental costs have been shunted from rich to poor, most notably though not exclusively from global warming. A recent report offers a very conservative estimate of the number of people harmed today by climate change at 325 million, every year. The number of deaths from weather changes alone is set to exceed 500,000 people per year (which is the number of women who die annually from breast cancer), and most of these deaths will happen among those who have had the least to do with causing the pollution, people whose countries were colonized by the very same powers that have caused this new catastrophe.[1] This does not mean that polluters shouldn't pay and that carbon dioxide has to be free because there's no good way to price it. Handing the matter over to capitalism is, however, likely to prove as good an idea as asking the iceberg to fix the *Titanic*. These are conclusions that come from the two investigations into "free" goods in the first half of this book, where we looked at what happens when corporations provide free goods, and what happens when governments do the same. In both cases, the rigid property schemes, profit-driven markets and corporations we've allowed to flourish create a deeply flawed system for valuing the world.

So where do we start to rebalance market society? Once we decide that exchanges are governed by the rules of the market, it is incredibly hard to put the genie back into the bottle. Neuroeconomic and sociological studies about the irreversibility of monetary-transaction relations confirm that markets can be a social toxin: After all, the day someone leaves money for a lover in payment for sex is the day that relationship ends. We face a far harder task, not just of removing the taint of money from specific transactions, but of removing corporate rapacity from government, and the bleak weight of consumerism from our political imaginations.

After the September 11 terrorist attacks, the only way that President Bush could think to begin the healing was to encourage Americans to fight terrorism with shopping, as if the damage and trauma could be neutralized through a sufficiently large spend. Luckily,

George W. Bush's philosophy isn't the only one. Some philosophies and religions have tried consciously to address the corrosive dangers of cupidity. Of those attempts, the most sophisticated of these, perhaps because of its central focus on the plucking out of desire from our hearts, is Buddhism. The prime exponent of Buddhist economics, E. F. Schumacher, was a colleague of John Maynard Keynes who, after long reflection on the theories that he once practiced, wrote a popular exposition of a more sustainable economics in *Small Is Beautiful*.[2] At the heart of Buddhist economics is a theory of want and greed, but one rather different from classical economics. Buddhism has a particular vision of what it is to be human—it is to be subject to desire. The source of human unhappiness is attachment. Buddha himself, born a prince, found that wealth brought him no joy. So he renounced his possessions and walked into the forest, to live a life of poverty. But he found that there was no happiness in poverty either. He came to understand that there is a Middle Path, one that plots a course between poverty and hedonism, one that doesn't reject the pleasures of the body, but merely observes that it is the craving for them that causes unhappiness.[3]

From this, it's possible to derive a Buddhist theory of value. The real value of something is not its ability to satisfy a craving, a desire, a vanity, but to meet the need for well-being. With this in mind, the baubles and fripperies that we're persuaded by advertisers are indispensible for our well-being—the luxury cars, the latest phones and footwear—turn out to be ashen.

If this were the sum total of the Buddhist insight, perhaps the only outcome would be some sort of lifestyle cult, in which we perform the daily calisthenics of desiring less. While such an exercise would certainly not be fruitless (and indeed, the practices of ancient Stoicism are exactly these sorts of spiritual exercises, "technologies of the self," to use a modern phrase),[4] there's also a bigger set of insights that Buddhism provides about the need to change in the wider world.

Flourishing happens in a social context, and engaging with that social context is a central feature of putting the genie of pecuniary values back into the bottle, and of developing a politics of value that comes from a particular vision of human nature. In Thailand, Buddhist monks have been active in supporting struggles for the protection of the environment (Thai forests are among the most denuded on the planet).[5] As part of that protest, they ordained a Bodhi tree, of the species under which Buddha attained enlightenment. The tree was part of a largely eviscerated forest, threatened by a large dam, upon which local communities depended for their survival. The act of ordaining the tree, by wrapping it in orange robes, made its sacred quality easier to see. In anointing the tree, the monks delivered their critique of commodification—the market exists within nature, and society and nature can and should provide boundaries to it. Many civilizations long ago came to a conclusion only recently rediscovered by ecologists: We belong to the earth, not the other way around.[6]

Of course, recognizing the embeddedness of market in society, and of market society in ecology, challenges the modern mechanics of value. It is perhaps for this reason that the Dalai Lama himself has taken a position on his preferred economic system. "I am a Marxist monk, a Buddhist Marxist," he said provocatively in a lecture at the Indian Institute of Management. "I belong to the Marxist camp, because unlike capitalism, Marxism is more ethical. Marxism, as an ideology, takes care of the welfare of its employees and believes in distribution of wealth among the people of the state."[7]

The Dalai Lama's views on economic justice aren't widely reported in the Global North, where he's portrayed as cuddly, apolitical and possessed of a wisdom that stretches to the next world without quite touching this one. But his position on economics is entirely compatible with Buddhism (and quite anathema to what the ostensibly Marxist Chinese government fosters). This might create cognitive dissonance within Europe and, much more, in North America, because of the immovable idea that to be a Marxist simply *means* wishing the Chinese or Soviet governments to take over. That the Dalai Lama finds value in a system in whose name he has been persecuted says much both about him, and about the misperceptions of Marxism. Buddhist economic and political models involve an approach to value that's very different from ethical consumerism, or even the act of voting once every four years. These are kinds of government that involve the daily political practice of controlling value, resources and distribution.

MAKING DEMOCRACY WORK

One shouldn't underestimate how hard this will be. Reclaiming the ability to engage market society, reclaiming the right to have rights, is difficult work. To begin with, it means regaining an appetite for conflict. It means understanding that some entities in the private sector are structurally part of the problem, not part of the solution, and that they need to be successfully challenged. Every philosophy of social change has had an understanding of enmity. Gandhian philosophy isn't, as some have reconstructed it, a big tent of beads and incense. Although it's nonviolent, it involves opposition and conflict—tender opposition no doubt, but opposition nonetheless. Movements around the world have developed the psychological tools to deal with conflict, guided by principles of equality and a desire to control the terms of inclusion.

Of course, this threatens the status quo, which is why many of the movements I've discussed—from peasants to shackdwellers—have been branded criminals and hooligans. Turning dissenters into criminals doesn't happen by magic—it happens because today's market society has an ideology in which those who challenge the fragile consensus around the role of the market cannot be tolerated. The activist Abbie Hoffman once observed, "You measure democracy by the freedom it gives its dissidents, not the freedom it gives its assimilated conformists." By that metric, there's not much democracy around.

Take, for instance, the case of the Kingsnorth Six, a group of six Greenpeace protesters who temporarily shut down a coal-fired power station in South East England, demanding an end to government plans for a new generation of similar power stations. They wanted to paint a message on the smokestack addressed to Prime Minister Brown: "Gordon, Bin It." Ultimately, they only managed to daub "Gordon," but it cost thirty thousand pounds to remove, and they were charged with criminal damage. At their trial, they argued that, yes, they'd damaged the power station, but they'd done so to prevent a greater harm. There's provision in law for this. If you smash the door of a burning house to save the people inside, you are breaking and entering to prevent a greater harm. When the jury was presented with the evidence of the harm that climate change was currently causing—shutting down the plant for a day prevented about $1.5 million in damage to human welfare worldwide—they agreed with the defense. The Kingsnorth Six were acquitted, the British government was forced to backtrack and the decision was even hailed by *The New York Times* as a milestone of 2008's life-changing ideas.

In moving to a more just and sustainable world, direct action that tests the boundaries of private property in the name of global justice will undoubtedly be necessary. Again, this isn't a terribly radical thing to say. Nobel laureate Al Gore observed that "we have reached the stage where it is time for civil disobedience to prevent the construction of new coal plants."[8] The Kingsnorth Six trial demonstrated where the power of direct action lies. The best kinds of political theater open up the world—educating, recruiting and entertaining in almost equal measure, making it possible for other people to act in new and daring ways. To talk only of the Kingsnorth Six defendants ignores others who made a difference in that trial. Of course the lawyers, activists and well-wishers mattered, but there were twelve others who turned the tide—the jurors.

It's no small matter that the game-changing legal decision lay in the hands not of government bureaucracy or the power company's accountants, but of twelve ordinary and anonymous men and women. In the jurors' deliberations, in their meetings, they exercised virtues of reason and freedom that hint at what a proper democracy, where people are able to craft the terms on which value is set, might look like.

Athens is democracy's overused Exhibit A, yet it might come as a surprise that the way Athenian democracy worked has little in common with the circus that shares the same name today.[9] There were no elections in Athens as we know them. Politics was not conducted by a self-selected group of power seekers, but by everyone, and involved drawing lots instead of elections. Twelve groups of five hundred people each were selected, and together the six thousand ruled the city, with each of the twelve groups trying cases themselves. Experts and lawyers were limited to advisory roles.

The idea behind the selection by lot was that no citizen should be excluded from the opportunity and responsibility of deliberative justice. That process of deliberation extended beyond the courtroom, where the remnants of this system apply to the twelve peers who judge cases. It can, and should, be extended elsewhere. As historian C. L. R. James argued in a wonderful 1956 essay titled "Every Cook Can Govern,"[10] it can and should be extended everywhere. Unlike today, where democracy has been reduced to a once-every-four-years chore, Athenians took their politics seriously. The term democracy was synonymous with *isonomia*—"equality"—and people who didn't want to be troubled by it were considered *idiotes*.[11] Today, the English descendent of this word just means "moron," but it once had far greater force.

Pericles' hymn to Athenian democracy sounds like a manifesto for the kinds of sovereignty that social movements are fighting for:

> Taking everything together then, I declare that our city is an education to Greece, and I declare that in my opinion each single one of our citizens, in all the manifold aspects of life, is able to show himself the rightful lord and owner of his own person, and do this, moreover, with exceptional grace and exceptional versatility.[12]

And you don't need to be Athenian to practice democracy. The University of Wuppertal in Germany has a planning group, and the Jefferson Center in Minneapolis a "policy jury," that select citizens at random who deliberate, hear expert testimony and come to democratic decisions, with "fairly consistent results."[13] Ultimately, though, no movement knows for sure how to build a functioning democracy. Dan Moshenberg's idea that the city unfolds in the fight for it, and Han Dongfang's wonder at not knowing how to make the first leap, would be familiar to the women and men of the Lacandon jungle, in Chiapas, Mexico. There, the Zapatistas are forging a new kind of democracy. The mistakes that get made along the way are part of that process of democracy; this process even has a name: *Preguntando caminamos*—Asking, we walk. To see it in action, I flew to Mexico.

Where I saw a lot of masks. At the airport in Mexico City, everyone wore a little blue surgical mask—I was given mine by a soldier who gestured with his gun that I'd be better off wearing it. We were protecting ourselves from one another. A fellow traveler could be a swine flu carrier—the outbreak had just begun. The masks were the most visible sign that Mexico was experiencing a massive externality that had everything to do with food, and would soon spread far beyond Mexico's borders.

Although it wasn't being reported in the mainstream English-language media,[14] the Mexican press had been writing about the horrific health conditions at Granjas Carroll, a subsidiary of the U.S.-based Smithfield meat-packing company, for some time.[15] At the company's operation in La Gloria, in Veracruz, they kill nearly one million pigs a year.[16] It was here, on March 30, 2009,[17] nearly a month before the outbreak hit Mexico City, that health officials recorded the first swine flu case. The virus that is currently in Mexico and the southern United States is a novel H1N1 virus, one that jumped species from pigs to humans.

Smithfield insists that it repeatedly tested its pigs and found them to be free of the virus, though *The New York Times* reports skepticism among some veterinary experts about whether these tests were meaningful. It's still an empirical question as to whether Smithfield factory played a role in the epidemic, and some federal officials have said the disease emerged in Asia, not Mexico. Still, some sort of confined animal operation remains a highly likely point of origin of the disease.[18]

Meanwhile, anyone in public space in Mexico had to walk around in blue masks. The most dangerous part of us was our mouths.[19] My destination, however, was not Mexico City but the country's southernmost state, Chiapas. There, I saw altogether different masks when I met with the Zapatistas, the insurgent group that declared war on the Mexican government in 1994. Here's how their proclamation formalized the state of affairs in their southernmost corner of Mexico over the past five hundred years:

> We are a product of 500 years of struggle: first against slavery, then during the War of Independence against Spain led by insurgents, then to avoid being absorbed by North American imperialism, then to promulgate our constitution and expel the French empire from our soil,

and later the dictatorship of Porfirio Díaz denied us the just application of the Reform laws and the people rebelled and leaders like Villa and Zapata emerged, poor men just like us. We have been denied the most elemental preparation so they can use us as cannon fodder and pillage the wealth of our country. They don't care that we have nothing, absolutely nothing, not even a roof over our heads, no land, no work, no health care, no food nor education. Nor are we able to freely and democratically elect our political representatives, nor is there independence from foreigners, nor is there peace or justice for ourselves and our children.[20]

In the fifteen years since that declaration, they've won land—by some estimates over half a million acres[21]—built primary health care facilities and made schools for the tens of thousands of people in their "liberated" territory. Their greatest victory, however, has been to build what has been hailed as a highly successful experiment in democracy and justice. I came to Chiapas to talk to the representatives of the Juntas de Buen Gobierno (the Good Government Councils, or Juntas for short). And when I met them, they were wearing their signature accessory—ski masks.

Beyond the rather obvious reason that they don't want to be hunted by the Mexican government—a fate that seems increasingly likely with the recent expansion of military forces in Chiapas—there's another explanation for the masks. The foundation of Zapatista democracy is the village, which is usually anywhere between fifteen and one hundred families. They hold regular assembly meetings that everyone is allowed to attend, and at which everyone is encouraged to speak. At the meeting, the village appoints two or sometimes four *responsables*, men and women equally represented, who act both as local authorities and as representatives to a regional municipality

(of about fifteen to one hundred villages). Together these municipalities select a pool of members from all villages to be on their Junta
de Buen Gobierno—there are five in total, covering all Zapatista-
controlled territory. Once selected, the members leave their villages
to serve at the Junta's headquarters for one week out of every six, for
a term of three years. After that, they'll never serve again. With constant rotation, faces change all the time, but the Junta's function remains the same.

The room of balaclavas is a sign that indigenous people are engaging in democracy without its most infectious symptom—elections.
Rather than sitting in individual air-conditioned offices in front of
large portraits of themselves, these democratic officials serve their
communities anonymously, with their faces hidden by the masks of
the office they have assumed. The ski masks also serve another political purpose. They are a reminder that when you visit the Junta,
you aren't there to see a particular person—you came to see *the
people*. The masks reveal that the most important face in the room is
yours. There's still accountability, though—the Juntas sometimes
publish *denuncias*, open letters denouncing a human-rights violation,
as they did recently when the Mexican army, allegedly looking for
marijuana fields while conducting "the war on drugs," destroyed the
main collective cornfield in the town of La Garrucha. In these cases,
the Junta members will sign their real names, but when they're working, the mask is a mantle of office.

At the entrance to the Zapatista territories, there's always a sign
that says *"Está usted en territorio rebelde zapatista. Aquí manda el
pueblo y el gobierno obedece."* (You are in rebel Zapatista territory.
Here the people lead and the government obeys.) This is in marked
contrast to the famously corrupt Mexican ruling party, the PRI (Institutional Revolutionary Party, which, despite its name, is structurally
more aligned with the U.S. Republican Party, or the British Conser-
vatives). As one Junta member explained, "In Mexico, the federal

government tries to buy your vote, the PRI gives out soda to buy your conscience. Here, we don't get paid—we do it because we have been chosen." They were at pains to stress that they weren't there by choice. When they are at the Junta's headquarters, they need to find someone to take care of their fields or their children, and yet, without exception, they said it was important to do.

Conducting an interview with a Junta is unusual. Names, ages, occupations and personal opinions are off-limits, because they're irrelevant (see above). I was asked to present a written list of questions, they privately pondered their collective response and I was invited back to hear every member of the Junta take a turn answering. This takes time. Not for nothing is the name of the five Zapatista Junta headquarters "Caracol," snail. I asked one of the Juntas why. "Three reasons—first, the snail walks slowly but surely; second, our ancestors blew through a conch shell to call a meeting together; third, the shape of the shell shows how information goes in and out of the Caracol, and that's how we work: by listening and exchanging."

Those familiar with the Slow Food movement will see some similarity here. Slow Food's philosophy rejects the acceleration that capitalism has brought to food, insisting that food should be produced in consonance with the environment and with a respect for the labor that produces it. Not fast food but Slow Food. If you've ever tried Slow Food, you'll know what a sublime and transformative experience it can be. Although the Slow Food movement has the reputation of being a middle-class supper club, its DNA is radical, and has a resonance with the Zapatistas—it shares the notion that *everyone* has the right to participate in, and enjoy, the world around them, and that genuine democracy takes time. The joke about the Zapatistas is this:

Q: How many Zapatistas does it take to change a lightbulb?
A: Come back in two weeks.

What Zapatistas are practicing is slow politics. Visitors and nongovernmental organizations trying to work with the Zapatistas can get a little impatient with the process of constant consultation, discussion and deliberation. It doesn't feel efficient, and NGOs get frustrated at being made to wait, but that's because they're making a mistake in valuing time. It's not as if the Zapatista government isn't capable of swift responses. You wouldn't want deliberative emergency service, and the Zapatistas have two ambulances and a clinic that provide prompt and universal coverage. But to decide justice and politics takes time—you wouldn't rush a criminal trial, or cut short the presentation of evidence in order to reach a verdict more swiftly, and it's the same with politics. Urgency is quick. Insurgency takes much longer.

It's a point I heard made rather clearly. "People know that we declared war fifteen years ago," one of the masked men offered. "But what people also know is that the shooting war lasted only twelve days. Much more important was the political war. It takes time to build a secondary school—first we had to build all the primary schools. There's nothing that happens overnight. It takes time to find the form."

And, again, the form isn't obvious, or even found the first time. "We didn't know what we were doing," said a woman whose eyes suggested she might be thirty. "We didn't know if a government run like ours was even possible. But we've shown that it can be." That the process works better if people spend more time on it is a finding only recently discovered by psychologists and behavioral economists. In one paper, researchers quote Henry Ford's autobiography, where he states that "time waste differs from material waste in that there can be no salvage."[22] What the economists demonstrate, and what the Zapatistas know, is that with a correctly structured system, you can build a great deal of trust between participants by taking time together.

The Juntas have been so successful in their deliberative democracy that ordinary non-Zapatista Mexicans seek their advice. The Zapatistas will receive anyone. Such is their reputation for impartial deliberation that their governing body is trusted by citizens and state alike to resolve cases ranging from divorce to grand theft. Local people prefer the Juntas' deliberations to the federal court system, where the case will be decided on the basis of which side was better able to bribe the officers of the court.[23] The justice that the Zapatistas offer is transformative justice rather than punitive. There is a jail that is mainly used for drunks, but incarceration is not the solution for most problems. The kinds of punishments that the Junta recommends are warnings, duties of care and community service. In one case involving the theft of over $40,000 from a truck carrying the salaries of local government employees, the Junta first tracked down the robbers, forced them to return the money to the government and then deliberated over their sentences. It was decided that sending them to jail would only hurt their families, who would have to work in the fields without the robbers' labor, so they were sentenced to 365 days of community service, with half the time allowed to tend to family fields, and the rest spent on public work. This is, of course, a million miles away from the prison industry in the United States, which leads the world in incarceration in the name of "public safety."

The Juntas are also involved in commoning, figuring how to share resources from land that they have reclaimed from large landholders. Balancing the economic needs of the community and the ecosystem's ability to sustain them is a delicate art. One Junta has restrictions on chopping down healthy trees (and, if it needs to be done, three are planted in each tree's stead). Revenues are shared between communities and the Junta.[24] Another Junta noticed declining yields on the land they'd been corralled onto by the Mexican government. Traditional methods of building soil fertility involved leaving land fallow for many years, but with the government reducing the amount of territory available, agriculture has needed to become more intensive. Nearby farmers adopted green revolution technologies, using seed and fertilizer, and after a few years, their soil was completely depleted. Seeing the need for an intensive agricultural system that didn't kill the soil, the junta started its own agroecological research and extension services, to teach their members how to farm in harmony with the environment and resources. As one of the Junta members said, "We come from nature and we know we can't live without it."

The ecological constraints, and the mounting aggression from the Mexican military, make life hard. "The economic situation isn't good and, yes, young people are leaving. When they come back, they're different—they don't respect their elders or siblings," said an elderly Junta member. "The government knows that if we're well organized, it's a danger to them. They would much rather keep young people confused and disoriented." The Junta suggests that the best weapon against this sort of disorientation is for people to become their government, rather than merely oppose it and leave governance to others. That requires both physical control of resources, and a constant dialogue about how the community should manage it.

The Zapatistas know too that the most dangerous part of us is our mouths.

OVERCOMING ANTON'S BLINDNESS

Zapatista democracy makes ours look decrepit and hollow. Our version is far removed from Athens, not so much a democracy as a complainocracy—a means of vacating the seat of power when the incumbent gets too troublesome. The emptiness of modern democratic politics explains why, from Mexico City's campaign to vote for *nulo* (null and void) to South Africa's "No Land, No House, No Vote" campaigns, people are responding to elections by choosing none of the above. Real, genuine control over power is not something many of us have ever really seen—we've suffered the blindness of thinking that what we practice is what we have been promised.

Bringing markets under control requires us to subdue governments and corporations, and there are ways to make that happen—but all of them will require us to overcome not only our current economic blindness but our political blindness as well, if we are to flourish and to save our planet from the destructive forces we've unleashed on it.

In Chuck Palahniuk's novel *Fight Club*, the first and second rules are that you don't talk about Fight Club. The cardinal rule of genuine democracy is that you *have* to talk about it. It needs meetings at which people can shape the terms on which value is set. Participating in these meetings isn't something you learn in school. Chinese workers, slum dwellers and hackers have all found that the skills they needed to become democratic citizens were ones they learned along the way. This isn't an unteachable craft—it's merely one that our market society has deemed superfluous. School is for learning how to be productive, follow instructions and respond to control—the last thing that today's standardized tests encourage is a healthy questioning about how to govern oneself. The Obama administration's education secretary, Arne Duncan, was clear about his portfolio: "There's a real sense of economic imperative. We have to educate our way [to] a better economy."[25] What the politics of sovereignty suggests is that everyone can be a teacher, an entrepreneur of change driven by something other than the profit motive.[26]

Not that the meetings are always exciting. Abbie Hoffman—writing under the name "Free"—had a good deal of experience with meetings, which he described as: information, meditation, experience, fun, trust, rehearsals and drama, but they're also "horseshit . . . meetings are a pain in the ass." But meetings are a venue in which we can set the rules so that when supply and demand meet, the consequences are not quite so devastating.[27]

Taking what we can from the sociology of the commons, a genuine democracy appears to involve changing the way we relate to the world around us, and moving beyond ownership to stewardship to commoning. This isn't a call to abandon all property—personal property is important, and no one should be denied it within reason. Nor is this a call to abandon markets—markets are good ways to decentralize decision making, and it's hard to imagine a functioning democracy where people are free without also having markets. British economist Diane Elson points out that even utopian community groups create some sort of market and tools of exchange—pure systems of barter are hard to manage, and democratically controlled markets make exchange easier, while leaving open the space to craft and adjust prices within those markets. What needs to be plucked out of markets is the perpetual and overriding hunger for expansion and profit that has brought us to the brink of ecological catastrophe; what needs to be plucked out of us is the belief that markets are the only way to value our world.

In developing new ways to respect the worth of the world around us, we need to understand that nothing is perfect—communities can fail, and democracy itself needs a safety net. Human rights are vital—although the process through which they have come to circulate may have been tainted, the idea of rights themselves has taken on a more democratic life. These demands level the playing field domestically, but also internationally—rights translate into a commitment from rich countries to pay back their debt to poor ones (and, obviously, cancel the debt that they are owed). What this adds up to isn't market socialism—Elson calls the vision one of socialized markets. If you don't like her term, perhaps Polanyi's might suit our times better—think of them as reembedded markets, markets driven by need, not profit.[28]

There are many barriers in the way of a fairer and more compassionate society. The concentration of resources and power in the hands of a few people and economic entities militates against a successful democracy. What we need is a more *plastic* idea of property, one in which property and markets are always subordinate to democratic concerns of equity and sustainability. That's exactly what the free software movement has been practicing—the hacking of market society, putting its power in everyone's hands. What their example also shows is that democracy isn't something that comes through its direct pursuit. The alibi of "democracy" has licensed a great deal of very antidemocratic politics, from Iraq to Afghanistan—but what free software, food sovereignty and shackdweller politics share is an idea that active and participatory democracy works not for its own sake, but as the best way of sharing the world's resources.

The basis for moving to more equitable and sustainable economies is already happening, not only in the fields and slums of the Global South but even in the world's most capitalist country. Despite the (sometimes self-inflicted) violence suffered by the U.S. union movement, some workers are taking control of their workplaces. When workers both own and participate in the governance of their corporations, these firms do much better than non-employee-owned-and-run firms.[29] Credit unions, for instance, are doing well for their owners—and the owners are everyone who saves with the union. Interest rates are higher for savers and lower for borrowers; the credit union is more responsive to community demands, and appears to have been less exposed to the travails of the financial crisis.

There are smaller examples every day of people getting together and working, sharing and giving things away for the common good. The free software movement is one example, and one that demonstrates better than most the contrasting meanings of "free." This open approach can work in the real world. Returning to a trend discussed earlier, many communities are losing their local newspapers. In Carbondale, Colorado, a local rural weekly, *The Valley Journal*, went out of business in February 2009. A small group of citizens decided to create their own replacement because, in the words of one of its founders, "It just beat the dickens out of sitting around whining that our paper was dead."[30] Of course, these sorts of volunteer operations struggle for financing, and the paper's collective is looking for any and all kinds of sponsorship. As one member of the local chamber of commerce puts it, "Every town should have a park, a library and a newspaper." This, of course, suggests where the resources might come from. Parks and libraries are generally not run by foundations or individual sponsors. They're run through public funding, and there's no reason why such important hubs of community engagement shouldn't be supported as they were in the last depression, by public funds.

But for that to happen, we need the imagination to reclaim both democracy and the economy—we need to understand the basic flaw in imagining that the two could be separated. This means telling ourselves different stories to replace the fantasies about the free market. Let's return to the Anton's blindness analogy, which, I admit, isn't the first medical metaphor for the economy. There's a history of using similes of disease and treatment to talk about the wider world, particularly when that world seems sick.[31] The earliest European theorists of money also used ideas of madness. John Locke wasn't only the intellectual godfather of modern liberal capitalism but a renowned physician too. He developed a controversial theory of madness that was applied in both medical and economic contexts. Unlike his contemporaries, Locke did not regard madness as a sign that the insane had no capacity for reason, but rather that their reason was being tricked by "bad input." For Locke, the cure was to tie down broken minds, sometimes literally, so that they could be retrained.

He dispensed similar advice for broken economies. In Locke's day, the great crisis of value lay in the falling value of money—coin clippers, counterfeiters and frauds of various kinds had altered and shaved the edges off silver coins so that the face value was more than 50 percent higher than its real worth. "It is no wonder, if the price and value of things be confounded, and uncertain, when the measure itself is lost. For we have now no lawful silver money current amongst us; and therefore cannot talk or judge right, by our present, uncertain, clipped money, of the value and price of things."[32] His solution was for the government to take a coin that claimed to be, say, a 10-ounce piece of silver, and reissue it as a more accurate 7-ounce piece. By turning coins into self-contained educational devices to correct the insanity of debauched currency, Locke sewed up both madness and money.

John Maynard Keynes saw the role of the economist as a particular kind of medical professional who fixes the economy and prescribes a preventive regime to keep it healthy. In his words, "If economists could manage to get themselves thought of as humble, competent people on a level with dentists, that would be splendid."[33] It's a model that, while rich in diagnosing the problems of the economy as ones resulting from the inevitable ups and downs of social psychology in the financial domain, still leaves the treatment of economic ill in the hands of a few sufficiently well-qualified social surgeons.

Naomi Klein's *The Shock Doctrine* has shown how this logic was updated by free market fundamentalists, who drew inspiration from ways of treating mental illness through electroshock therapy. The walk from electroshock therapy to the shock therapy of free markets is one that we are still experiencing, and one with a painfully long history.

The Anton's blindness analogy isn't a call for an army of neurologists to fix us. Invariably, there is no cure to the disease of believing you can see when, in fact, you cannot. Patients have to learn to distrust what they see in their heads, to develop ways of living without sight, relying on other senses, and other people, to live a full life. Rather than hoping for a cure to prices getting it wrong, we'll need to appreciate that prices can, at best, only give a blurry sense of priorities and possibilities. We'll never be able to see the world clearly through the glass of the market. And that's no bad thing. Armed with this knowledge, we can train ourselves to use our other senses, to know the world in different ways. The same thing needs to happen with the way we approach our economy and society. We've been socialized into thinking only in terms of the money value of something, but thinking this way shrinks us. We need to admit that prices don't signal what we believe—only after we've stopped confabulating about prices will we be on the road to recovery.

Discussion, regulation, trust, generosity and forbearance are ways to reclaim what the market has taken from us psychologically. If we exercise those faculties, as Harvard political philosopher Michael Sandel suggests, they'll grow stronger. Which begs the question about how to body-build our political selves. Every activist in this book has said that there's no guarantee, that we make the road only by walking. And that's what we'll need to do, to confront inequalities in power, especially those spawned by the artificial people, corporations and governments, that surround us. This will undoubtedly mean direct action to make the world fairer. If the prospect seems unnerving, it should—it is anathema to the politics of patience and passivity that we've been encouraged to believe in. The shattering of illusions is never easy, but to see beyond the limitations of the market we will need to experiment with ways of sharing the world, and of figuring out the boundaries of how we pool resources. That means nationalization, in cases like health care or the banking system.[34] In other cases, it means developing new ways of sharing, and of stinting. In all cases, it involves building collectivities that respect human rights, while helping us to value the world differently.

Talk of developing our blunted faculties might sound a little too much like science fiction, or "using the force" from the *Star Wars* universe. Octavia Butler, one of the few African American women science fiction writers, defended her craft in ways that are very relevant to us. Responding to the question "What good is science fiction to black people?" she wrote:

> What good is science fiction's thinking about the present, the future, and the past? What good is its tendency to warn or to consider alternative ways of thinking and doing? What good is its examination of the possible effects of science and technology, or social organization and political direction? At its best, science fiction stimulates imagination and creativity. It gets reader and writer off the beaten track, off the narrow, narrow footpath of what "everyone" is saying, doing, thinking—whoever "everyone" happens to be this year.
>
> And what good is all this to Black people?[35]

In order to reclaim politics, we too will need more imagination, creativity and courage. We will need to remember that democracy's triumphs come not from the ballot box but from the circumstances that make democracy possible: equality, accountability, and the possibility of politics. We will need to understand that our collective and individual happiness is only damaged by becoming Greenspan's monsters, the role for which most of us have been groomed since birth, christened in consumer culture and loaded with material desire until we die. A sustainable future will need markets, but ones that are kept firmly in their place lest the motives, passions and resources that a few people are able to derive from them continue to corrupt the rest of society and the planet. We need to see, value and steward the world in more democratic ways, realize that property and government can be much more plastic than we'd ever thought possible. This, ultimately, will be a collective enterprise, tough but infinitely more rewarding than today's market society. Our happiness cannot come from its solitary pursuit, but from the liberty of living together and engaging in the democratic politics that will help us value our common future.

NOTES

1. THE FLAW

1. Alan Greenspan, "Testimony of Dr. Alan Greenspan to the Committee of Government Oversight and Reform, October 23, 2008," http://oversight.house.gov/documents/20081023100438.pdf.

2. Edward Luce and Chrystia Freeland, "Summers Calls for Boost to Demand," *Financial Times*, March 9, 2009.

3. *Time*, "10 Questions for Jim Cramer," May 14, 2009.

4. If you remember *The Metamorphosis* beginning with Samsa waking up as a beetle, that's right too. The original German word for what Samsa turns into is *Ungeziefer*, which translates into English as "vermin." Translators have taken the liberty of interpreting it as something six-legged. Vladimir Nabokov, in a famed essay, suggested that beneath the carapace, Samsa had wings, but never realized it: "This is a very nice observation on my part to be treasured all your lives. Some Gregors, some Joes and Janes, do not know that they have wings." Vladimir Vladimirovich Nabokov and Fredson Bowers, *Vladimir Nabokov: Lectures on Literature* (London: Weidenfeld and Nicolson, 1980), 259.

5. This is an accounting practice that, laughably, has been introduced by the U.S. Securities and Exchange Commission as a tool for "protecting investors." This accounting technique was widespread in the Enron fraud and the failure of Long-Term Capital Management.

6. Sanford J. Grossman and Joseph E. Stiglitz, "On the Impossibility of Informationally Efficient Markets," *The American Economic Review* 70, no. 3 (1980).

7. Behavioral economists are now trying to patch up these models by factoring in the fact that investors can be irrational. It's a reflection on the discipline that when financial models failed, economists decided that the models were fine, but that the world was flawed: The real-life changes

that need to be factored into these models are called "imperfections." The discipline is waking up to the behavior of irrational people, possessed of imperfect information, in imperfect markets.

8. See Justin Fox, *The Myth of the Rational Market: A History of Risk, Reward, and Delusion on Wall Street* (New York: HarperBusiness, 2009), for more.

9. Greg Farrell and Sarah O'Connor, "Goldman Sachs Staff Set for Record Pay," *FT.Com*, July 15, 2009.

10. Andrew Clark, "Indiana Tries to Halt Chrysler Deal," *Guardian*, April 6, 2009; Matt Taibbi, "The Great American Bubble Machine," *Rolling Stone*, July 2009.

11. Nassim Nicholas Taleb, "Ten Principles for a Black Swan–Proof World," *Financial Times*, April 8, 2009.

12. The analyst with the strongest claim to seeing this coming is the sociologist Giovanni Arrighi, who died as this book went to press. The author of *The Long Twentieth Century*, he argued that capitalism spurts forward in these periods of financial crisis, with one combination of government and financial capital crumbling as another rises: first the Genoese (1340s to 1630s), then the Dutch (1560s to 1780s), then the British (1740s to 1930s), then the American (from about 1870s to now). Granted, Arrighi thought when he finished his book in 1994 that the likely successor after the U.S. system collapsed would be Japan. But with China and India now major international financial centers, and with the emergence of multibillion-dollar sovereign wealth funds, it looks as if states and finance are indeed recombining in novel ways. A new multipolar financial world is already being fixed into place, but it remains a world subject to the whims of finance, where a trillion dollars is just an electronic credit in the ether that can make or break entire countries. For more, see Giovanni Arrighi, *The Long Twentieth Century: Money, Power and the Origins of Our Times* (London: Verso, 1994).

13. The Great Depression mattered in Europe and North America undoubtedly, but today's globe is far bigger, and because the global economy is more tightly integrated than it was eighty years ago and involves far more people, the scale of today's economic crisis is far greater.

14. Cited in Mark P. Mostert, "Useless Eaters: Disability as Genocidal Marker in Nazi Germany," *The Journal of Special Education* 36, no. 3 (2002).

15. Joseph E. Stiglitz and Linda Bilmes, *The Three Trillion Dollar War: The True Cost of the Iraq Conflict,* 1st ed. (New York: W. W. Norton, 2008), 138. To see why international comparisons of this sort are fraught, see Thomas Pogge and Sanjay G. Reddy, "How Not to Count the Poor," Social Science Research Network, October 29, 2005, http://ssrn.com/abstract=893159 (accessed December 6, 2007).

16. Millennium Ecosystem Assessment, *Ecosystems and Human Well-Being: Synthesis* (Washington, D.C.: Island Press, 2005).

17. Though see George Monbiot for sensible reasons why we should reduce CO_2 to below 350 parts per million in any case. George Monbiot, "If We Behave as If It's Too Late, Then Our Prophecy Is Bound to Come True," *Guardian*, March 17, 2009.

18. Daly's views on population, including "birth licences," are worrisome. For more on the troubling politics of population control, see Jacqueline Rorabeck Kasun, *The War Against Population: The Economics and Ideology of World Population Control.* San Francisco: Ignatius Press, 1988.

19. Herman E. Daly, "In Defense of a Steady-State Economy," *American Journal of Agricultural Economics* 54, no. 5 (1972): 950–51.

20. Luke D. Kartsounis, Merle James-Galton and Gordon T. Plant, "Anton Syndrome, with Vivid Visual Hallucinations, Associated with Radiation Induced Leucocncephalopathy," *Journal of Neurology, Neurosurgery, and Psychiatry* (2009), http://jnnp.bmj.com/cgi/content/short/jnnp.2008.151118vl.

21. V. S. Ramachandran and Diane Rogers-Ramachandran, "Denial of Disabilities in Anosognosia," *Nature* 382 (1996).

22. Albert O. Hirschman, *Exit, Voice, and Loyalty: Responses to Decline in Firms, Organizations, and States* (Cambridge, MA: Harvard University Press, 1970).

23. Indeed, one of the ideological functions of contemporary economic theory is to obscure this difference, to conflate need with profit, facilitating the construction of a world in which everything is for sale.

2. BECOMING *HOMO ECONOMICUS*

1. John Stuart Mill, *Essays on Some Unsettled Questions of Political Economy*, 2nd ed. ([S.l.]: Longmans, Green, Reader, and Dyer, 1874), 144.

2. Ibid., 145 (italics added).

3. Gary S. Becker, *The Economic Approach to Human Behavior* (Chicago: University of Chicago Press, 1976), 14 (italics in original).

4. Tore Frängsmyr, ed., *Les Prix Nobel. The Nobel Prizes 1992* (Stockholm: Nobel Foundation, 1993).

5. See in particular Alexander Rosenberg, "Review Symposium: Can Economic Theory Explain Everything?," *Philosophy of the Social Sciences* 9, no. 4 (1979), for a thoughtful discussion.

6. Gary S. Becker, "Competition and Democracy," *Journal of Law and Economics* 1 (1958): 106.

7. Gary S. Becker, "A Theory of Marriage: Part I," *Journal of Political Economy* 81 (1973): 819. Becker is, as some critics have observed, extremely heteronormative—since one of the transhistorical purposes of getting married is to have your own children with someone of the opposite sex, there's only room for straight people in Becker's families. For critiques of Becker on this issue, see Friederike Haberman, *Der homo oeconomicus und das Andere Hegemonie, Identität und Emanzipation*, Feminist and Critical Political Economy 1 (Baden-Baden, Germany: Nomos 2008); Colin Danby, "Political Economy and the Closet: Heteronormativity in *Feminist Economics*" 13 no. 2 (2007), 29–53.

8. Ibid., 822.

9. Gary S. Becker, *A Treatise on the Family*, enl. ed. (Cambridge, MA: Harvard University Press, 1991), 117.

10. See Barbara R. Bergmann, "Becker's Theory of the Family: Preposterous Conclusions," *Feminist Economics* 1, no. 1 (1995), for more.

11. Ibid., 145.

12. Martin Brokenleg, "Native American Perspectives on Generosity," *Reclaiming Children and Youth* 8, no. 2 (1999).

13. Gerald Marwell and Ruth E. Ames, "Economists Free Ride, Does Anyone Else?: Experiments on the Provision of Public Goods, IV," *Journal of Public Economics* 15, no. 3 (1981). There's a debate among economists today about whether their graduates make poorer citizens—the most convincing arguments tilt toward yes, which again augurs ill, given that the tailors of global economics policy are themselves cut from this very cloth. Robert H. Frank et al., "Do Economists Make Bad Citizens?," *The Journal of Economic Perspectives (1986–1998)* 10, no. 1 (1996).

14. Joseph Henrich et al., "'Economic Man' in Cross-Cultural Perspective: Behavioral Experiments in 15 Small-Scale Societies," *Behavioral and Brain Sciences* 28, no. 6 (2005).

15. Although this outcome is still far better than the predictions of *Homo economicus*, it also serves as an antidote to some of the more overtly misty-eyed (and covertly racist) blanket notions of the innate generosity of indigenous people that permeate much "alternative'" Western culture.

16. Edward Vul et al., "Puzzlingly High Correlations in fMRI Studies of Emotion, Personality, and Social Cognition," *Perspectives on Psychological Science* (forthcoming). An important disclaimer: Experiments conducted recently at Yale found that people are very apt to be blown away by impressive-sounding science. Researchers inserted the words "Brain scans indicate that . . . because of the frontal lobe brain circuitry involved in self-knowledge . . ." into good and bad explanations. They found that without the brain scan

preface, people were pretty good at telling apart good and bad explanations. But when the brain scan suggestion was made, people threw up their hands and let the neuroscientists do the thinking for them. My wife's a neuroscientist, and although experience shows that I should let her do the thinking for me far more often than I do, she too is suspicious of the technology and conclusions drawn by her colleagues and their big machines. The resolution of functional Magnetic Resonance Imaging (fMRI) scans is so low, it's hard really to tell what's going on inside our heads—it's like trying to appreciate the *Mona Lisa* from a mile away.

17. Jorge Moll et al., "Human Fronto-Mesolimbic Networks Guide Decisions About Charitable Donation," *Proceedings of the National Academy of Sciences* 103 (2006).

18. M. Bekoff, "Wild Justice and Fair Play: Cooperation, Forgiveness, and Morality in Animals," *Biology and Philosophy* 19, no. 4 (2004).

19. Frans B. M. de Waal, "How Selfish an Animal? The Case of Primate Cooperation," in *Moral Markets: The Critical Role of Values in the Economy*, ed. Paul Zak (Princeton: Princeton University Press, 2008), 69.

20. See Sarah F. Brosnan, "Fairness and Other-Regarding Preferences in Nonhuman Primates," in *Moral Markets*, ed. Paul Zak.

21. When dogs were trained to give out their paw in exchange for a treat, but when one dog was given a treat in view of a dog that wasn't being treated for holding out a paw, the second dog became far less cooperative. Friederike Range et al., "The Absence of Reward Induces Inequity Aversion in Dogs," *Proceedings of the National Academy of Sciences* 106, no. 1 (2009).

22. See Ernst Fehr and Bettina Rockenbach, "Detrimental Effects of Sanctions on Human Altruism," *Nature* 422, no. 6928 (2003), cited in Samuel Bowles, "Policies Designed for Self-Interested Citizens May Undermine 'The Moral Sentiments': Evidence from Economic Experiments," *Science* 320, no. 5883 (2008).

23. Becker, *Economic Approach to Human Behavior*, 132.

24. Adam Smith thought not: "When Providence divided the earth among a few lordly masters, it neither forgot nor abandoned those who seemed to have been left out in the partition. These last too enjoy their share of all that it produces. In what constitutes the real happiness of human life, they are in no respect inferior to those who would seem so much above them. In ease of body and peace of mind, all the different ranks of life are nearly upon a level, and the beggar, who suns himself by the side of the highway, possesses that security which kings are fighting for." Adam Smith, *The Theory of Moral Sentiments* (1759; repr., Oxford: Clarendon, 1976), part 4, chap. 1.

25. Carol Nickerson et al., "Zeroing in on the Dark Side of the American Dream: A Closer Look at the Negative Consequences of the Goal for Financial Success," *Psychological Science* 14, no. 6 (2003).

26. Ibid.

27. Abhishek Srivastava et al., "Money and Subjective Well-Being: It's Not the Money, It's the Motives," *Journal of Personality and Social Psychology* 80, no. 6 (2001).

28. What's important here, though, is that there's a disconnect between happiness and money, and if that's the case, markets aren't going to be the best way of ensuring that happiness is maximized. Here's a slightly mathematical example, but one that I think is intriguing, and suggested by Gavin McCormick. Imagine that Radhika and Apple-mart are both selling apples. Let's further imagine that Radhika has a net worth of ten dollars (and one apple), that Apple-mart is entirely owned by Bill Bates (net worth ten million dollars and lots of apples), and that along comes Mr. Jones (net worth ten thousand dollars and no apples) to buy lunch. If Radhika can sell her apple for twenty cents, but Apple-mart can undercut her and sell for ten cents due to economies of scale, then Mr. Jones (whose willingness to pay for an apple is fifty cents) will buy from Apple-mart. Measured in dollars, this generates the highest possible surplus—forty cents. But dollars are just a proxy for value, and measured in value, things look quite different, because the value of those twenty cents to Radhika (log $10.20 − log $10) would have been far greater than the value of ten cents to Apple-mart's owner (log $10 million and $0.10 − log $10 million) plus an additional ten cents from Mr. Jones (log $9,999.90 − log $9,999.80).

Similarly, willingness to pay is a terrible proxy for value. Suppose Mr. Bates and Radhika are both dying in different deserts. Let's be unbelievably crass and assume their lives have no value except what happiness their money brings them, so Mr. Bates's life is worth log(10 million) = 7 utils, and Radhika's life is worth log(10) = 1 util. Further assume that Mr. Jones could go rescue them for a little effort, equal to one tenth of a util. If the market dealt in utils, it would be clear to see that Mr. Jones should go rescue both of them, and they could work out a going market rate for rescue somewhere between 0.1 utils and 1.0 utils. But since the market deals in dollars, the transaction cannot go through: 0.1 utils for someone of Mr. Jones's income level is equal to about $2,055. So since Radhika can trade only with her paltry $10, not her more valuable supply of 1 util, she cannot buy a rescue.

29. Arloc Sherman and Aviva Aron-Dine, *New CBO Data Show Income Inequality Continues to Widen* (Washington, D.C.: Center on Budget and Policy Priorities, 2007).

30. Robert H. Frank, *Falling Behind: How Rising Inequality Harms the Middle Class*, The Aaron Wildavsky Forum for Public Policy 4 (Berkeley: University of California Press, 2007).

31. United Nations Department of Economic and Social Affairs, *The Inequality Predicament: Report on the World Social Situation 2005* [a/60/117/Rev.1 St/Esa/299] (New York: UNDESA, 2005).

32. William Langley, "Profile: The King of Bhutan," *The Sunday Telegraph*, November 9, 2008.

33. And that's assuming we were comparing like with like in international GDP data—but we're not. Again, see Pogge and Reddy, "How Not to Count the Poor."

34. Juliet Michaelson et al., *National Accounts of Well-Being: Bringing Real Wealth onto the Balance Sheet* (London: New Economics Foundation, 2009).

35. James Konow and Joseph Earley, "The Hedonistic Paradox: Is Homo Economicus Happier?," *Journal of Public Economics* 92, no. 1–2 (2008).

36. John Stuart Mill, *The Autobiography of John Stuart Mill* (Sioux Falls, SD: NuVision Publications, 1997), 73.

37. Michel Foucault and Michel Senellart, *The Birth of Biopolitics: Lectures at the Collège de France, 1978–79* (Basingstoke: Palgrave Macmillan, 2008).

38. Datamonitor, *Life Insurance: Global Industry Guide* (London: Datamonitor: An Informa Business, 2009).

39. Viviana A. Rotman Zelizer, *Morals and Markets: The Development of Life Insurance in the United States* (New Brunswick, NJ: Transaction, 1983); Viviana A. Rotman Zelizer, *Pricing the Priceless Child: The Changing Social Value of Children* (New York: Basic, 1985).

3. THE CORPORATION

1. Joel Bakan, *The Corporation: The Pathological Pursuit of Profit and Power* (New York: The New Press, 2004). Using the same idea, academic Lynn Stout has applied similar thinking to the question of *Homo economicus*, and come to the same conclusion. Lynn A. Stout, "Taking Conscience Seriously," in *Moral Markets*, ed. Paul Zak.

2. Michael Grunwald, "Monsanto Hid Decades of Pollution; PCBs Drenched Ala. Town, but No One Was Ever Told," *Washington Post*, January 1, 2002.

3. *Wired*, "The Future of Food: How Science Will Solve the Next Global Crises," October 28, 2008.

4. Nancy Dunne, "Why a Hamburger Should Cost 200 Dollars—The Call for Prices to Reflect Ecological Factors," *Financial Times*, January 12, 1994.

5. Alicia Harvie and Timothy A. Wise, "Sweetening the Pot: Implicit Subsidies to Corn Sweeteners and the U.S. Obesity Epidemic," in *Policy Brief 09-01*, Global Development and Environment Institute, Tufts University, 2009.

6. Environmental Working Group, "Corn Subsidies in the United States," *Environmental Working Group's Farm Subsidies Database*, 2009, http://farm.ewg.org/farm/progdetail.php?fips=00000&progcode=corn (accessed March 4, 2009).

7. Bureau of Labor Statistics, "Combined Food Preparation and Serving Workers, Including Fast Food," *Occupational Employment and Wages*, May 2007, http://www.bls.gov/oes/2007/may/oes353021.htm (accessed March 14, 2009).

8. SEIU, "SEIU Beyond the Bonuses: Tarp," 2009, http://www.seiu.org/a/change-that-works/bank-of-america/beyond-the-bonuses-tarp.php (accessed March 4, 2009); Piet Van Lier, *Public Benefits Subsidize Major Ohio Employers: A 2008 Update* (Cleveland, OH: Policy Matters Ohio, 2008).

9. See Tom Lotshaw, "Working for Welfare," *Marietta Register*, January 6, 2009.

10. D. Barnard et al., "The Medical Costs Attributable to Meat Consumption," *Preventive Medicine* 24, no. 6 (1995).

11. Barry M. Popkin, "The Nutrition Transition and Its Health Implications in Lower-Income Countries," *Public Health Nutrition* 1, no. 1 (1998).

12. SEI, "Price Per Ton of Carbon Offset: Voluntary Carbon Offset Information Portal," Stockholm Environment Institute and the Tufts University Climate Initiative, 2009, http://www.tufts.edu/tie/carbonoffsets/price.htm (accessed March 5, 2009).

13. Weiqi Chen et al., "Estimation of Environmental Cost Incurred by Pesticide Application in Coastal Agricultural Region and Management Measures," *Environmental Informatics Archives* 4 (2006).

14. Jules N. Pretty et al., "A Preliminary Assessment of the Environmental Costs of the Eutrophication of Fresh Waters in England and Wales" (paper, Centre for Environment and Society and Department of Biological Sciences, University of Essex, Colchester, UK, 2002).

15. See Partha Dasgupta, "Comments on the Stern Review's Economics of Climate Change" (comments were prepared for a seminar on the Stern Review's Economics of Climate Change, organized by the Foundation for Science and Technology at the Royal Society, London, on November 8, 2006; available from www.econ.cam.ac.uk/faculty/dasgupta/STERN.pdf.)

16. Erin M. Tegtmeier and Michael D. Duffy, "External Costs of Agricultural Production in the United States," *International Journal of Agricultural Sustainability* 2 (2004).

17. J. N. Pretty et al., "An Assessment of the Total External Costs of UK Agriculture," *Agricultural Systems* 65, no. 2 (2000).

18. *Economist*, "A Survey of China's Quest for Resources: Negative Externalities," *Economist Special Reports*, March 13, 2008.

19. *People's Daily Online*, "Desertification Causes Yearly Loss of 54 Billion Yuan in China," November 26, 2008.

20. Ibid.

21. Pacific Institute, "Reign of Sand: Inner Mongolia. A Vast Chinese Grassland, a Way of Life Turns to Dust," *Circle of Blue*, 2008, http://www.circleofblue.org/reign/article_main_2.php (accessed March 15, 2008).

22. Peter Ford, "Drought Threatens China's Wheat Crop," *Christian Science Monitor*, February 11, 2009.

23. Ibid.

24. Scott M. Swinton et al., "Ecosystem Services and Agriculture: Cultivating Agricultural Ecosystems for Diverse Benefits," *Ecological Economics* 64, no. 2 (2007).

25. Harpinder S. Sandhu et al., "The Future of Farming: The Value of Ecosystem Services in Conventional and Organic Arable Land: An Experimental Approach," *Ecological Economics* 64, no. 4 (2008).

26. Leo Horrigan et al., "How Sustainable Agriculture Can Address the Environmental and Human Health Harms of Industrial Agriculture," *Environmental Health Perspectives* 110, no. 5 (2002).

27. Juan Martinez-Alier, *The Environmentalism of the Poor: A Study of Ecological Conflicts and Valuation* (Cheltenham, UK: Edward Elgar, 2002).

28. U. Thara Srinivasan et al., "The Debt of Nations and the Distribution of Ecological Impacts from Human Activities," *Proceedings of the National Academy of Sciences* 105, no. 5 (2008).

29. Lawrence Mishel and Jared Bernstein, *Economy's Gains Fail to Reach Most Workers' Paychecks* (Washington, D.C.: Economic Policy Institute, 2007)

30. There's an extensive literature on why and whether we're duped by the difference between, say, $1 and $0.99; those who'd like to hang on to the idea that we're being at least a little bit rational will argue that although it may feel like the difference between $1 and $0.99 is more than, say the difference between $1.01 and $1, that's because we're used to ignoring the last digit, as a rational way of saving our brain's scarce computing

power for better things. See Dan Ariely, *Predictably Irrational: The Hidden Forces That Shape Our Decisions* (New York: HarperCollins, 2008), for instance.

31. Which gives you some sense of the profit margin—at full retail price, they'd have turned over $12 million.

32. Bruce Horovitz, "2 Million Enjoy Free Breakfast at Denny's," *USA Today*, February 3, 2009.

33. Rudyard Kipling, *American Notes* (Boston: Brown and Company, 1899), 18. I'm very happy to acknowledge that Wikipedia pointed me toward this source.

34. Richard B. McKenzie, *Why Popcorn Costs So Much at the Movies: And Other Pricing Puzzles* (New York: Copernicus Books, 2008).

35. Dominique Soguel, "Mining Interests Tied to Rape Impunity in Congo," *Women's eNews*, June 3, 2009.

36. Raj Patel, *Stuffed and Starved: Markets, Power and the Hidden Battle for the World Food System* (London: Portobello Books, 2007), 280.

37. Shin-Yi Chou et al., "Fast Food Restaurant Advertising on Television and Its Influence on Childhood Obesity," *The Journal of Law and Economics* 51, no. 4 (2008).

38. Steve Stecklow, "Microsoft Battles Low-Cost Rival for Africa," *Wall Street Journal*, October 28, 2008.

39. Annelies Allain and Yeong Joo Kean, "The Youngest Market: Baby Food Peddlers Undermine Breastfeeding," *Multinational Monitor* 30, no. 1 (2008). The figure for infant mortality estimates from infant formula relates to 2004, and comes from http://www.unicef.org/nutrition/index_22657.html, cited in George Kent, "WIC's Promotion of Infant Formula in the United States," *International Breastfeeding Journal* 1, no.8 (2006), doi:10.1186/1746 4358-1-8.

40. Allain and Kean, "The Youngest Market."

41. Michael Sandel, *Reith Lectures: A New Citizenship* (British Broadcasting Corporation, 2009) http://www.bbc.co.uk/programmes/b00kt7rg (accessed August 10, 2009).

4. ON DIAMONDS AND WATER

1. As quoted in Michael Albert, *Moving Forward: Programme for a Participatory Economy* (Edinburgh: AK, 2000), 128.

2. The part of *The Wealth of Nations* that "invisible hand" has come to represent is this one: "man has almost constant occasion for the help of his

brethren, and it is in vain for him to expect it from their benevolence only. He will be more likely to prevail if he can interest their self-love in his favour, and show them that it is for their own advantage to do for him what he requires of them. Whoever offers to another a bargain of any kind, proposes to do this. Give me that which I want, and you shall have this which you want, is the meaning of every such offer; and it is in this manner that we obtain from one another the far greater part of those good offices which we stand in need of. It is not from the benevolence of the butcher, the brewer, or the baker, that we expect our dinner, but from their regard to their own interest. We address ourselves, not to their humanity but to their self-love, and never talk to them of our own necessities but of their advantages." Adam Smith, *An Inquiry into the Nature and Causes of the Wealth of Nations*, 5th ed. (1776; rep., London: Methuen, 1904), 44.

3. Incidentally, he writes this immediately after the only reference to the invisible hand in his *Theory of Moral Sentiments*.

4. Smith, *Wealth of Nations*, bk. 1, p. 13.

5. Paul Anthony Samuelson, *Economics: An Introductory Analysis* (New York: McGraw-Hill, 1948).

6. Adam Smith, *Glasgow Edition of the Works and Correspondence Vol. 5 Lectures on Jurisprudence* (1762; repr., Indianapolis: Liberty Fund, 1982), Monday, March 28, 1763.

7. Smith, *Wealth of Nations*, bk. 1, p. 2.

8. Ibid., bk. 1, p. 7.

9. This might look like an analytical get-out-of-jail-free card, because it runs the risk of circularity: How much labor time is socially necessary, after all? But there's no God-given normal level of productivity. The number of work hours it takes to make a car today, for instance, is very different to a century ago. This is why productivity is a "social" phenomenon.

10. This also explains why, in the long run, capitalists are doomed. Capitalists increase profits by lowering labor costs, and they do this by having better machines. But this lowers the profit rate over the long term, because surplus value comes by exploiting labor, of which now less is needed to produce the same output.

11. The profit is possible because workers can't stop working when they have made enough to pay their wages—the control of working time is essential. Neoclassical economics assumes that workers can choose exactly when they will stop working.

12. See volume 2 of Karl Marx, *Capital: A Critique of Political Economy* (Harmondsworth, UK: Penguin, 1978), for more on his thought here.

13. United Nations Development Programme, *Human Development*

Report 1995: Gender and Human Development (New York: Oxford University Press, 1995).

14. Jean Gardiner, "Women's Domestic Labour," *New Left Review* I/89 (1975).

15. International Labour Organization, *Global Wage Report 2008/09: Minimum Wages and Collective Bargaining; Towards Policy Coherence.* (Geneva: International Labour Office, 2008). A further consideration, and one that deserves greater attention than space allows here, is the link between energy and unpaid labor. Today's economy substitutes energy for labor—as the price of energy increases, the downward pressure on wages will increase too, pushing more work into the realm of the unpaid. For more on this, keep an eye out for work by scholar/activist Kolya Abramsky.

16. See footnote 10 above, which explains Marx's idea of a declining rate of profit. Marx also has sophisticated ideas about the contradictions within financial capitalism in volume 2 of *Capital.*

17. See the recent pamphlet from the Midnight Notes collective for more: Midnight Notes Collective and Friends, *Promissory Notes: From Crisis to Commons* (New York: Autonomedia, 2009).

18. John Maynard Keynes, *A General Theory of Employment, Interest and Money* (New York: Harcourt, Brace and World, 1936), 383.

19. Ibid., 9.

20. Ibid., 161–62.

21. Ibid., 202.

22. Ibid., 156.

23. Ibid., 158–59.

24. Mark Zandi, "Testimony before the House Committee on Small Business Hearing on 'Economic Stimulus for Small Business: A Look Back and Assessing Need for Additional Relief,'" http://www.house.gov/smbiz/hearings/hearing-07-24-08-stimulus/Zandi.pdf (accessed December 18, 2008).

5. ANTI-ECONOMIC MAN

1. WorldPublicOpinion.org, *World Public Opinion and the Universal Declaration of Human Rights* (Washington, D.C.: WorldPublicOpinion.org, 2008).

2. Department for International Development, "Free Education Means a Future for Rwanda's Children," October 15, 2007, http://www.dfid.gov.uk/Media-Room/Case-Studies/2007/Free-education-means-a-future-for-Rwan

das-children/ (accessed July 12, 2009). But note even here there are ambiguities. The extension of education is part of a fraught political process of state building that is far from untainted by the politics that spawned the genocide.

3. Ibid.

4. In the language of economics, this is talk about rivalrous and excludable goods.

5. Jeremy Scahill, *Blackwater: The Rise of the World's Most Powerful Mercenary Army* (London: Serpent's Tail, 2007).

6. Jenny Tomkins, "Xe Is the Problem," *In These Times,* May 20, 2009.

7. Stockholm International Peace Research Institute, *SIPRI Yearbook 2009: Armaments, Disarmament and International Security* (Oxford: Oxford University Press, 2009), chap. 5.

8. Nick Turse, *The Complex: How the Military Invades Our Everyday Lives,* 1st ed. (New York: Metropolitan Books, 2008).

9. Travis Sharp, *U.S. Defense Spending vs. Global Defense Spending* (Washington, D.C.: Center for Arms Control and Non-Proliferation, 2009).

10. Smith, *Wealth of Nations,* bk. 5, p. 7.

11. Ibid., bk. 1, p. 264.

12. Karl Marx and Friedrich Engels, *The Communist Manifesto,* (London: Penguin, 2002), 202.

13. Alexander Hamilton, John Jay and James Madison, *The Federal Convention,* ed. Henry Cabot Lodge (New York: G. P. Putnam's Sons, The Knickerbocker Press, 1902), 204.

14. TRAC IRS, "IRS Audit Rate for Millionaires Plummets," Transactional Records Access Clearinghouse, 2009, http://trac.syr.edu/tracirs/latest/204/ (accessed July 20, 2009). For more, see Radhika Balakrishnan et al., *Rethinking Macro Economic Strategies from a Human Rights Perspective (Why MES with Human Rights II)* (Atlanta: US Human Rights Network, 2009).

15. Ben Stein, "In Class Warfare, Guess Which Class Is Winning," *New York Times,* November 26, 2006.

16. Andrew Cockburn, "The Wall Street White House," *CounterPunch,* July 2, 2009.

17. Fernand Braudel, *The Wheels of Commerce* (London: Collins, 1992), 229–30. For a general discussion of this, see David Harvey, *A Brief History of Neoliberalism* (Oxford: Oxford University Press, 2005). For a fine discussion of how this relates to the food system, see Michael S. Carolan, "Disciplining Nature: The Homogenising and Constraining Forces of Anti-Markets on the Food System," *Environmental Values* 14 (2005).

18. Except, curiously, Jordan—see WorldPublicOpinion.org et al., *World Public Opinion on Governance and Democracy* (Washington, D.C.: WorldPublicOpinion.org, 2008).

19. GlobeScan for the BBC, "Economic System Needs 'Major Changes': Global Poll," GlobeScan/BBC, 2009.

20. Jesse Washington, "Some Say Holocaust Memorial Shooting Signals a Broader War," *The Philadelphia Inquirer*, June 14, 2009.

21. Thomas Hobbes and Richard Tuck, *Leviathan*, rev. ed. (Cambridge: Cambridge University Press, 1996), 89.

22. Basil H. Johnston, *The Manitous: The Spiritual World of the Ojibway* (New York: HarperPerennial, 1996), 221–37.

23. T. S. Eliot, *The Complete Poems and Plays, 1909–1950* (New York: Harcourt, Brace & Co. 1960), 283.

24. Alfred Nobel himself never dignified economics with a prize—the Nobel Prize in Economics was endowed in 1969 by the Swedish central bank so that the discipline might share some of the glory Nobel had bestowed on Medicine, Physics, Chemistry, Literature and Peace.

25. See Elinor Ostrom, *Governing the Commons: The Evolution of Institutions for Collective Action* (New York: Cambridge University Press, 1990). But also see Peter Linebaugh's work and George Caffentzis's predictably thoughtful and challenging 2004 essay, "A Tale of Two Conferences: Globalization, the Crisis of Neoliberalism and Question of the Commons," http://www.globaljusticecenter.org/papers/caffentzis.htm.

6. WE ARE ALL COMMONERS

1. *Oxford English Dictionary*, 2nd ed., 1992, s.v. "common," http://dictionary.oed.com /cgi/entry/50045107 (accessed June 1, 2009).

2. Garrett Hardin, "The Tragedy of the Commons," *Science* 162, no. 3859 (1968).

3. I'm happy that, today, Friends of the Earth is a great deal wiser, not least because it has decentralized its decision making.

4. At least Hardin was consistent—he and his wife were members of the right-to-die Hemlock Society, and took their own lives soon after their sixty-second wedding anniversary. I'd very much like to see advocates of population control become advocates of feminism, but I suspect that they're coming from a place where women's empowerment isn't their top priority.

5. David Feeny et al., "Questioning the Assumptions of the 'Tragedy of the Commons' Model of Fisheries," *Land Economics* 72, no. 2 (1996).

6. Boris Worm et al., "Impacts of Biodiversity Loss on Ocean Ecosystem Services," *Science* 314, no. 5800 (2006).

7. Alex Wijeratna, *Taking the Fish—Fishing Communities Lose Out to Big Trawlers in Pakistan* (Johannesburg: ActionAid International, 2007).

8. Ann Kelley, "Net Losses," *Guardian*, April 11, 2007.

9. R. W. D. Davies et al., "Defining and Estimating Global Marine Fisheries Bycatch," *Marine Policy* 33 (2009).

10. Food and Agriculture Organization of the United Nations, "The Islamic Republic of Pakistan. Fishery and Aquaculture Country Profile," Fisheries and Aquaculture Department, 2009, http://www.fao.org/fishery/countrysector/FI-CP_PK/en (accessed April 21, 2009).

11. Henry Makori, "Why Belief in Witchcraft Remains Strong among Africans," *Catholic Information Service for Africa*, April 6, 2009.

12. See, for example, Silvia Federici, *Caliban and the Witch* (New York: Autonomedia, 2004).

13. Robin Briggs, *Witches and Neighbours: The Social and Cultural Context of European Witchcraft*, 2nd ed. (Oxford: Blackwell Publishers, 2002); Brian P. Levack, *The Witch-Hunt in Early Modern Europe*, 3rd ed. (Harlow: Pearson Longman, 2006).

14. This isn't an argument that all women everywhere were resisting enclosure, and that this is specifically the only reason why there were witch hunts. If that were true, then one might expect witch hunts to be directly correlated with enclosures, and the historical record is much messier than that. But it is to suggest that some women died defending their right to control resources in ways inimical to the market.

15. This is the logic that makes Arthur Miller's *The Crucible* such a powerful indictment of McCarthyism.

16. Peter Linebaugh, *The Magna Carta Manifesto: Liberties and Commons for All* (Berkeley: University of California Press, 2008). See also Massimo De Angelis, *The Beginning of History: Value Struggles and Global Capital* (London: Pluto, 2007).

17. Linebaugh, *Magna Carta Manifesto*, 27.

18. I am grateful for Edward Vallance's excellent *Radical History of Britain* for this background: Edward Vallance, *A Radical History of Britain: Visionaries, Rebels and Revolutionaries—the Men and Women Who Fought for Our Freedoms* (London: Little, Brown, 2009).

19. Smith, *Wealth of Nations*, bk. 1, p. 8.

20. David E. Stannard, *American Holocaust: The Conquest of the New World* (New York: Oxford University Press, 1993), quoted in Federici, *Caliban and the Witch*, 85.

21. John Locke, *Two Treatises of Government* (London: Whitmore and Fenn, 1821), 259.

22. For a fuller discussion of how capitalism, animals and property work together, see Bob Torres, *Making a Killing: The Political Economy of Animal Rights* (Edinburgh: AK Press, 2007).

23. Gilbert Malcolm Sproat to the Superintendent-General of Indian Affairs, October 27, 1879, RG 10, vol. 3669, f. 10961; quoted in Tina Loo, "Dan Cranmer's Potlach: Law as Coercion, Symbol, and Rhetoric in British Columbia, 1884–1951," *Canadian Historical Review* 73, no. 2 (1992).

24. The hunt for land on which to grow agrofuels offers a painful demonstration of this. See Gaia Foundation et al., *Agrofuels and the Myth of the Marginal Lands* (London: Gaia Foundation, 2008).

25. One source is Richard Petratis, "The Witch Killers of Africa" (2003?), http://www.infidels.org/library/modern/richard_petraitis/witch_killers. shtml. (accessed March 1, 2009), whose well-referenced sources include a report from Tanzania claiming five thousand deaths alone between 1994 and 1998.

26. Officially, Safari Club International calls this "the Big Five Grand Slam." Of course, animals have been commodities for longer than people, but it's surprising how recently that transformation has been completed— see Giorgio Agamben, *The Open: Man and Animal* (Stanford, CA: Stanford University Press, 2004).

27. Environmental Rights Action, "Field Report #172: Michelin Converts Prime Forest to Plantation" (Environmental Rights Action/Friends of the Earth, Lagos, Nigeria, 2008).

28. World Rainforest Movement, *Women Raise Their Voices Against Tree Plantations: The Role of the European Union in Disempowering Women in the South* (Montevideo: World Rainforest Movement, 2009).

29. J. M. Lobo Orensanz et al., "What Are the Key Elements for the Sustainability of 'S-Fisheries'? Insights from South America," *Bulletin of Marine Science* 76, no. 2 (2005).

30. George Monbiot, "These Are Not the Mariners of Old but Pirates Who Make Bureaucrats Blanch," *Guardian*, June 1, 2009.

7. THE COUNTERMOVEMENT AND THE RIGHT TO HAVE RIGHTS

1. World Health Organization. "World Health Organization Statistical Information System," WHO, 2009, http://www.who.int/whosis/ (accessed July 19, 2009); (all figures refer to 2005).

2. World Bank, *World Development Indicators* (Washington, D.C.: World Bank, 2007).

3. Charlotte Cooper, "Online Chat Spotlights Most-Ailing Millennium Goal," *Women's eNews*, March 29, 2009.

4. You can find the full declaration online at the United Nations' Web site: http://www.un.org/en/documents/udhr/.

5. For more on this, see the excellent Sam Pizzigati, *Greed and Good: Understanding and Overcoming the Inequality That Limits Our Lives* (New York: Apex Press, 2004).

6. For more, including a discussion of how rights were, in some ways, a regression to Victorian approaches to international relations, see Mark Mazower, "The Strange Triumph of Human Rights, 1933–1950," *The Historical Journal* 47, no. 2 (2004).

7. Saul David Alinsky, *Rules for Radicals: A Practical Primer for Realistic Radicals* (New York: Random House, 1971), xxiii.

8. See Michael Neocosmos, "Development, Social Citizenship and Human Rights: Re-Thinking the Political Core of an Emancipatory Project in Africa," *Africa Development* 32, no. 4 (2007), for a thoughtful treatment of this in the African context. In many cases, this simultaneous call for individual patience has been facilitated by elite NGOs with the effect of postponing immediate, collective and democratic action. See Harri Englund, *Prisoners of Freedom: Human Rights and the African Poor*, California Series in Public Anthropology 14 (Berkeley: University of California Press, 2006).

9. See Patel, *Stuffed and Starved*.

10. See John Perkins, *Confessions of an Economic Hit Man* (London: Ebury Press, 2005), for the "crook" part.

11. See Vandana Shiva, *Biopiracy: The Plunder of Nature and Knowledge* (Dartington: Green Books in association with The Gaia Foundation, 1998) and Richard Stallman's short and pointed think piece about biopiracy, "Biopiracy or Bioprivateering," available at http://stallman.org/articles/biopiracy.html.

12. World Bank, *World Bank Assistance to Agriculture in Sub Saharan Africa: An Independent Evaluation Group Review* (Washington, D.C.: World Bank, 2007).

13. Lyla Mehta, "The World Bank and Its Emerging Knowledge Empire," *Human Organization* 60, no. 2 (2001); Pauline E. Peters, *Development Encounters: Sites of Participation and Knowledge*, Harvard Studies in International Development (Cambridge, MA: Harvard Institute for International Development, 2000).

14. Hannah Arendt, *The Origins of Totalitarianism*, 3rd ed. (London: Allen & Unwin, 1967), 177.

15. For more on popular will, see the excellent essay by Peter Hallward: Peter Hallward, "The Will of the People: Notes Towards a Dialectical Voluntarism," *Radical Philosophy* 155 (May/June 2009).

16. Although attributed to Forster, it appears to be a remark Forster overheard. W. H. Auden, *The Dyer's Hand, and Other Essays* (New York: Random House, 1962), 22.

17. Gloria Jacobs, *Not a Minute More: Ending Violence Against Women* (New York: UNIFEM, 2003). There is evidence that the recession has seen an increase in the prevalence of domestic violence.

18. For more on this use of "violence," see both Slavoj Zizek, *Violence: Six Sideways Reflections, Big Ideas* (London: Profile, 2008); and Frantz Fanon, *The Wretched of the Earth*, trans. Constance Farrington (London: Penguin, 1965).

19. Eric Schlosser, "A Side Order of Human Rights," *New York Times*, April 6, 2005.

20. Bill Maxwell, "Eating That Tomato Can Put You in Moral Peril," *St. Petersburg (FL) Times*, July 13, 2008.

21. Jane Black, "A Squeeze for Tomato Growers; Boycott vs. Higher Wages," *Washington Post*, April 29, 2009.

22. Katrina vanden Heuvel, "In the Trenches and Fighting Slavery," *TheNation.com*, December 28, 2008, http://www.thenation.com/blogs/edcut/391546/in_the_trenches_and_fighting_slavery (accessed March 14, 2009).

8. DEMOCRACY IN THE CITY

1. For more on food rebellions, see Eric Holt-Giménez and Raj Patel, *Food Rebellions! Crisis and the Hunger for Justice* (Oxford: Fahamu, 2009).

2. Building on the "Treaty for Democratic, Equitable and Sustainable Cities, Towns and Villages" approved in 1992 at the Earth Summit in Rio de Janeiro, and the formal recognition of the "right to the city" by the 2001 City Statute in Brazil, several NGOs and urban social movements, especially from Brazil and other Latin American countries, started drafting a text called the "World Charter on the Human Right to the City." The draft was expanded (and the "Human" was dropped) following discussion at the July 2004 Social Forum of the Americas in Quito, and the September 2004 World Urban Forum in Barcelona. For more on the Brazilian context, see Edesio Fernandes, "Constructing the 'Right to the City' in Brazil," *Social*

Legal Studies 16, no. 2 (2007). The United Nations Educational, Scientific and Cultural Organization hosts a copy of the document at http://portal.unesco.org/shs/en/ev.php-URL_ID=8218&URL_DO=DO_TOPIC&URL_SECTION=201.html.

3. Desmond Tutu, "The Second Nelson Mandela Foundation Lecture" (Johannesburg, South Africa, November 23, 2004); http://www.nelsonmandela.org/index.php/news/article/look_to_the_rock_from_which_you_were_hewn/ (accessed November 20, 2005).

4. Full disclosure—I manage the Web site for the organization.

5. Mike Davis, "Planet of Slums: Urban Involution and the Informal Proletariat," *New Left Review* 26 (2004), Robert Neuwirth, *Shadow Cities: A Billion Squatters, a New Urban World* (New York: Routledge, 2005).

6. Rafael Di Tella et al., "The Formation of Beliefs: Evidence from the Allocation of Land Titles to Squatters," *Quarterly Journal of Economics* 122, no. 1 (2007).

7. Rikke B. Broegaard, "Land Access and Titling in Nicaragua," *Development and Change* 40, no. 1 (2009); Christopher Woodruff, "Review of De Soto's 'The Mystery of Capital,'" *Journal of Economic Literature* 39, no. 4 (2001); and Timothy Mitchell, "The Properties of Markets," in the enjoyable collection *Do Economists Make Markets? On the Performativity of Economics*, eds. Donald Mackenzie, Fabian Muniesa and Lucia Siu (Princeton: Princeton University Press, 2007).

8. To watch some of this thinking, see the forthcoming film *Dear Mandela*, directed by Dara Kell and Christopher Nizza, produced by Sleeping Giant Films.

9. For more about where this photo was taken, and the politics of the meeting, see Raj Patel, "A Short Course in Politics at the University of Abahlali BaseMjondolo," *Journal of Asian and African Studies* 43, no. 1 (2008): 95–112.

10. I am grateful to Richard Pithouse for his permission to quote from his interviews with Abahlali representatives.

11. Kerry Chance, "'Broke-on-Broke Violence': What the U.S. Press Got Wrong About South Africa's Xenophobic Riots," *Slate.com*, June 20, 2008, http://www.slate.com/id/2193949/ (accessed January 1, 2009); and, more recently, see Richard Pithouse, "Burning Message to the State in the Fire of Poor's Rebellion," *Business Day*, July 23, 2009.

12. Rousseau would have been pleased. See also the work of Alain Badiou and Jacques Rancière: Alain Badiou, *Ethics: An Essay on the Understanding of Evil*, trans. Peter Hallward (London: Verso, 2001); Alain Badiou, *Metapolitics*, trans. Jason Barker (London: Verso, 2005); Jacques Rancière, *On the*

Shores of Politics, Radical Thinkers 21 (London: Verso, 2007); Jacques Rancière and Steve Corcoran, *Hatred of Democracy* (London: Verso, 2006).

13. Yes, this is the group who put thousands of disenfranchised voters back on the rolls in the last election and which, while clearly staffed in some places by the unscrupulous, is also involved in vital work supporting poor American families.

14. And that out of undergraduates who had taken an economics class, only 7 percent got it right. Paul J. Ferraro and Laura O. Taylor, "Do Economists Recognize an Opportunity Cost When They See One? A Dismal Performance from the Dismal Science," *Contributions to Economic Analysis & Policy* 4, no. 1, Article 7 (2005).

15. *Economist*, "Let Them Eat Pollution," February 8, 1992.

16. Najad Abdullahi, "'Toxic Waste' Behind Somali Piracy," *Al Jazeera in English*, October 11, 2008.

17. Janaina Rochido, "Brazilian Cities Pioneer Democratic Budgeting," *City Mayors*, November 18, 2006.

18. Iain Bruce, *The Porto Alegre Alternative: Direct Democracy in Action*, IIRE, Notebook for Study and Research, no. 35–36 (London: Pluto Press with the International Institute for Research and Education [IIRE], 2004), 6; see also the introduction to Boaventura de Sousa Santos, *Democratizing Democracy: Beyond the Liberal Democratic Canon*. Reinventing Social Emancipation, vol. 1 (London: Verso, 2005).

19. Bruce, *The Porto Alegre Alternative*, 45.

20. Carl Bergstrom, Ben Kerr and Michael Lachmann, "Building Trust by Wasting Time," in *Moral Markets*, ed. Paul Zak.

21. Bruce, *The Porto Alegre Alternative*, 10.

22. For more on participatory budgeting, see Gianpaolo Baiocchi, *Radicals in Power: The Workers' Party (Pt) and Experiments in Urban Democracy in Brazil* (London: Zed Books, 2003). Rebecca Abers, "Learning Democratic Practice: Distributing Government Resources through Popular Participation in Porto Alegre, Brazil," in *The Challenge of Urban Government: Policies and Practices*, eds. Maria Emilia Freire and Richard Stren (Washington, D.C.: World Bank, 2001); Patrick Heller, "Moving the State: The Politics of Democratic Decentralization in Kerala, South Africa, and Porto Alegre," *Politics Society* 29, no. 1 (2001); Archon Fung and Erik Olin Wright, "Deepening Democracy: Innovations in Empowered Participatory Governance," *Politics Society* 29, no. 1 (2001).

23. Sharon K. Hom and Stacy Mosher, *Challenging China: Struggle and Hope in an Era of Change* (New York: New Press, 2007). See also http://chinaworker.info/en/content/news/722/.

24. Han Dongfang, "Chinese Labour Struggles," *New Left Review* 34 (2005).

25. China Labour Bulletin, "The Case of China: The Challenge of Labour Unrest in a Communist-Run Capitalist Economy" (paper presented at the International Seminar on Business and Human Rights, Paris, December 4, 2008).

26. More on the Yirenping Center's work is available at http://www.yirenping.org/english/eng.htm, including documentation of its legal filings (see 2007 Annual Report for more); *China Pharmaceuticals & Health Technologies Weekly*, "About 80 Pct of Multinationals Discriminate against Chinese Hep B," July 4, 2007, reports the broader trends in hepatitis B discrimination.

27. This idea is more fully explored in Jacques Rancière's work, e.g., Jacques Rancière, *Disagreement: Politics and Philosophy* (Minneapolis: University of Minnesota Press, 1998).

28. Instead of private property here, then, we have a more flexible and plastic idea of who owns knowledge, with attribution—that's what makes this a commons.

9. BACK TO FOOD SOVEREIGNTY

1. Larry Lohmann, *Financialization, Quantism and Carbon Markets: Variations on Polanyian Themes* (Sturminster Newton, Dorset: The Corner House, 2009), 19.

2. Taibbi, "The Great American Bubble Machine."

3. Gwyn Prins and Steve Rayner, "Time to Ditch Kyoto," *Nature* 449, no. 7165 (2007).

4. The report led by Robert Watson, the International Assessment of Agricultural Knowledge Science and Technology for Development (IAASTD), is published as a series of documents by Island Press, and the original report is available at http://agassessment.org. For more on the carbon sequestration potential of organic farming, see Tim J. LaSalle and Paul Hepperly, *Regenerative Organic Farming: A Solution to Global Warming* (Kutztown, PA: Rodale Institute, 2008).

5. Daniel Maxwell et al., "Does Urban Agriculture Help Prevent Malnutrition? Evidence from Kampala," *Food Policy* 23, no. 5 (1998).

6. Rob Hopkins, *The Transition Handbook: From Oil Dependency to Local Resilience* (Totnes: Green, 2008) is the bible of the transition town movement. See also TRAPESE Collective, "The Rocky Road to a Real Transition: The Transition Towns Movement and What It Means for Social

Change," *The Commoner* 13 (2009), http://www.commoner.org.uk/N13/11-Trapese.pdf (accessed August 17, 2009).

7. Juan Forero, "In Ecuador, High Stakes in Case against Chevron," *Washington Post*, April 28, 2009. Ben Casselman, "Chevron Expects to Fight Ecuador Lawsuit in U.S.," *Wall Street Journal*, July 20, 2009.

8. Jeffrey Kaplan, "Consent of the Governed: The Reign of Corporations and the Fight for Democracy," *Orion Magazine*, November/December 2003.

9. One of the most widely overlooked heroes of the Indian Independence struggle, B. R. Ambedkar (who was to the Indian constitution what Jefferson was to the United States'), a Dalit leader who fostered a Buddhist revival.

10. I am grateful to the work of P. V. Satheesh, Gayatri Menon, Bina Agarwal and Katharine Ainger in understanding the Deccan Development Society better.

11. The figures for women's participation have always been underestimated, but according to the Food and Agriculture Organization's database, from a rate of women "economically active" in agriculture at 66 percent of male rates in 1961, the figure is nearer 80 percent today.

12. Gayatri A. Menon, "Re-Negotiating Gender: Enabling Women to Claim Their Right to Land Resources" (paper presented at the Panel on Best Practices on Gender and Land/Property Rights, NGO Forum of the United Nations Conference on Human Settlements—Habitat II, Istanbul, June 1996).

13. I've written elsewhere about how green revolution technologies were ways to allow landlords to hang on to their land and still increase productivity, rather than for the government to engage in land reform—one of the most robust technologies for increasing agricultural productivity. Patel, *Stuffed and Starved.*

14. Given that these sorts of farming systems thrive under intensive smaller-scale agriculture, the battle against climate change will also involve land reform to redistribute larger landholdings to small-scale farmers. For more, see forthcoming work by Annie Shattuck, a policy analyst at the Institute for Food and Development Policy.

15. And, of course, what needs management needs management consultants.

10. ANTON'S BLINDNESS

1. Global Humanitarian Forum, *Anatomy of a Silent Crisis* (Geneva: Global Humanitarian Foundation, 2009).

2. Though see Phra (Prayut) Thepwethi et al., *Buddhist Economics: A Middle Way for the Market Place* (Bangkok: Buddhadhamma Foundation, 1994) for more.

3. In this, I'm aware that I'm running counter to some Buddhist lore here—some texts prescribe that food only be eaten as nourishment, not as the end of desire. But if that were true, then Buddhist food in China, Japan and Thailand wouldn't taste so damn good. I'm not seeing anything wrong with the pleasure of eating, just as long as one doesn't lust after it.

4. William Braxton Irvine, *A Guide to the Good Life: The Ancient Art of Stoic Joy* (Oxford: Oxford University Press, 2009), offers more.

5. Susan M. Darlington, "The Ordination of a Tree: The Buddhist Ecology Movement in Thailand," *Ethnology* 37, no. 1 (1998).

6. This isn't a claim about blood and soil or nationalism—it's a conclusion about the relationship between our species and every other one.

7. Express News Service, "'I Am a Marxist Monk,' Says Dalai Lama," *Indian Express*, January 19, 2008.

8. And for those who aren't minded to engage in direct action themselves, the artists/activists The Yes Men have developed a splendid system of "Action Offsets," where you can support the work of people who are more able to put themselves in harm's way. More at www.beyondtalk.net.

9. The question of slavery often prevents any sensible discussion of democracy based on the Athenian model. Yet, as Ellen Meiksins Wood argues (Ellen Meiksins Wood, "Demos Versus 'We the People': Freedom and Democracy Ancient and Modern," in *Demokratia: A Conversation on Democracies, Ancient and Modern*, eds. Josiah Ober and Charles W. Hedrick, 121–38 [Princeton, NJ: Princeton University Press, 1996]; Ellen Meiksins Wood, *Peasant-Citizen and Slave: The Foundations of Athenian Democracy* [London: Verso, 1988]), it was because of the democratic engagement of Athenian peasants that slavery was not *more* widespread. And the lessons that Athenian democracy has to offer are ones that don't demand an underclass in order to work, and work well.

10. C. L. R. James, "Every Cook Can Govern: A Study of Democracy in Ancient Greece: Its Meaning for Today," *Correspondence* 2, no. 12 (1956). See also Josiah Ober and Charles W. Hedrick, eds., *Demokratia: A Conversation on Democracies, Ancient and Modern* (Princeton, NJ: Princeton University

Press, 1996); especially the essays by Sheldon S. Wolin, "Transgression, Equality and Voice" and Wood, "Demos Versus 'We the People': Freedom and Democracy Ancient and Modern" in *Demokratia*.

11. Robert Milton Everton, "'This Is What Democracy Looks Like!' Democracy in Action: Communicative Action" (Ph.D. diss., Simon Fraser University, 2003).

12. Thucydides and Henry Dale, *The History of the Peloponnesian War* (London: H. G. Bohn, 1848), cited by James, "Every Cook Can Govern."

13. With thanks to Mindy Peden for directing me to these examples.

14. Tom Philpott at *Grist* is a notable exception.

15. Andrés Timoteo Morales, "En Veracruz, Oponerse a Operación de Granjas Carroll Se Castiga Con Cárcel," *La Jornada*, April 12, 2009, for instance.

16. Pigs account for only part of the plant's profitability—the operation is also allowed to issue carbon credits for the methane that they could be producing but aren't.

17. Diego Cevallos, "New Influenza Strain Has Led to the Closure of Schools," *IPS (Latin America)*, April 28, 2009.

18. Donald G. McNeil Jr., "In New Theory, Swine Flu Started in Asia, Not Mexico," *New York Times*, June 23, 2009.

19. The death toll has already passed one hundred. Meanwhile, there's money to be made. Reuters reported that a venture capital company has done well from the outbreak, and that "shares of the two public companies in the firm's portfolio of eight Pandemic and Bio Defense companies— BioCryst Pharmaceuticals (BCRX.O) and Novavax (NVAX.O)—jumped Friday on news that the swine flu killed a reported 60 people in Mexico and has infected people in the United States." Death is a business, and with this virus, business is good; Alexander Haislip, "Venture Capital Firm Set to Reap Rewards on Swine Flu," Reuters, April 24, 2009.

20. Tom Hayden, ed., *The Zapatista Reader* (New York: Nation Books, 2001) 218.

21. Kristen Bricker, "In Defense of Land and Territory: Zapatistas Take on Paramilitaries," *Left Turn*, June 1, 2008.

22. Bergstrom et al., "Building Trust by Wasting Time."

23. See the excellent Mariana Mora, "Decolonizing Politics: Zapatista Indigenous Autonomy in an Era of Neoliberal Governance and Low Intensity Warfare" (Ph.D. diss., University of Texas at Austin, 2008) for more.

24. Although no one in the Junta gets paid, the Junta has expenses for food, bus fares and accommodation, though the accommodation is purposely kept minimal, and the meals meager, to prevent serving on the Junta

becoming some sort of sinecure. The Junta members invariably eat better when they're at home than at work.

25. Dana Goldstein, "The Selling of School Reform," *Nation*, May 27, 2009.

26. See, for instance, Ivan Illich, *Deschooling Society* (Harmondsworth, UK: Penguin Education, 1973).

27. Churchill put it more succinctly—democracy is the worst form of government except for all those others—but his experience of democracy was rather different to one in which citizens are able to control government.

28. Diane Elson, "Socializing Markets, Not Market Socialism," *Socialist Register*, 2000.

29. A summary of studies is available at the Web site of the National Center for Employee Ownership—http://www.nceo.org/library/corpperf.html

30. DeeDee Correll, "Fine, They'll Just Publish the Newspaper Themselves," *Los Angeles Times*, March 23, 2009.

31. See the excellent George Caffentzis, "Medical Metaphors and Monetary Strategies in the Political Economy of Locke and Berkeley," *History of Political Economy* 5, no. 2 (2003), for instance.

32. Constantine George Caffentzis, *Clipped Coins, Abused Words, and Civil Government: John Locke's Philosophy of Money* (Brooklyn, NY: Autonomedia, 1989), 28.

33. John Maynard Keynes, *Essays in Persuasion* (London: Macmillan, 1931), 373.

34. In off-record conversation after off-record conversation, financial insiders have said they're astounded that governments haven't yet nationalized banks, since it is so obviously the right thing for governments to do. In a recent and powerful statement on health care, Paul Krugman has laid out rather well the case for nationalized health care: Paul Krugman, "Health Care Realities," *New York Times*, July 30, 2009.

35. Octavia E. Butler, "Positive Obsession," in *Bloodchild and Other Stories* (New York: Seven Stories Press, 1996), 134–35.

BIBLIOGRAPHY

Abdullahi, Najad "'Toxic Waste' Behind Somali Piracy." *Al Jazeera in English*, October 11, 2008.

Abers, Rebecca. "Learning Democratic Practice: Distributing Government Resources Through Popular Participation in Porto Alegre, Brazil." In *The Challenge of Urban Government: Policies and Practices*, edited by Maria Emilia Freire and Richard Stren, 129–44. Washington, D.C.: World Bank, 2001.

Agamben, Giorgio. *The Open: Man and Animal.* Stanford, CA: Stanford University Press, 2004.

Albert, Michael. *Moving Forward: Programme for a Participatory Economy.* Edinburgh: AK, 2000.

Alinsky, Saul David. *Rules for Radicals: A Practical Primer for Realistic Radicals.* New York: Random House, 1971.

Allain, Annelies, and Yeong Joo Kean. "The Youngest Market: Baby Food Peddlers Undermine Breastfeeding." *Multinational Monitor* 30, no. 1 (2008).

Arendt, Hannah. *The Origins of Totalitarianism*, 3rd ed. London: Allen & Unwin, 1967.

Ariely, Dan. *Predictably Irrational: The Hidden Forces That Shape Our Decisions.* New York: HarperCollins, 2008.

Arrighi, Giovanni. *The Long Twentieth Century: Money, Power and the Origins of Our Times.* London: Verso, 1994.

Auden, W. H. *The Dyer's Hand, and Other Essays.* New York: Random House, 1962.

Badiou, Alain. *Ethics: An Essay on the Understanding of Evil.* Translated and introduced by Peter Hallward. London: Verso, 2001.

———. *Metapolitics.* Translated by Jason Barker. London: Verso, 2005.

Baiocchi, Gianpaolo. *Radicals in Power: The Workers' Party (Pt) and Experiments in Urban Democracy in Brazil.* London: Zed Books, 2003.

Bakan, Joel. *The Corporation: The Pathological Pursuit of Profit and Power.* New York: The New Press, 2004.

Balakrishnan, Radhika, Diane Elson and Raj Patel. *Rethinking Macro Economic Strategies from a Human Rights Perspective (Why MES with Human Rights II).* Atlanta: US Human Rights Network, 2009.

Barnard, D, A. Nicholson and J. L. Howard. "The Medical Costs Attributable to Meat Consumption." *Preventive Medicine* 24, no. 6 (1995): 646–55.

——. "Competition and Democracy." *Journal of Law and Economics* 1 (1958): 105–109.

——. *The Economic Approach to Human Behavior.* Chicago: University of Chicago Press, 1976.

Becker, Gary S. "A Theory of Marriage: Part I." *Journal of Political Economy* 81 (1973): 813–46.

——. *A Treatise on the Family.* Enl. ed. Cambridge: Harvard University Press, 1991.

Bekoff, M. "Wild Justice and Fair Play: Cooperation, Forgiveness, and Morality in Animals." *Biology and Philosophy* 19, no. 4 (2004): 489–520.

Bergmann, Barbara R. "Becker's Theory of the Family: Preposterous Conclusions." *Feminist Economics* 1, no. 1 (1995): 141–50.

Bergstrom, Carl, Ben Kerr and Michael Lachmann. "Building Trust by Wasting Time." In *Moral Markets: The Critical Role of Values in the Economy,* edited by Paul Zak, 142–56. Princeton, NJ: Princeton University Press, 2008.

Black, Jane. "A Squeeze for Tomato Growers; Boycott vs. Higher Wages." *Washington Post,* April 29, 2009.

Bowles, Samuel. "Policies Designed for Self-Interested Citizens May Undermine 'The Moral Sentiments': Evidence from Economic Experiments." *Science* 320, no. 5883 (2008): 1605–1609.

Braudel, Fernand. *The Wheels of Commerce.* London: Collins, 1982.

Bricker, Kristen. "In Defense of Land and Territory: Zapatistas Take on Paramilitaries." *Left Turn,* June 1, 2008.

Briggs, Robin. *Witches and Neighbours: The Social and Cultural Context of European Witchcraft,* 2nd ed. Oxford: Blackwell Publishers, 2002.

Broegaard, Rikke B. "Land Access and Titling in Nicaragua." *Development and Change* 40, no. 1 (2009): 149–69.

Brokenleg, Martin. "Native American Perspectives on Generosity." *Reclaiming Children and Youth* 8, no. 2 (1999): 66–68.

Brosnan, Sarah F. "Fairness and Other-Regarding Preferences in Nonhuman Primates." In *Moral Markets: The Critical Role of Values in the*

Economy, edited by Paul Zak, 77–104. Princeton: Princeton University Press, 2008.

Bruce, Iain. *The Porto Alegre Alternative: Direct Democracy in Action,* IIRE Notebook for Study and Research, no. 35-36. London: Pluto Press with the International Institute for Research and Education (IIRE), 2004.

Bureau of Labor Statistics. "Combined Food Preparation and Serving Workers, Including Fast Food." *Occupational Employment and Wages,* May 2007. http://www.bls.gov/oes/2007/may/oes353021.htm (accessed March 14, 2009).

Caffentzis, Constantine George. *Clipped Coins, Abused Words, and Civil Government: John Locke's Philosophy of Money.* Brooklyn, NY: Autonomedia, 1989.

Caffentzis, George. "Medical Metaphors and Monetary Strategies in the Political Economy of Locke and Berkeley." *History of Political Economy* 5, no. 2 (2003): 204–33.

———. "A Tale of Two Conferences: Globalization, the Crisis of Neoliberalism and Question of the Commons." Presented at Alternatives to Globalisation conference, hosted by the Center for Global Justice, 2004. http://www.globaljusticecenter.org/papers/caffentzis.htm (accessed August 1, 2009).

Carolan, Michael S. "Disciplining Nature: The Homogenising and Constraining Forces of Anti-Markets on the Food System." *Environmental Values* 14 (2005): 363–87.

Casselman, Ben. "Chevron Expects to Fight Ecuador Lawsuit in U.S." *Wall Street Journal,* July 20, 2009.

Cevallos, Diego. "New Influenza Strain Has Led to the Closure of Schools." *IPS (Latin America),* April 28, 2009.

Chance, Kerry. "'Broke-on-Broke Violence': What the U.S. Press Got Wrong About South Africa's Xenophobic Riots." *Slate.com,* June 20, 2008. http://www.slate.com/id/2193949/ (accessed January 1, 2009).

Chen, Weiqi, Luoping Zhang and Xiaofeng Hou. "Estimation of Environmental Cost Incurred by Pesticide Application in Coastal Agricultural Region and Management Measures." *Environmental Informatics Archives* 4 (2006): 490–501.

China Labour Bulletin. "The Case of China: The Challenge of Labour Unrest in a Communist-Run Capitalist Economy." Paper presented at the International Seminar on Business and Human Rights, Paris, December 4, 2008.

China Pharmaceuticals & Health Technologies Weekly. "About 80 Pct of Multinationals Discriminate against Chinese Hep B," July 4, 2007.

Chou, Shin-Yi, Inas Rashad and Michael Grossman. "Fast Food Restaurant Advertising on Television and Its Influence on Childhood Obesity." *The Journal of Law and Economics* 51, no. 4 (2008): 599–618.

Clark, Andrew. "Indiana Tries to Halt Chrysler Deal." *Guardian*, April 6, 2009.

Cockburn, Andrew. "The Wall Street White House." *CounterPunch*, July 2, 2009.

Cooper, Charlotte. "Online Chat Spotlights Most-Ailing Millennium Goal." *Women's eNews*, March 29, 2009.

Daly, Herman E. "In Defense of a Steady-State Economy." *American Journal of Agricultural Economics* 54, no. 5 (1972): 945–54.

Danby, Colin. "Political economy and the closet: heteronormativity in feminist economics." *Feminist Economics* 13, no. 2 (2007): 29–53.

Darlington, Susan M. "The Ordination of a Tree: The Buddhist Ecology Movement in Thailand." *Ethnology* 37, no. 1 (1998): 1–15.

Dasgupta, Partha. 2006. "Comments on the Stern Review's Economics of Climate Change." Comments were prepared for a seminar on the Stern Review's Economics of Climate Change, organized by the Foundation for Science and Technology at the Royal Society, London, on November 8, 2006. www.econ.cam.ac.uk/faculty/dasgupta/STERN.pdf (accessed March 20, 2009).

Datamonitor. *Life Insurance: Global Industry Guide*. London: Datamonitor: An Informa Business, 2009.

Davies, R. W. D., S. J. Cripps, A. Nickson and G. Porter. "Defining and Estimating Global Marine Fisheries Bycatch." *Marine Policy* 33 (2009): 661–72.

Davis, Mike. "Planet of Slums: Urban Involution and the Informal Proletariat." *New Left Review* 26 (2004): 5–34.

De Angelis, Massimo. *The Beginning of History: Value Struggles and Global Capital*. London: Pluto, 2007.

de Waal, Frans B. M. "How Selfish an Animal? The Case of Primate Cooperation." In *Moral Markets: The Critical Role of Values in the Economy*, edited by Paul Zak, 63–76. Princeton, NJ: Princeton University Press, 2008.

Department for International Development. "Free Education Means a Future for Rwanda's Children." October 15, 2007. http://www.dfid.gov.uk/Media-Room/Case-Studies/2007/Free-education-means-a-future-for-Rwandas-children/ (accessed July 12, 2009).

Di Tella, Rafael, Sebastian Galiani and Ernesto Schargrodsky. "The Formation of Beliefs: Evidence from the Allocation of Land Titles to Squatters." *Quarterly Journal of Economics* 122, no. 1 (2007): 209–41.

Dunne, Nancy. "Why a Hamburger Should Cost 200 Dollars—The Call for Prices to Reflect Ecological Factors." *Financial Times*, January 12, 1994.

Economist. "Let Them Eat Pollution," February 8, 1992.

———. "A Survey of China's Quest for Resources: Negative Externalities." *Economist Special Reports*, March 13, 2008.

Eliot, T. S. *The Complete Poems and Plays, 1909–1950*. New York: Harcourt, Brace & Co., 1960.

Elson, Diane. "Socializing Markets, Not Market Socialism." *Socialist Register* (2000): 67–86.

Englund, Harri. *Prisoners of Freedom: Human Rights and the African Poor*. California Series in Public Anthropology 14. Berkeley: University of California Press, 2006.

Environmental Rights Action. "Field Report #172: Michelin Converts Prime Forest to Plantation." Environmental Rights Action/Friends of the Earth, Lagos, Nigeria, 2008.

Environmental Working Group. "Corn Subsidies in the United States." *Environmental Working Group's Farm Subsidies Database*. http://farm.ewg.org/farm/progdetail.php?fips=00000&progcode=corn (accessed March 4, 2009).

Express News Service. "'I Am a Marxist Monk,' Says Dalai Lama." *Indian Express*, January 19, 2008.

Everton, Robert Milton. "'This Is What Democracy Looks Like!' Democracy in Action: Communicative Action." Ph.D diss., Simon Fraser University, 2003.

Fanon, Frantz. *The Wretched of the Earth*. Translated by Constance Farrington. London: Penguin, 1965.

Farrell, Greg , and Sarah O'Connor. "Goldman Sachs Staff Set for Record Pay." *FT.Com*, July 15, 2009.

Federici, Silvia. *Caliban and the Witch*. New York: Autonomedia, 2004.

Feeny, David, Susan Hanna and Arthur F. McEvoy. "Questioning the Assumptions of the 'Tragedy of the Commons' Model of Fisheries." *Land Economics* 72, no. 2 (1996): 187–205.

Fehr, Ernst, and Bettina Rockenbach. "Detrimental Effects of Sanctions on Human Altruism." *Nature* 422, no. 6928 (2003): 137–40. Quoted in Samuel Bowles, "Policies Designed for Self-Interested Citizens May Undermine 'The Moral Sentiments': Evidence from Economic Experiments," *Science* 320, no. 5883 (2008).

Fernandes, Edesio. "Constructing the 'Right to the City' in Brazil." *Social Legal Studies* 16, no. 2 (2007): 201–19.

Ferraro, Paul J., and Laura O. Taylor. "Do Economists Recognize an Opportunity Cost When They See One? A Dismal Performance from the Dismal Science." *Contributions to Economic Analysis & Policy* 4, no. 1 (2005).

Food and Agriculture Organization of the United Nations. "The Islamic Republic of Pakistan. Fishery and Aquaculture Country Profile." Fisheries and Aquaculture Department, 2009. http://www.fao.org/fishery/country sector/FI-CP_PK/en (accessed April 21, 2009).

Ford, Peter. "Drought Threatens China's Wheat Crop." *Christian Science Monitor*, February 11, 2009.

Forero, Juan. "In Ecuador, High Stakes in Case Against Chevron." *Washington Post*, Tuesday, April 28, 2009.

Foucault, Michel, and Michel Senellart. *The Birth of Biopolitics: Lectures at the Collège De France, 1978–79.* Basingstoke: Palgrave Macmillan, 2008.

Fox, Justin. *The Myth of the Rational Market: A History of Risk, Reward, and Delusion on Wall Street.* New York: HarperBusiness, 2009.

Frängsmyr, Tore, ed. *Les Prix Nobel. The Nobel Prizes 1992.* Stockholm: Nobel Foundation, 1993.

Frank, Robert H. *Falling Behind: How Rising Inequality Harms the Middle Class.* The Aaron Wildavsky Forum for Public Policy 4. Berkeley: University of California Press, 2007.

Frank, Robert H., Thomas D. Gilovich and Dennis T. Regan. "Do Economists Make Bad Citizens?" *The Journal of Economic Perspectives (1986–1998)* 10, no. 1 (1996): 187–92.

Fung, Archon, and Erik Olin Wright. "Deepening Democracy: Innovations in Empowered Participatory Governance." *Politics & Society* 29, no. 1 (2001): 5–41.

Gaia Foundation, BiofuelWatch, African Biodiversity Network, Salva La Selva, Watch Indonesia, and EcoNexus. *Agrofuels and the Myth of the Marginal Lands.* London: Gaia Foundation, 2008.

Gardiner, Jean. "Women's Domestic Labour." *New Left Review* I/89 (1975).

Global Humanitarian Forum. *Anatomy of a Silent Crisis.* Geneva: Global Humanitarian Foundation, 2009.

GlobeScan for the BBC. "Economic System Needs 'Major Changes': Global Poll." GlobeScan/BBC, 2009.

Goldstein, Dana. "The Selling of School Reform." *Nation*, May 27, 2009.

Greenspan, Alan. "Testimony of Dr. Alan Greenspan to the Committee of Government Oversight and Reform, October 23, 2008." http://oversight .house.gov/documents/20081023100438.pdf (accessed February 12, 2009).

Grossman, Sanford J., and Joseph E. Stiglitz. "On the Impossibility of Informationally Efficient Markets." *The American Economic Review* 70, no. 3 (1980): 393–408.

Grunwald, Michael. "Monsanto Hid Decades of Pollution; PCBs Drenched Ala. Town, but No One Was Ever Told." *Washington Post,* January 1, 2002.

Habermann, Friederike. *Der homo oeconomicus und das Andere. Hegemonie, Identität und Emanzipation.* Feminist and Critical Political Economy 1. Baden-Baden, Germany: Nomos, 2008.

Haislip, Alexander. "Venture Capital Firm Set to Reap Rewards on Swine Flu." Reuters, April 24, 2009.

Hallward, Peter. "The Will of the People: Notes Towards a Dialectical Voluntarism." *Radical Philosophy* 155 (May/June 2009): 17–29.

Hamilton, Alexander, John Jay and James Madison. *The Federal Convention.* Edited by Henry Cabot Lodge. New York: G. P. Putnam's Sons, The Knickerbocker Press, 1902.

Han, Dongfang. "Chinese Labour Struggles." *New Left Review* 34 (2005).

Hardin, Garrett. "The Tragedy of the Commons." *Science* 162, no. 3859 (1968): 1243–48.

Harvey, David. *A Brief History of Neoliberalism.* Oxford: Oxford University Press, 2005.

Harvie, Alicia, and Timothy A. Wise. "Sweetening the Pot: Implicit Subsidies to Corn Sweeteners and the U.S. Obesity Epidemic." In *Policy Brief 09-01,* Global Development and Environment Institute, Tufts University, 2009.

Hayden, Tom, ed. *The Zapatista Reader.* New York: Nation Books, 2001.

Heller, Patrick. "Moving the State: The Politics of Democratic Decentralization in Kerala, South Africa, and Porto Alegre." *Politics & Society* 29, no. 1 (2001): 131–63.

Henrich, Joseph, Robert Boyd, Samuel Bowles, Colin Camerer, Ernst Fehr, Herbert Gintis, Richard McElreath, Michael Alvard, Abigail Barr, Jean Ensminger, Natalie Smith Henrich, Kim Hill, Francisco Gil-White, Michael Gurven, Frank W. Marlowe, John Q. Patton and David Tracer. "'Economic Man' in Cross-Cultural Perspective: Behavioral Experiments in 15 Small-Scale Societies." *Behavioral and Brain Sciences* 28, no. 6 (2005): 795–815.

Hirschman, Albert O. *Exit, Voice, and Loyalty: Responses to Decline in Firms, Organizations, and States.* Cambridge, MA: Harvard University Press, 1970.

Hobbes, Thomas, and Richard Tuck. *Leviathan,* rev. ed. Cambridge: Cambridge University Press, 1996.

Holt-Giménez, Eric, and Raj Patel. *Food Rebellions!: Crisis and the Hunger for Justice.* Oxford: Fahamu, 2009.

Hom, Sharon K., and Stacy Mosher. *Challenging China: Struggle and Hope in an Era of Change.* New York: New Press, 2007.

Hopkins, Rob. *The Transition Handbook: From Oil Dependency to Local Resilience.* Totnes: Green, 2008.

Horovitz, Bruce. "2 Million Enjoy Free Breakfast at Denny's." *USA Today,* February 3, 2009.

Horrigan, Leo, Robert S. Lawrence and Polly Walker. "How Sustainable Agriculture Can Address the Environmental and Human Health Harms of Industrial Agriculture." *Environmental Health Perspectives* 110, no. 5 (2002): 445–56.

Illich, Ivan. *Deschooling Society.* Harmondsworth, UK: Penguin Education, 1973.

International Labour Organization. *Global Wage Report 2008/09: Minimum Wages and Collective Bargaining; Towards Policy Coherence.* Geneva: International Labour Office, 2008.

Irvine, William Braxton. *A Guide to the Good Life: The Ancient Art of Stoic Joy.* Oxford: Oxford University Press, 2009.

Jacobs, Gloria. *Not a Minute More: Ending Violence Against Women.* New York: UNIFEM, 2003.

James, C. L. R. "Every Cook Can Govern: A Study of Democracy in Ancient Greece: Its Meaning for Today." *Correspondence* 2, no. 12 (1956).

Johnston, Basil H. *The Manitous: The Spiritual World of the Ojibway.* New York: HarperPerennial, 1996.

Kaplan, Jeffrey. "Consent of the Governed: The Reign of Corporations and the Fight for Democracy." *Orion Magazine,* November/December 2003.

Kartsounis, Luke D., Merle James-Galton and Gordon T. Plant. "Anton Syndrome, with Vivid Visual Hallucinations, Associated with Radiation Induced Leucoencephalopathy." *Jounral of Neurology, Neurosurgery, and Psychiatry* (2009): http://jnnp.bmj.com/cgi/content/short/jnnp.2008.151118v1.

Kasun, Jacqueline Rorabeck. *The War Against Population: The Economics and Ideology of World Population Control.* San Francisco: Ignatius Press, 1988.

Kelley, Ann. "Net Losses." *Guardian,* April 11, 2007.

Kent, George. "WIC's Promotion of Infant Formula in the United States." *International Breastfeeding Journal* 1, no. 8 (2006).

Keynes, John Maynard. *A General Theory of Employment, Interest and Money.* New York: Harcourt, Brace and World, 1936.

Kipling, Rudyard. *American Notes*. Boston: Brown and Company, 1899.

Kofman, Eleonore, and Elizabeth Lebas. *Writings on Cities*. Oxford: Blackwell Publishers, 1996.

Konow, James, and Joseph Earley. "The Hedonistic Paradox: Is Homo Economicus Happier?" *Journal of Public Economics* 92, no. 1 2 (2008): 1–33.

Krugman, Paul. "Health Care Realities." *New York Times*, July 30, 2009.

Langley, William "Profile: The King of Bhutan." *Sunday Telegraph*, November 9, 2008.

LaSalle, Tim J., and Paul Hepperly. *Regenerative Organic Farming: A Solution to Global Warming*. Kutztown, PA: Rodale Institute, 2008.

Levack, Brian P. *The Witch-Hunt in Early Modern Europe*, 3rd ed. Harlow: Pearson Longman, 2006.

Linebaugh, Peter. *The Magna Carta Manifesto: Liberties and Commons for All*. Berkeley: University of California Press, 2008.

Locke, John. *Two Treatises of Government*. London: Whitmore and Fenn, 1821.

Lohmann, Larry. *Financialization, Quantism and Carbon Markets: Variations on Polanyian Themes*. Sturminster Newton, Dorset: The Corner House, 2009.

Loo, Tina. "Dan Cranmer's Potlach: Law as Coercion, Symbol, and Rhetoric in British Columbia, 1884–1951." *Canadian Historical Review* 73, no. 2 (1992): 125–65.

Lotshaw, Tom. "Working for Welfare." *Marietta Register*, January 6, 2009.

Luce, Edward, and Chrystia Freeland. "Summers Calls for Boost to Demand." *Financial Times*, March 9, 2009.

MacKenzie, Donald A., Fabian Muniesa and Lucia Siu. *Do Economists Make Markets?: On the Performativity of Economics*. Princeton, NJ: Princeton University Press, 2007.

Makori, Henry. "Why Belief in Witchcraft Remains Strong among Africans." *Catholic Information Service for Africa*, April 6, 2009.

Martinez-Alier, Juan. *The Environmentalism of the Poor: A Study of Ecological Conflicts and Valuation*. Cheltenham, UK: Edward Elgar, 2002.

Marwell, Gerald, and Ruth E. Ames. "Economists Free Ride, Does Anyone Else?: Experiments on the Provision of Public Goods, IV." *Journal of Public Economics* 15, no. 3 (1981): 295–310.

Marx, Karl. *Capital: A Critique of Political Economy*. Harmondsworth: Penguin; London: New Left Review, 1978.

Marx, Karl and Friedrich Engels. *The Communist Manifesto*. Edited by Gareth Stedman Jones. London: Penguin, 2002.

Maxwell, Bill. "Eating That Tomato Can Put You in Moral Peril." *St. Petersburg (FL) Times,* July 13, 2008.

Maxwell, Daniel, Carol Levin and Joanne Csete. "Does Urban Agriculture Help Prevent Malnutrition? Evidence from Kampala." *Food Policy* 23, no. 5 (1998): 411–24.

Mazower, Mark. "The Strange Triumph of Human Rights, 1933–1950." *The Historical Journal* 47, no. 2 (2004): 379–78.

McKenzie, Richard B. *Why Popcorn Costs So Much at the Movies: And Other Pricing Puzzles.* New York: Copernicus Books, 2008.

McNeil Jr., Donald G. "In New Theory, Swine Flu Started in Asia, Not Mexico." *New York Times,* June 23, 2009.

Mehta, Lyla. "The World Bank and Its Emerging Knowledge Empire." *Human Organization* 60, no. 2 (2001): 189.

Menon, Gayatri A. "Re-Negotiating Gender: Enabling Women to Claim Their Right to Land Resources." Paper presented at Panel on Best Practices on Gender and Land/Property Rights, NGO Forum of the United Nations Conference on Human Settlements—Habitat II, Istanbul, June 1996.

Michaelson, Juliet, Saamah Abdallah, Nicola Steuer, Sam Thompson and Nic Marks. *National Accounts of Well-Being: Bringing Real Wealth onto the Balance Sheet.* London: New Economics Foundation, 2009.

Midnight Notes Collective and Friends. *Promissory Notes: From Crisis to Commons.* New York: Autonomedia, 2009.

Mill, John Stuart. *The Autobiography of John Stuart Mill.* Sioux Falls, SD: NuVision Publications, 1997.

——. *Essays on Some Unsettled Questions of Political Economy,* 2nd ed. [S.l.]: Longmans, Green, Reader, and Dyer, 1874.

Millennium Ecosystem Assessment. *Ecosystems and Human Well-Being: Synthesis.* Washington, D.C.: Island Press, 2005.

Mishel, Lawrence, and Jared Bernstein. *Economy's Gains Fail to Reach Most Workers' Paychecks.* Washington, D.C.: Economic Policy Institute, 2007.

Mitchell, Timothy. "The Properties of Markets." In *Do Economists Make Markets? On the Performativity of Economics,* edited by Donald Mackenzie, Fabian Muniesa and Lucia Siu, 244–75. Princeton: Princeton University Press, 2007.

Moll, Jorge, Frank Krueger, Roland Zahn, Matteo Pardini, Ricardo de Oliveira-Souza and Jordan Grafman. "Human Fronto–Mesolimbic Networks Guide Decisions About Charitable Donation." *Proceedings of the National Academy of Sciences* 103 (2006): 15623–28.

Monbiot, George. "If We Behave as If It's Too Late, Then Our Prophecy Is Bound to Come True." *Guardian*, March 17, 2009.

———. "These Are Not the Mariners of Old but Pirates Who Make Bureaucrats Blanch." *Guardian*, June 1, 2009.

Mora, Mariana. "Decolonizing Politics: Zapatista Indigenous Autonomy in an Era of Neoliberal Governance and Low Intensity Warfare." Ph.D. dissertation, University of Texas at Austin, 2008.

Morales, Andrés Timoteo. "En Veracruz, Oponerse a Operación de Granjas Carroll Se Castiga Con Cárcel." *La Jornada*, April 12, 2009.

Mostert, Mark P. "Useless Eaters: Disability as Genocidal Marker in Nazi Germany." *The Journal of Special Education* 36, no. 3 (2002): 155–68.

Nabokov, Vladimir Vladimirovich, and Fredson Bowers. *Vladimir Nabokov: Lectures on Literature*. London: Weidenfeld and Nicolson, 1980.

Neocosmos, Michael. "Development, Social Citizenship and Human Rights: Re-Thinking the Political Core of an Emancipatory Project in Africa." *Africa Development* 32, no. 4 (2007): 35–70.

Neuwirth, Robert. *Shadow Cities: A Billion Squatters, a New Urban World*. New York: Routledge, 2005.

Nickerson, Carol, Norbert Schwarz, Ed Diener and Daniel Kahneman. "Zeroing in on the Dark Side of the American Dream: A Closer Look at the Negative Consequences of the Goal for Financial Success." *Psychological Science* 14, no. 6 (2003): 531–36.

Ober, Josiah, and Charles W. Hedrick. *Demokratia: A Conversation on Democracies, Ancient and Modern*. Princeton, NJ: Chichester: Princeton University Press, 1996.

Orensanz, J. M. Lobo, Ana M. Parma, Gabriel Jerez, Nancy Barahona, Mario Montecinos and Ines Elias. "What Are the Key Elements for the Sustainability of 'S-Fisheries'? Insights from South America." *Bulletin of Marine Science* 76, no. 2 (2005): 527–56.

Ostrom, Elinor. *Governing the Commons: The Evolution of Institutions for Collective Action*. New York: Carmbridge University Press, 1990.

The Oxford English Dictionary, 2nd ed. 1992. S.v. "common." http://dictionary.oed.com /cgi/entry/50045107 (accessed June 1, 2009).

Pacific Institute. "Reign of Sand: Inner Mongolia. A Vast Chinese Grassland, a Way of Life Turns to Dust." *Circle of Blue*, 2008. http://www.circleofblue.org/reign/article_main_2.php (accessed March 15, 2009).

Patel, Raj. "A Short Course in Politics at the University of Abahlali BaseMjondolo." *Journal of Asian and African Studies* 43, no. 1 (2008): 95–112.

——. *Stuffed and Starved: Markets, Power and the Hidden Battle for the World Food System.* London: Portobello Books, 2007.

People's Daily Online. "Desertification Causes Yearly Loss of 54 Billion Yuan in China." November 26, 2008.

Perkins, John. *Confessions of an Economic Hit Man.* London: Ebury Press, 2005.

Peters, Pauline E. *Development Encounters: Sites of Participation and Knowledge,* Harvard Studies in International Development. Cambridge: MA: Harvard Institute for International Development, 2000. Distributed by Harvard University Press.

Petratis, Richard. "The Witch Killers of Africa." [2003?] http://www.infidels.org/library/modern/richard_petraitis/witch_killers.shtml (accessed March 1, 2009).

Pithouse, Richard. "Burning Message to the State in the Fire of Poor's Rebellion." *Business Day,* July 23, 2009.

Pizzigati, Sam. *Greed and Good: Understanding and Overcoming the Inequality That Limits Our Lives.* New York: Apex Press, 2004.

Pogge, Thomas, and Sanjay G. Reddy. "How Not to Count the Poor." Social Science Research Network, October 29, 2005. http://ssrn.com/abstract= 893159 (accessed December 6, 2007).

Popkin, Barry M. "The Nutrition Transition and Its Health Implications in Lower-Income Countries." *Public Health Nutrition* 1, no. 1 (1998): 5–21.

Pretty, J. N., C. Brett, D. Gee, R. E. Hine, C. F. Mason, J. I. L. Morison, H. Raven, M. D. Rayment and G. van der Bij. "An Assessment of the Total External Costs of UK Agriculture." *Agricultural Systems* 65, no. 2 (2000): 113–36.

Pretty, Jules N., C. F. Mason, D. B. Nedwell and R. E. Hine. "A Preliminary Assessment of the Environmental Costs of the Eutrophication of Fresh Waters in England and Wales." Paper, Centre for Environment and Society and Department of Biological Sciences, University of Essex, Colchester, UK, 2002.

Prins, Gwyn, and Steve Rayner. "Time to Ditch Kyoto." *Nature* 449, no. 7165 (2007): 973–75.

Ramachandran, V. S., and Diane Rogers-Ramachandran. "Denial of Disabilities in Anosognosia." *Nature* 382 (1996): 501.

Rancière, Jacques. *Disagreement: Politics and Philosophy.* Minneapolis: University of Minnesota Press, 1998.

——. *On the Shores of Politics.* Radical Thinkers 21. London: Verso, 2007.

Rancière, Jacques, and Steve Corcoran. *Hatred of Democracy.* London: Verso, 2006.

Range, Friederike, Lisa Horn, Zsófia Viranyi and Ludwig Huber. "The Absence of Reward Induces Inequity Aversion in Dogs." *Proceedings of the National Academy of Sciences* 106, no. 1 (2009): 340–45.

Rochido, Janaina. "Brazilian Cities Pioneer Democratic Budgeting." *City Mayors*, November 18, 2006.

Rosenberg, Alexander. "Review Symposium: Can Economic Theory Explain Everything?" *Philosophy of the Social Sciences* 9, no. 4 (1979): 509–29.

Samuelson, Paul Anthony. *Economics: An Introductory Analysis*. New York: McGraw-Hill, 1948.

Sandel, Michael. *Reith Lectures: A New Citizenship*. British Broadcasting Corporation, 2009. http://www.bbc.co.uk/programmes/b00kt7rg (accessed August 10, 2009).

Sandhu, Harpinder S., Stephen D. Wratten, Ross Cullen and Brad Case. "The Future of Farming: The Value of Ecosystem Services in Conventional and Organic Arable Land: An Experimental Approach." *Ecological Economics* 64, no. 4 (2008): 835–48.

Santos, Boaventura de Sousa. *Democratizing Democracy: Beyond the Liberal Democratic Canon*. Reinventing Social Emancipation, vol. 1. London: Verso, 2005.

Scahill, Jeremy. *Blackwater: The Rise of the World's Most Powerful Mercenary Army*. London: Serpent's Tail, 2007.

Schlosser, Eric. "A Side Order of Human Rights." *New York Times*, April 6, 2005.

SEI. "Price Per Ton of Carbon Offset: Voluntary Carbon Offset Information Portal." Stockholm Environment Institute and the Tufts University Climate Initiative, 2009. http://www.tufts.edu/tie/carbonoffsets/price.htm (accessed March 5, 2009).

SEIU. "SEIU Beyond the Bonuses: Tarp." 2009. http://www.seiu.org/a/change-that-works/bank-of-america/beyond-the-bonuses-tarp.php (accessed March 4, 2009).

Sharp, Travis. *U.S. Defense Spending vs. Global Defense Spending*. Washington, D.C.: Center for Arms Control and Non-Proliferation, 2009.

Sherman, Arloc, and Aviva Aron-Dine. *New CBO Data Show Income Inequality Continues to Widen*. Washington, D.C.: Center on Budget and Policy Priorities, 2007.

Shiva, Vandana. *Biopiracy: The Plunder of Nature and Knowledge*. Dartington: Green Books, in association with The Gaia Foundation, 1998.

Smith, Adam. *Glasgow Edition of the Works and Correspondence Vol. 5 Lectures on Jurisprudence*. 1762. Reprint. Indianapolis: Liberty Fund, 1982.

———. *An Inquiry into the Nature and Causes of the Wealth of Nations.* 5th ed. 1776. Reprint, London: Methuen, 1904.

———. *The Theory of Moral Sentiments.* 1759. Reprint. Oxford: Clarendon, 1976.

Soguel, Dominique. "Mining Interests Tied to Rape Impunity in Congo." *Women's eNews,* June 3, 2009.

Srinivasan, U. Thara, Susan P. Carey, Eric Hallstein, Paul A. T. Higgins, Amber C. Kerr, Laura E. Koteen, Adam B. Smith, Reg Watson, John Harte and Richard B. Norgaard. "The Debt of Nations and the Distribution of Ecological Impacts from Human Activities." *Proceedings of the National Academy of Sciences* 105, no. 5 (2008): 1768–73.

Srivastava, Abhishek, Edwin A. Locke and Kathryn M. Bartol. "Money and Subjective Well-Being: It's Not the Money, It's the Motives." *Journal of Personality and Social Psychology* 80, no. 6 (2001): 959–71.

Stannard, David E. *American Holocaust: The Conquest of the New World.* New York: Oxford University Press, 1993.

Stecklow, Steve. "Microsoft Battles Low-Cost Rival for Africa." *Wall Street Journal,* October 28, 2008.

Stein, Ben. "In Class Warfare, Guess Which Class Is Winning." *New York Times,* November 26, 2006.

Stiglitz, Joseph E., and Linda Bilmes. *The Three Trillion Dollar War: The True Cost of the Iraq Conflict.* 1st ed. New York: W. W. Norton, 2008.

Stockholm International Peace Research Institute. *SIPRI Yearbook 2009: Armaments, Disarmament and International Security.* Oxford: Oxford University Press, 2009.

Stout, Lynn A. "Taking Conscience Seriously." In *Moral Markets: The Critical Role of Values in the Economy,* edited by Paul Zak, 157–72. Princeton: Princeton University Press, 2008.

Swinton, Scott M., G. Frank Lupi, Philip Robertson and Stephen K. Hamilton. "Ecosystem Services and Agriculture: Cultivating Agricultural Ecosystems for Diverse Benefits." *Ecological Economics* 64, no. 2 (2007): 245–52.

Taibbi, Matt. "The Great American Bubble Machine." *Rolling Stone,* July 2009: 52–101.

Taleb, Nassim Nicholas. "Ten Principles for a Black Swan–Proof World." *Financial Times,* April 8, 2009.

Tegtmeier, Erin M., and Michael D. Duffy. "External Costs of Agricultural Production in the United States." *International Journal of Agricultural Sustainability* 2 (2004): 1–20.

Thepwethi, Phra (Prayut), Bruce Evans, Dhammavijaya, Jourdan Arenson and Mūnnithi Phutthatham. *Buddhist Economics: A Middle Way for the Market Place*. Bangkok: Buddhadhamma Foundation, 1994.

Thucydides, and Henry Dale. *The History of the Peloponnesian War*. London: H. G. Bohn, 1848.

Time magazine. "10 Questions for Jim Cramer." May 14, 2009.

Tomkins, Jenny. "Xe Is the Problem." *In These Times*, May 20, 2009.

Torres, Bob. *Making a Killing: The Political Economy of Animal Rights*. Edinburgh: AK Press, 2007.

TRAC IRS. "IRS Audit Rate for Millionaires Plummets." Transactional Records Access Clearinghouse, 2009. http://trac.syr.edu/tracirs/latest/204/ (accessed July 20, 2009).

TRAPESE Collective. "The Rocky Road to a Real Transition: The Transition Towns Movement and What It Means for Social Change." *The Commoner* 13 (2009). http://www.commoner.org.uk/N13/11Trapese.pdf (accessed August 17, 2009).

Turse, Nick. *The Complex: How the Military Invades Our Everyday Lives*. 1st ed. New York: Metropolitan Books, 2008.

Tutu, Desmond. 2004. "The Second Nelson Mandela Foundation Lecture." Given in Johannesburg, South Africa, November 23, 2004. http://www.nelsonmandela.org/index.php/news/article/look_to_the_rock_from_which_you_were_hewn/ (accessed November 20, 2005).

United Nations Department of Economic and Social Affairs. *The Inequality Predicament: Report on the World Social Situation 2005* [a/60/117/Rev.1 St/Esa/299]. New York: UNDESA, 2005.

United Nations Development Programme. *Human Development Report 1995: Gender and Human Development*. New York: Oxford University Press, 1995.

Vallance, Edward. *A Radical History of Britain: Visionaries, Rebels and Revolutionaries—the Men and Women Who Fought for Our Freedoms*. London: Little, Brown, 2009.

Vanden Heuvel, Katrina. "In the Trenches and Fighting Slavery." *The Nation.com*, December 28, 2008. http://www.thenation.com/blogs/edcut/391546/in_the_trenches_and_fighting_slavery (accessed March 14, 2009).

Van Lier, Piet. *Public Benefits Subsidize Major Ohio Employers: A 2008 Update*. Cleveland, OH: Policy Matters Ohio, 2008.

Vul, Edward, Christine Harris, Piotr Winkielman and Harold Pashler. "Puzzlingly High Correlations in fMRI Studies of Emotion, Personality, and Social Cognition." *Perspectives on Psychological Science* (forthcoming).

Washington, Jesse. "Some Say Holocaust Memorial Shooting Signals a Broader War." *Philadelphia Inquirer,* June 14, 2009.

Wijeratna, Alex. *Taking the Fish—Fishing Communities Lose Out to Big Trawlers in Pakistan.* Johannesburg: ActionAid International, 2007.

Wired. "The Future of Food: How Science Will Solve the Next Global Crises." October 20, 2008.

Wolin, Sheldon S. "Transgression, Equality and Voice." In *Demokratia: A Conversation on Democracies, Ancient and Modern,* edited by Josiah Ober and Charles W. Hedrick, 63–90. Princeton, NJ: Princeton University Press, 1996.

Wood, Ellen Meiksins. "Demos Versus 'We the People': Freedom and Democracy Ancient and Modern." In *Demokratia: A Conversation on Democracies, Ancient and Modern,* edited by Josiah Ober and Charles W. Hedrick, 121–38. Princeton, NJ: Princeton University Press, 1996.

———. *Peasant-Citizen and Slave: The Foundations of Athenian Democracy.* London: Verso, 1988.

Woodruff, Christopher. "Review of De Soto's 'The Mystery of Capital.'" *Journal of Economic Literature* 39, no. 4 (2001): 1215–23.

World Bank. *World Bank Assistance to Agriculture in Sub Saharan Africa: An Independent Evaluation Group Review.* Washington, D.C.: World Bank, 2007.

———. *World Development Indicators.* Washington, D.C.: World Bank, 2007.

World Health Organization. "World Health Organization Statistical Information System. "WHO, 2009. http://www.who.int/whosis/" (accessed July 19, 2009).

WorldPublicOpinion.org. *World Public Opinion and the Universal Declaration of Human Rights.* Washington, D.C.: WorldPublicOpinion.org, 2008.

WorldPublicOpinion.org, Steven Kull, Clay Ramsay, Stephen Weber, Evan Lewis, Melinda Brouwer, Melanie Ciolek and Abe Medoff. *World Public Opinion on Governance and Democracy.* Washington, D.C.: WorldPublicOpinion.org, 2008.

World Rainforest Movement. *Women Raise Their Voices Against Tree Plantations: The Role of the European Union in Disempowering Women in the South.* Montevideo: World Rainforest Movement, 2009.

Worm, Boris, Edward B. Barbier, Nicola Beaumont, J. Emmett Duffy, Carl Folke, Benjamin S. Halpern, Jeremy B. C. Jackson, Heike K. Lotze, Fiorenza Micheli, Stephen R. Palumbi, Enric Sala, Kimberley A. Selkoe,

John J. Stachowicz, and Reg Watson. "Impacts of Biodiversity Loss on Ocean Ecosystem Services." *Science* 314, no. 5800 (2006): 787.

Zandi, Mark. "Testimony before the House Committee on Small Business Hearing on 'Economic Stimulus for Small Business: A Look Back and Assessing Need for Additional Relief.'" July 24, 2008. http://www.house.gov/smbiz/hearings/hearing-07-24-08-stimulus/Zandi.pdf (accessed December 18, 2008).

Zelizer, Viviana, and A. Rotman. *Morals and Markets: The Development of Life Insurance in the United States.* New Brunswick, NJ: Transaction, 1983.

——. *Pricing the Priceless Child: The Changing Social Value of Children.* New York: Basic, 1985.

Zizek, Slavoj. *Violence: Six Sideways Reflections, Big Ideas.* London: Profile, 2008.

ACKNOWLEDGMENTS

It's only appropriate for a book that argues the merits of collective valuing that so many university communities opened their doors to me during this book's conception. I'm grateful to the Center for Social Theory and Comparative History at UCLA, the Center for African Studies at Berkeley, the Department of Political Science at John Carroll University, the University of Saskatchewan, the School of Journalism and South Asia Institute at the University of Texas at Austin, the Polson Institute for Global Development, and the Department of Development Sociology at Cornell University and the Norwegian University of Life Sciences for conversations, meals and the opportunity to share ideas.

Collective valuation isn't anonymous, though, and I cannot begin to compass the debt I owe to my research team, friends, comrades, sherpas, well-wishers and fellow travelers. For inspiration, correction, suggestion, translation, perspiration and enervation, I'm grateful to Abahlali baseMjondolo, Adam Shapiro, Alex Peake-Tomkinson, Alice Waters, Andrea Ismert, Anna Zalik, Annie Shattuck, Bob Jensen, Carol Park, Chad Futrell, the Coalition of Immokalee Workers, Damara Luce, Dan Lowenstein, Dan Moshenberg, David Lindsay, Debby Krant, Diane Elson, Elisa Oceguera, Eric Holt-Gimenez, Eric Vanhaute, Gavin McCormick, Gayatri Menon, George Caffentzis, Gerardo Reyes, Greg Asbed, Hannah Wittman, Haroon Akram-Lodi, Hilary Klein, Iain Boal, Jacques Depelchin, Jamie Johnston, Jamie McCallum, Jim Gifford, Jim Rigby, Joe Quirk, John Wildman, Jonathan Brumberg-Kraus, Josephine Crawley, Julia Flynn Syler, Jun Borras, Kamala Visverswaran, Kara Holmstrom, Karalei Nunn, Kemble Scott, Kerry Chance, Kevin Smith, Kolya Abramsky, Kris Dahl, Kristin Becker, Larry Lohmann, Laura Barber, Laura Neely, Lucas Benitez, Marcia Ishii-Eiteman, Marco Flavio Marinucci, Maria Elena Martinez, Mariana Mora, Mark Fowler, Martha Saavedra, Matt Birkinshaw, Medha Chandra, Michael Kamerick, Michael Lyon, Michael Pollan, Mike Linksvayer, Mindy Peden, Nely Rodriguez,

Nigel Gibson, Pat Youngblood, Pauline Wynter, Peter Rosset, Philip Gwyn-Jones, Phil McMichael, Radhika Balakrishnan, Riaz Ansary, Richard Bensel, Richard Pithouse, Rob Firing, Robin Chang, Ryan Hagen, Ryan Ismert, Sabina Alkire, Sally Smyth, Sam Grey, Sanjay Reddy, Sasha Abramsky, S'bu Zikode, several masked men and women in Chiapas, Shae Davidson, Shalmali Guttal, Sharad Chari, Silvia Federici, Staughton Lynd, Summer Brenner, Sunita Narain, Susie Lyon, Tamim Ansary, Ted Vallance, Tim Lang, Vashna Jagarnath, Will Jones, Will Kopp and Yasser Toor.

Members of two San Francisco institutions provided almost unlimited funds of advice. First, the denizens of the Sanchez Grotto—Sean Beaudoin, Alison Bing, Michael Chorost, Joshua Citrak, Michelle Gagnon, Scott James, Ammi Keller, Jeff Kirschner, Paul Linde, Shana Mahaffey, Eric Tipler, Diane Weipert and Doug Wilkins. Second, the staff at the San Francisco Public Library, especially at the Mission Bay branch, which became a home away from home. Meanwhile, on the other side of the continent, I was supported by the able team of magicians at Picador—Danielle Schlang, Darin Keesler, David Logsdon, Heather Kirkpatrick, James Meader, Kelsey Smith, Tanya Farrell and Sara Sarver.

Finally, in the writing of this book, three people were invaluable. I couldn't have hoped for a more supportive and intelligent writing partner than Chris Brooke, nor a wiser mentor through the world of publishing than Karolina Sutton, nor an editor who could so patiently, generously and beautifully turn my wormy prose into silk than Frances Coady.

But before I could be a writer, I needed to be able to write, and for that I thank my family, scattered across continents. Most of all, always and for everything, Mini Kahlon.

INDEX